FRENCH-AMER

Remembering D-Day after September 11

Eric Touya de Marenne

University Press of America,® Inc.
Lanham · Boulder · New York · Toronto · Plymouth, UK

Copyright © 2008 by
University Press of America®, Inc.
4501 Forbes Boulevard
Suite 200
Lanham, Maryland 20706
UPA Acquisitions Department (301) 459-3366

Estover Road
Plymouth PL6 7PY
United Kingdom

Library of Congress Control Number: 2007940297
ISBN-13: 978-0-7618-3968-2 (paperback : alk. paper)
ISBN-10: 0-7618-3968-2 (paperback : alk. paper)

Table of Contents

Preface

Recent discussions on French-American relations have revealed a certain degree of ambivalence. From admiration to opposition, comprehension to criticism, they have shed light on the paradoxical nature of this historical alliance. In the aftermath of September 11, the French people forcefully expressed their solidarity and compassion illustrated through the headlines of *Le Monde* newspaper titled the day after: "We are all Americans." After France's opposition to the war in Iraq, however, some Americans reminded their compatriots about what France owed the United States and about the eminent role played by its soldiers during the two world wars of the 20th Century. Did they *forget*, many of them asked, the *sacrifice* made by the GIs on French soil for the cause of *liberty*?

This question held within itself three fundamental facets of human experience. It alluded to the memory of the past which carries the heritage and tradition imbedded in the collective consciousness of nations; the ultimate abnegation and offering of the self, which, according to ancient traditions, constitutes the most noble act of humankind; and finally, conquered in the name of justice, the freedom that we all cherish. Like the land they conquered to liberate, the sacrifice of the "citizen soldiers" has become a sacred space; as such, both the soldiers and the D-Day beaches of Normandy, the United States and France, share a common past and destiny. Knowing what that destiny entails, and what it might hold for the future, is in fact one of the aims of this book.

The American experience in Normandy and beyond allows us to explore the character of the American people but also the intangible yet fundamental plane of sentiment through which a special bond exists between two countries. Our aim, in this respect, is to examine how such a dialogue is critical in the current state of world affairs. The conversations with WWII veterans divulge the differences that exist on both sides of the Atlantic, but also the common heritage, history and values that the two nations share. Thus, revisiting D-Day after September 11 enables us to question and envision the future of both France and America in a way that honors the memory of the WWII generation's purpose, courage and sacrifice. To what extent should the most important country in the world remain open to France's vision of international relations? Have the common ideals that brought the two countries together from Yorktown to the beaches of Normandy faded away? Has a shift occurred in their relation since the end of the Cold War and the aftermath of September 11? How can the two countries face and meet the global challenges of the 21st Century?

This book attempts to shed light on these questions by way of a series of *tête-à-têtes* conducted with American and French veterans who were actively involved in the liberation of Europe and the defeat of Nazism in 1939–1945. The veterans have much to teach us about the world today and the reflection that emerges from their diverse witness accounts give a new meaning to the debates scholars and historians have partaken in on the subject of French-American relations, from Alexis de Tocqueville to, more recently, Jean-François Revel and Bernard Henri-Lévy. Their testimonies center on the most essential debates of our time: the role freedom, patriotism, heroism, humanism and faith play in a modern democracy, the significance of the transformation of French and American societies, the dialogues among cultures, and the challenges humanity faces in the post-September 11 era with the emergence of terrorism. The considerations of those who fought for a democratic world, while experiencing its possible demise, project all of us into the future.

From this perspective *Remembering D-Day after September 11* gives us the chance to learn from each other, across boundaries, stories and generations. We learn from the past what we need to understand for the future. Landing under fire on the shores of Normandy, the young citizen soldiers, often aged 18 to 21, have left us a legacy we must measure through the prism of a present world in which the principles of democracy, tolerance and civilization are still undermined. The 21st Century, perhaps more than ever, presents itself with extraordinary challenges that the lessons of the past can help us overcome. The world that had been destroyed by an ideology of hatred and systematic destruction was redeemed through the concerted efforts of the greatest generation, in a way that elevated the whole of humanity.

Eric Touya de Marenne
New York, New York
July 4, 2007

Acknowledgments

I wish to thank Madame Létizia de Linares of the *Fondation Charles De Gaulle*, for her very génerous assistance during my stay in Paris and for guiding me to the Free-French veterans, members of the *Fondation Charles De Gaulle*, *Fondation de la France Libre*, and *Fondation du Maréchal Leclerc*. I also wish to extend my gratitude to Mr. Tom Gaukel, Chairman of the *59th Annual National Convention of the 82nd Airborne Division Association*, for facilitating my meetings and interviews with the WWII veterans of the 82nd Airborne Division who attended the Conference in Milwaukee, Wisconsin, and to Mr. John Robert Slaughter who welcomed me in Roanoke, Virginia, during the annual reunion of the WWII veterans of the 116th Infantry Regiment, 29th Division, who landed on Omaha Beach on June 6, 1944.

This book would not have been possible without the participation of the veterans. I wish to express to all of them my profound gratitude. French-American relations have been an academic interest of mine for many years. I am indebted to the late François Furet, member of the French Academy and renowned historian, with whom I had the opportunity to study Alexis de Tocqueville's *Democracy in America* while pursuing my Ph.D. at the University of Chicago. I am also very grateful to the Adelphi Faculty Development Grant Committee for its support in this project, and to the faculty members of Adelphi University, Diane Della Croce and Igor Webb, who agreed to read parts of the manuscript and share with me their invaluable comments. It is my pleasure to express my appreciation to Nora Wizenberg who contributed to the preparation of the manuscript, and to the dedicated students of Adelphi who provided their assistance. Finally, I wish to thank my wife Lucile Luo for her unyielding support. I dedicate this book in memory of my grandparents, Madeleine and Maurice (wounded in the Battle of Verdun, 1916), and Marie and Jean-Baptiste (wounded in the Battle of France, 1940).

Introduction

The questions we seek to answer in this book are as follows: To what extent should the most important country in the world remain open to France's vision of international relations? Have the common ideals that brought the two countries together from Yorktown to the beaches of Normandy faded away? Has a shift occurred in their relation since the end of the Cold War and the aftermath of September 11? How can the two countries face and meet the global challenges of the 21st Century? These questions will be examined in this introduction through four themes and perspectives: first, the discovery of America by French explorers, the analogous purpose and democratic ideals of the French and American Revolutions, and the common heritage and destiny that the two people share; second, the understanding of French and American historians, literary figures and journalists about both countries, from the time of Lincoln to today, including the points of contention that may exist among them; third, the significance of D-Day in a post-September 11 world taking into account what has brought the two people together in their struggle against Nazism and in seeking a response to the challenges of the future; fourth, the return to the future implies that learning about the past through dialogue and reflection, and honoring the memory of those who died in Normandy, can inspire us to reinvent the present and create a better world.

The French-American Experience (1562–1865)

Traveling to the New World, the French saw the North American continent as a land of promise. Born in Caen in 1735, Jean de Crèvecœur defined its inhabitants as survivors of European injustice and intolerance. Regenerated by a new system of laws and a new way of life, he predicted that the Americans would guide human destiny toward global unity: "Here individuals of all nations are melted into a new race of men, whose labors and posterity will one day cause great changes in the world. Americans are the western pilgrims who are carrying along with them that great mass of arts, sciences, vigor, and industry which began long since in the East; they will finish the great circle."[1] Driven forward by progress, the birth of the American nation presaged a new era for the universal mind and spirit.

Early on, the French had a fascination with America. They searched for and discovered its lands and rivers as no other explorers had. Gripped by the stories told by the Natives, they were the first Europeans to conceive of a passage on the continent from the Atlantic to the Pacific oceans. Landing in the New World in 1530, Jacques Cartier believed that the St. Lawrence River could lead to India. The path to the riches of the Orient lay in the West, as did the way to religious freedom. A French Huguenot exploratory group led by Jean Ribault landed in 1562 on the Atlantic shores of Florida to found the first European settlement on the North American continent at Fort Caroline on the shores of the St. Johns River. There, Jacques Lemoyne sketched and engraved the life and customs of the Timucuan natives.

While the settlers of Jamestown had explored only their immediate surroundings, Samuel de Champlain, founder of Québec, had, by 1615, reached the borders of the Georgian Bay and Lake Huron, via the Ottawa River and Lake Nipissing. Supported by Colbert and Louis XIV, expeditions to the Great Lakes were conducted during the following decades into present-day Illinois and Ohio. French explorers, trappers, and missionaries were the first Europeans to reach the Great Lakes region in the early 1600s before Jean Nicolet, originally from Cherbourg, discovered Lake Michigan in 1634.

The mapping of America entered the French consciousness at an early stage. It merged with and influenced, geographically and intellectually, the discourse of its literature and history. Louis Joliet's and Jacques Marquette's narratives and interactions with the Natives played an essential role in this process. Well versed in the languages of the Algonquin, Hurons and Illinois, they led in 1673 their expedition to unexplored land out West, in search of the Mississippi River. Obtaining from the Wild Oats, Miamis, Maskoutens and Kikabous information about the people and places they encountered, and resources such as corn, fish and buffalo, they discovered a land unknown to Europeans. During his journey, Marquette noted in his diary: "Two Miamis who were given us as guides embarked with us, in the sight of a great crowd, who could not sufficiently express their astonishment at the sight of seven Frenchmen, alone in two canoes, daring to undertake so extraordinary and so hazardous an expedition. . . . At 42 and a half degrees of latitude, we safely entered the Mississippi on the 17th of June, with a joy that I cannot express."[2]

Uncovering the natural beauty of the land, the deer and cattle, bustards and swans, and "a herd of four hundreds buffaloes," they pursued their journey cautiously until the 25th of June, when they "perceived on the water's edge some tracks of men, and a narrow and somewhat beaten path leading to a fine prairie." Marquette recalled that "we silently followed the narrow path, and after walking about two leagues, we discovered a village on the bank of a river, and two others on a hill. We commanded ourselves to God. Two Indians advanced with tobacco pipes raised toward the sun and offered them to smoke. We were invited to enter their village. At the door of the cabin in which we were to be received was an old man who stood erect, and stark naked, with his hands extended and lifted toward the sun. When we came near him, he declared: 'How beautiful the sun is when you come to visit us! Our village awaits you and you shall enter all our cabins in peace.' Having said this, he made us enter his own in which were a crowd of people; they devoured us with their eyes, but, nevertheless, observed profound silence. We could, however, hear these words, which were addressed to us from time to time in a low voice: 'How good it is, my brothers, that you should visit us.'"

"These people had never seen any Frenchmen and could not cease looking at them; they lay on the grass along the road, they ran ahead and then back for another look. All this was done in silence. The reception by the leader of the Illinois was similar to the first welcome: 'I thank you for having taken so much trouble to come to visit us. Never has the earth been so beautiful, or the sun so bright, as today; never has our river been so calm, or so clear of rocks, which your canoes have removed in passing; never has our tobacco tasted so good, or our corn appeared so fine, as we now see them.' He begged us [however] on behalf of his nation not to go farther, on account of the great dangers to which we exposed ourselves. I replied that I feared no death and that I regarded no happiness as greater than that of losing my life for the glory of the one who has made all." [3]

Reaching as far south as today's Arkansas, Marquette and Joliet began their return on the 17th of July by way of the Illinois River and Lake Michigan. Eyewitness accounts such as the ones they gave of their journey influenced the image that the French had of North America and its inhabitants. Both natives and settlers were thought to be living in harmony with nature, and freed from what the new Americans perceived as the corruption of European society. La Salle later reached the fork of the Mississippi Delta in 1681 where the city of New Orleans would be founded by a small French colony in 1717. Going in the opposite direction, Pierre Le Sueur journeyed in 1700 from the mouth of the Mississippi to the country of the Sioux, in what is now Minnesota, and, seeking a passage to the Pacific, the La Verendyres, father and sons, reached the foothills of the Rocky Mountains in 1742. The image of the New World was particularly imprinted in the minds of the French authors and philosophers who sought to legitimize through the laws of nature a new political and social order. By 1770, it was believed that in their aspiration for liberty, the American insurgents were guided by natural virtues at a time when France was still ruled by a monarchy prone to intolerance and injustice.

The New World was seen as a land of promise where democratic ideals reconceived in 18th Century political thought could be made a reality. In *Histoire et politique des établissements et du commerce des Européens dans les deux Indes, Recherches sur les Américains*, published in 1770, Guillaume-Thomas Raynal predicted that as European powers grew weaker and succumbed one to another, America, sprung from nothing, would assume a leadership role on the face of the Earth. It is in this context that Benjamin Franklin was welcomed with open arms in Paris by members of high French society such as Mme Du Deffand and Mme Helvétius, and by the scientists and *philosophes*, among them Cabanis, d'Alembert and Voltaire, who fully adhered to the principles upon which the

American Declaration of Independence was founded. Much of French society had embraced their cause for no other reason than to help them attain a comprehensive liberty of which many of the French were deprived.

The cultural shock between the American insurgents hostile to the European monarchies and the French liberal[4] aristocracy dwindled when the French Expeditionary Corps led by Comte de Rochambeau landed in Newport and exhibited the grace and heroism of its military youth. The strength, courage and decency of their conduct astonished and attracted the admiration of the Americans. Fervent supporters of the cause of liberty, the leaders of French army and navy who played a pivotal role in the American Independence, the Marquis de Lafayette, the Comte d'Estaing and the Admiral François de Grasse, belonged to a generation that, in spite of its membership in high society, would later contribute and give its full support to the changes brought forth by the French Revolution in 1789, among them, the abolition of privileges and the Declaration of the Rights of Man and Citizens. This fringe of the French nobility influenced by Voltaire and Montesquieu recognized in principle that the ideals and aspirations of the American Revolution, at the forefront of the movement for liberty, were legitimate and desirable for all humankind.

The French fascination with the American continent and the plight of its people continued. The New World offered a space in which the new democratic ideals could be put into practice as a political system of governance. The French elite therefore anxiously followed the progress of the War of Independence. They sensed that their fate and the very fate of their country were at stake. Through these events, a communion of spirit was seeded between the two people and grew over time through France's decisive aid to the Americans in 1781 to the early June landing of 1944 on the beaches of Normandy. Significantly, the sacrifice of French soldiers at Yorktown corresponded with the Americans' in that both shared an analogous purpose. The crucial role played by the American GIs and Rochambeau's Army fulfilled what Franklin and Lafayette had envisioned for the future of their nations.

In spite of their distinctive heritage and history of 1,300 years of monarchical and imperial regimes, the French remained attentive to the birth of democracy on the other side of the Atlantic. Having witnessed in 1783 at age 15 the military parade of the victorious French fleet returning to Brest from America, and having listened to the accounts of the sailors' journey to the New World, François-René de Chateaubriand was, by 1790, fleeing the instability generated by the French Revolution. Born of a liberal aristocratic Breton family, he embarked in 1790 at Saint-Malo for America, synonymous in his mind with spiritual and individual freedom. Beyond his scattered hopes about his country's future, he celebrated in the American wilderness the natural abundance, scenic grandeur and unspoiled landscape in which his dreams and ideals could be reborn: "Primitive liberty, I find you at last! [He wrote during his voyage.] I pass as that bird that flies before me, who travels haphazardly, who has only an embarrassment of riches among the shadows. Here I am as the Almighty created me, the sovereign of nature. . . . Not a single beat of my heart will be constrained, not a single one of my thoughts will be enchained; I shall be free as nature; I shall recognize as sovereign only Him who lit the flame of the suns and who with one movement of His hand set in motion all the worlds."[5]

The future author of *The Genius of Christianity* left his homeland to recreate, by way of his travels, an imaginary universe in which a freed humanity could be reconciled with an innocent nature. This longing for harmony would later give rise to the American transcendentalism of Emerson and Thoreau. Upon his return to Paris in 1792, however, Chateaubriand witnessed the decline of the monarchy and the steady rise of the Reign of Terror, the dictatorship of the people, and the guillotine's massacres. Disillusioned, he turned his back from the secular Enlightenment that had condemned the abuses of the Church in the Old Regime, to reconcile Christianity with liberty. The error of the revolutionaries in France was to have been persuaded that democratic societies should be hostile to religion, an assertion that Tocqueville would also contradict a few decades later. Unlike liberty, he maintained, despotism could survive without religious faith and morality.

A striking contrast existed between the political destinies of Washingtonian democracy and the French Revolution. The fate of the French heroes of the American Revolution who had favored and even initiated the political changes of 1789 illustrated the gap that separated the outcome of the two revolutions. Having led the American campaign of 1781 alongside Washington, Jean-Baptiste de Rochambeau barely escaped the guillotine in 1794, and the Comte d'Estaing was, for his part, executed on unfounded accusations. In his attempt to reconcile the maintenance of the parliamentary monarchy with the exigencies of the French Revolution, the Marquis de Lafayette, playing a pivotal role in the party of the liberal aristocracy, gradually found himself in a perilous position. Threatened from the outside by the monarchical powers of Europe who wanted to reinstate a regime of absolute monarchy in France, and from within, by those who were leading the Revolution to extremes, he could in the end only surrender to one of the two parties, spending five years of his life under arrest in a Prussian jail under precarious conditions. An opponent of slavery and a friend of liberty, it was he who on July 11, 1789, had introduced the project of the Declaration of the Rights of Man and Citizens to the French Assembly in an attempt to restate the American Revolution. A few days later on July 16, he had ordered the destruction of the Bastille.

When he returned to America in 1824–1825, Lafayette was welcomed as a hero. A warm greeting awaited the persistent supporter of the American cause. At every stage of his tour, from Boston to Alabama, the whole nation, from the common farmer to the President, celebrated the one who, upon hearing of the defeats of the insurgents in New York, came to Philadelphia in 1776 to pledge his allegiance and support. But although the American founding fathers and the liberal French aristocracy were animated by the same ideals, they could not achieve the same aims under different political and historical circumstances. The basic precepts of the French Revolution were signed into law in France as in America, but the definite emergence of democracy in France would have to await the birth of the Third Republic.

A descendent of an old French noble family from Normandy, Tocqueville belonged to a society that had been defeated by the French Revolution. As a witness of European political instability, he saw a few years later in the New World an example of how subdued democratic progress in France could be awakened. In the footsteps of Chateaubriand, his nephew by alliance, he would explore during his trip to the New World in 1831 the extent to which liberty and equality coexisted in a unique equilibrium. What distinguished the two continents, in his views, was that the Americans coalesced the principles of Christianity and liberty so intimately that it was impossible for them to conceive one without the other. In France, by comparison, the spirit of religion and freedom were marching in opposite directions. Hence, the greatness of America was not in its fertile fields and boundless forests, in its rich mines and vast commerce, or in its public school system and institutions of learning. Its pre-eminence resided in the deep faith of its citizens: "Americans show by their practice that they are fully aware of the need to instill morality into democracy by way of religion. What they think about themselves in this respect is a truth in which every democratic nation ought to be steeped."[6]

Also originating from Normandy, Ernest Duvergier de Hauranne had read Tocqueville who was a close friend of his father and had spoken in his presence about his journey in America. Appalled by the inhuman treatment of African Americans and by the abject poverty of the Natives, he witnessed from Washington and Boston ("the center of philosophical liberalism") to La Crosse, Chicago, and Saint Louis, the extent to which the rise of liberty and progress might be sacrificed by the outcome of the Civil War.

The portrait he made of Lincoln attested to his admiration for a "man who has raised himself by his own unaided efforts from a log cabin deep in the Indian woods to the presidency of the United States. . . . He needed a great deal more than intelligence . . . he also needed that moral force, these virtues of perseverance and resolution which are, indeed, the American virtues par excellence." Informed of his oratorical abilities, Hauranne summed up the great leader on the occasion of what was to be remembered as one of the most important speeches in American history: "I do not believe that modern eloquence has ever produced anything more noble than the address he delivered over the graves of the soldiers who died at Gettysburg. He attained the sublime simplicity, the inspired detachment of antique patriotism, but one feels at the same time the emotion of a human being and a Christian, face to face with the horrors of the Civil War."[7]

Tenaciously, the visitor from France raised his voice against Lincoln's critics who attempted to diminish his importance: "I have been told that this 'illiterate buffoon' or, as the New York Herald scornfully calls him 'our very classical president', knows by heart all of Shakespeare and I also hear that when he goes to hear it performed, no one is more quick to notice omissions from the original text or to catch mistakes by the actors. I begin to believe that his only fault was to have been a lumberjack, a rail splitter, and a man of all work. For my part, I only honor him the more for it."[8]

Introduced to Lincoln by Senator Charles Sumner of Massachusetts on January 20, 1865, Duvergier de Hauranne noted that although the White House "possesses a certain prestige . . . its doors stand open to every American: like a church, it is everybody's house . . . you may think that a policeman or at least a guard has been posted. Not at all! There is only a notice asking visitors to respect the furnishings which belong to the government. We went up the flight of stairs, we opened a door and suddenly we were in the majestic presence of the President . . . 'Father Abraham' was seated on a low chair and writing on his knees with his long legs bent double." In front of him stood five or six people, soldiers and women who were silently awaiting their turn "and the President rose to receive us; it was then that his great height was revealed." "Strangely penetrating," his eyes had a "sardonic expression . . . he seemed sad and preoccupied, bent under the burden of his immense task. . . . In order to judge people rightly it is first of all necessary to understand the realities of life and remember that in a democracy nobody has any use for the pomp and circumstance of high society. Despotism holds up little idols for the crowd's adoration; but republics fill positions of general esteem and power with carpenters like Abraham Lincoln."[9]

Visions of America: from Hauranne to Revel

Duvergier de Hauranne's portrait of Lincoln alluded to the old adage that no one is a prophet in his own country. It also conveyed the great admiration that a visitor can have for a foreign leader and his nation. Furthermore, this portrait taught important lessons, still valid today, for journalists and historians of all ages who seek to understand the fabric and soul of a nation. Hauranne's integrity and vision showed how to make sense of people from other lands and how to interpret their life experience and history.

Hauranne's message was that even the atrocities of the Civil War had not permanently imperiled American democracy: "The shock which was expected to annihilate the American nation has served instead to prove its strength and vitality. That freedom which was to have perished at the slightest test has come without mishap through five years of revolution, political turmoil and civil war. Many have said that democratic and federal institutions were perhaps good for a time of calm and prosperity, but that they would be powerless to resist a violent revolutionary onslaught; yet these same institutions have once more shown their solidity and adaptability." In contrast with the reputation it suffered in some European circles, the strength and character of the American people was unaltered: "This anarchic people, ungovernable, impelled, it is said, toward barbarism, by an excess of selfishness and individual freedom, has suddenly displayed a spirit of order and discipline, a patriotic unanimity, a devotion and perseverance of which the great military and monarchical nations of the Old World would not always have been capable."[10]

On his journey, Hauranne recognized the necessity to question the rigidity and fixity of one's predictable point of view : "I did not want to impose a logical and hence artificial order. . . . I thought it would be better to give to the reader my impressions of each day, the groping and even the contradictions of my thoughts, and have him or her take part in the formation of my judgment, than to give a dogmatic conclusion which would only show one side of the truth. I wanted to oppose my sincere impressions to preconceived theories." The latter line of reasoning encouraged the readers to move away from facile misconceptions: "Now, when one can go from New York to Paris or London in ten days, America should no longer be for us an object of astonishment or dread, or admiration or exaggerated aversion; nor should it be a battlefield of ideals where the friends and enemies of modern democracies are engaged in combat. Rather, it should be viewed as a vast storehouse of experience from which to gather warnings and examples with an open mind."[11]

Arguing that "the one which sees nothing but evil in American democracy, is at the same time the enemy of freedom," Hauranne revealed among those who both admire and condemn America, the existence of two groups outside of which there was no salvation for the independent thinker. Hence, the judgment we make of other people and cultures demands both inquisitiveness and self-examination: "In truth, what repels us is perhaps not so much the vice itself as the costume in which it is dressed and the language, more or less familiar or strange, which it speaks to us. Virtue itself needs to be fashionable in order to be admired and when it wears odd or outmoded clothes; it runs a great risk of displeasing us or of being taken for a fault. I have been no more free of this tendency than anyone else. . . . I saw things only through the prism of habit."[12]

Underlining the subjectivity and relativity of one's interpretation, Duvergier de Hauranne shed light on the fragility of our models of perception. Today's use of email and the Internet has not necessarily set in motion the process of demystification of the other in order to bring the world together. In a book that was neither a condemnation nor an apologia of the United States, Hauranne reminded his readers about the responsibility that we share: "If we find in America whose greatness we cannot deny some shortcomings that displease us and deserve our blame, how many faults that revolt their conscience and baffle their understanding might Americans not discover in France!"[13]

Today, this cautionary note should be examined by journalists and politicians in France and the United States who systematically pass judgment on each other. This consideration matters all the more if one takes into account the sacrifices of the D-Day veterans, the historical role of France in the making of America, and the challenges and hopes that both nations share for the future. Taking into account that our perception of each other's reality is too often based on pre-judged assumptions, and determined by our ways of seeing the world (our view of what is natural and logical to us), our aim should be to comprehend the reality of the other, and go beyond what we perceive as normal or outside the norm in our own culture.[14]

Since the end of the Cold War era, studies on trans-Atlantic relations have reexamined the meaning of America and its place in the world.[15] As seen earlier, such queries have been at the heart of debates among French historians and intellectuals since the 18th Century because they were inseparable from a reflection on France itself, before and after the Revolution, on the nature of democracy, on the relationship between liberty and equality, and on the contradictions that lay between the rise of individualism and the search for the common good. Needless to say, the debate continues today, and has extended itself to the rest of the world through questions of justice and human rights.

A contrasting image emerges from these considerations in both the United States and France. As the greatest power in the world, the former is portrayed by some as the embodiment of an economic, cultural and military empire whose actions contradict the ideals to which its founders aspired. As an example, Michael Lind explores in *The Next American Nation* the consequences of "the weakening of democracy in its birthplace": "This passage of the United States into a new oligarchical stage [implies that] a free and democratic order is slowly being sapped of its substance within the United States [and that as a result] the country's goal can hardly be to defend such an order abroad."[16] Emmanuel Todd asserts in *After the Empire. The Breakdown of the American Order* that the unilateral action of the new superpower endangers the world's stability. In spite of its industrial and military force, the political scientist argues that "far from being a sign of increasing power," the American expansion in military activity served in fact "to mask a decline": "The size of the opponent chosen by the United States is the true indicator of its current power. Attacking the weak is hardly a convincing proof of one's own strength."[17]

One could maintain that combating terrorism and fundamentalism, whatever its source may be, is by no means a sign of weakness, and point to the contradictions in Todd's reasoning. He makes the case that "Georges W. Bush and his neoconservative helpers will go down in history as the grave diggers of the American empire," an empire which he strongly condemns, and that Europeans need "to understand why America refuses to resolve the Israeli-Palestinian question since it clearly has the power to do so." Earlier, he explained that the United States' influence was weakening. Such a paradoxical interpretation systematically places the United States as either irrelevant ("If democracy triumphs everywhere, we arrive at an endpoint wherein the United States would be of no further use to the rest of the world as a military power and would have to accept being no more than one democracy among others") or an impediment to global security ("Such a strategy, never resolve a problem to justify military action around the world and trigger arms race, makes the United States a new and unexpected obstacle to world peace."[18]).

Not all the "intellectuals" in France present such an unwelcoming view of the country in which Tocqueville witnessed the modern renaissance of democracy. Among them is Jean-François Revel, author of *Anti-Americanism* (the French title is *L'Obsession anti-américaine*), who questions the systematic downgrading of the United States. Other well known critics who have a favorable opinion of the United States include André Glucksmann, Guy Millère, Pierre Rigoulot and Yves Roucaute, to name a few. In his book, Revel alleges that the systematic bashing of America among certain groups of intellectuals and politicians exceeds the bounds of reasonable criticism. Underlining the contradictions of anti-Americanism and its link to anti-globalization, he gives a voice to the many in France who consider the United States and the American people, friends, even though they may disagree at times with its government's policy.

Overall, Jean-François Revel asserts that "we" in Europe desire to "project our faults onto America as to absolve ourselves." On the social and economic functioning of the world, he measures the different views between two nations such as France and the United States who consider themselves charged with the task of enlightening the rest of the world. As an example, to do away with a globalization *à l'américaine*, Lionel Jospin, former Socialist prime minister, proposed to promote a globalization *à la française* (or a "globalization with a human face"), where capitalism would play a lesser role.

In opposition to America's critics, Revel also sheds a positive light on the historical contribution of the United States for the betterment of humanity: "As for the American 'hyperpower' that causes Europeans so many sleepless nights, they should look to their own history and ask themselves how far they themselves are responsible for that predominance; for it was they who turned the twentieth century into the grimmest in history. It was they who brought about the two apocalypses of the World Wars and invented the two most absurd and criminal political regimes ever inflicted in the human race. If Western Europe in 1945 and Eastern Europe in 1990 were ruined, whose fault was it? . . . Yet, it has become habitual to turn the situation around and constantly indict the United States."[19]

Faced with the challenge of terrorism, France and the United States have worked together with the same sense of commitment and purpose. France supported the Enduring Freedom operation in Afghanistan by sending 5,500 troops into the region and provided training to the new Afghan army. It was second only to the United States in contributing troops to NATO operations in Afghanistan, the Balkans and Africa; it worked in cooperation with American agencies against terrorism and in providing humanitarian assistance around the world. From this standpoint, we should distinguish between a constructive criticism of American or French policy and a systematic rejection of what the two nations stand for, and we should remain open to their respective vision of the world.

American and French people may not agree with the current Administration's foreign policy but this does not make them "anti-Americans." We need clarification concerning the French perception of Americans, and to underline the fact that even in the course of the disagreement over Iraq, the American people themselves continued to enjoy a favorable and positive opinion among the French (72 percent on average, 80 percent for the people on the right) according to a study conducted by Sofres for *Le Monde* newspaper on September 28–29, 2004. Furthermore, according to the same study, 41 percent on the left and 64 percent on the right stated that it is important that the United States play a leadership role in the world, and 90 percent of French people judged that it is important to keep good relations with the United States. The May 2007 election of President Sarkozy who voiced in his campaign his esteem for the United States corroborated the findings of these polls.

Real points of contention do not lie between two nations as much as between the hopes and ideals of their citizens and the realities they experience, between the universal and humanistic principles on which the French and American democracies were founded and the perception that their promises are not fulfilled for everyone. From this standpoint, the dynamics of attraction and repulsion that at times characterize the relationship between France and the United States also originate from each people's views of their own country. When it manifests itself in France, the criticism of American policy does not necessarily translate into a systematic rejection of America, but rather expresses a concern about international policies of which the French government itself partakes, and for which the United States is not solely responsible.

Considering the variety of judgments that exist in both countries, the points of contention are not confined to national differences as some in the media would like us to believe. They are based on global apprehension and distress: How do we create a just and peaceful world? What is a just and democratic society? How do we improve the dialogue among cultures and overcome the challenge of terrorism? A broad range of opinions are expressed in each country, and from this perspective, what unites our two people is far greater than what separates them. If one spent a year in Paris amid its protests, one would be convinced that the French are more anti-French than they are anti-American.

Criticism and the existence of an opposition are essential to the subsistence of a democracy. It was Theodore Roosevelt who affirmed that standing by the president or any other public official, right or wrong, is not only unpatriotic and servile, but is morally treasonable to the American public. Franklin Delano Roosevelt acted democratically and patriotically when he denounced laissez faire policy and initiated a set of social programs that led the country to squarely face the Depression and improve the lives of millions of unemployed people. And it was also right for then Senator Harry S. Truman to investigate the fraud and wastefulness of military expenditure in the war effort. By opposing what was business as usual and the norm for the people in power, they pursued the truth, aimed toward impartiality, and served their country.

Democratic progress and justice can only be achieved when the political reality is questioned. It is essential, therefore, in a democracy that the people be allowed to express their views, be they supportive or in opposition. In this respect, what is valid for domestic issues is necessary and legitimate internationally. What is also desirable today is to seek a better understanding of the people who partake in debates worldwide. Some publications have, for example, seen collaborative efforts between journalists and scholars on both sides of the Atlantic. Michael Brenner and Guillaume Parmentier have explored the differences that exist between a "uni-polar" and "multi-polar" vision of the world while they share their convictions that building a stable world order must be grounded on principles of democracy.

As they examined transatlantic partnership, the two authors sought to interpret "France's questioning of American dominance [which] expressed more than an impulse to clip the wings of the American eagle. It brought to the surface the core question of what practical meaning was attached to the concept of the

West."[20] Such a reflection is indispensable today because in combating terrorism, we must ensure that our ideals and actions do not contradict one another. As "powerful nations" we should also measure the perceptions and consequences of our efforts around the world. These real challenges should not be overshadowed by the "injured pride, feelings of ingratitude, real or imagined offenses, all the negatives intertwined with the positive experience as comrades in arms in the great tests of the twentieth century."[21]

The French tendency to scrutinize the most powerful nation's policy must be considered in the context of a shared history. We have traced the French reflection on America back to the 18th Century and examined the extent to which it is for many people in France inseparable from their own existence and aspirations as members of the world community. As we face in common the tribulations of the years to come, themes of this meditation find a resonance in the United States. One of them centers on the question of power. In *The Paradox of American Power*, Joseph Nye distinguished between military and economic strength and the preponderance of openness and diplomacy that in his view is needed in American foreign policy.[22] At the opposite side of the spectrum, discussing the military and geopolitical might of the United States, Robert Kagan claimed in *Of Paradise and Power* that European countries like France are turning away from military power at the cost of global security.

One could underline that France's Defense budget has continuously increased in the past few years and that it could never match the American budget for military expenditure, which is larger than all of the nations' military budgets in the world combined. There is no question that weapons and armies win wars and that without the power of the United States Army in World War II, the fate of freedom and democracy in Europe would not have been secured. However, it cannot be the only source of power at our disposals today. Like all human inventions, weapons have limits. Another of Kagan's lines of reasoning could be questioned, when he claims for example that "Americans and Europeans no longer share a common strategic culture." Finally, when he makes the following judgment, "Americans are idealists. In some matters, they may be more idealistic than Europeans. But they have no experience of promoting ideals successfully without power,"[23] one must wonder what kind of "power" Robert Kagan has in mind, and whether he considered the size of Washington's army in 1776 when American ideals began to spread around the world by way of the Declaration of Independence.

As we remember the sacrifices of the American GIs in Normandy, we ought not to lose sight of Benjamin Franklin's vision that America's cause is the cause of mankind. Hence, the lack of knowledge of the other on both sides of the Atlantic or anywhere else must lead to a growing interest in exchanges among policy makers, elites and common citizens around the world. As Jean-François Revel writes: "It is not difficult to get to know the United States as she really is, with her virtues and her faults, both as a society and as an externally projected superpower. . . . And given the available resources, whoever remains poorly informed, even after frequent visits to the US must simply want to be so." To this, Duvergier de Hauranne would have concurred: "It is up to [opinion makers] to share this knowledge in digestible form. Journalists are both historians of the present and educators. If they use their forums narcissistically to trumpet their own preconceived ideas instead of serving facts, they are betraying their public. But spinning out prejudice-inspired resentments is futile, and the likely result is powerlessness. No society is fault-free of course. America has made her share of foreign policy mistakes. What country hasn't? . . . Meanwhile, critics should never lose sight of America's achievements."[24]

Remembering D-Day after September 11

One of the contentions of this book is that the role played in Normandy by "the greatest generation" in the struggle against one of the most horrific forms of despotic and barbaric regime that was Nazism, can indeed be examined in light of the providential role that the United States of America has played in world history. It reaffirmed and gave new meaning to Jefferson, Franklin and Abraham Lincoln's vision of a government of, by and for the people. The sacrifice of the GIs whose blood reddened the shore of France on that morning of June 6, 1944 redeemed humanity: "It was in Normandy . . . that the Western democracies made their fury manifest. The success of this great and noble undertaking was a triumph of democracy over totalitarianism."[25]

This event brought about a decisive change. It put an end to the atrocious deaths of millions of people and to the calamity of war. The aftermath of the conflict revealed the shocking existence of concentration camps. In this gloomy context, it was American leadership that set in motion the trial of the Nazi regime in Nuremberg, the generosity of the Marshall Plan, and the foundation of the United Nations. War ultimately brings out the worst and the best of human-kind. The testimonies of each veteran's courageous actions serve to illustrate American greatness at a time when the world was desperately in need of a leadership that would reconcile power and moral principles. The lessons of history to be learned, from this perspective, are that peace and liberty are fragile, that they are precious gifts that we must work to preserve, and that we must remain vigilant that their defense will not endanger or contradict the standards of human dignity.

Animated by the bravery and the audacity of the American spirit, the young GIs responded to the call. They rose above their fears and moved forward to destroy an evil regime in order to liberate the world. The landing in Normandy necessitated preparation and performance, a turn around and conquest through which they had to face, in a dramatic fashion, the four elements of the world: air, earth, fire and water. It also required on the part of each individual a strong sense of purpose and faith: "No one in the plane spoke [recalled Tom Porcella]. I could feel a chill come over me. . . . The silence was broken and we finally jumped up and snapped our hooks on to the wire. Then the sergeant called. My heart started pounding as I started saying a prayer to myself. I was so scared that my knees were shaking and just to relieve the tension, I knew I had to say something. So, I shouted 'What time is it?' Somebody answered me and told me it was about 2:30. All of a sudden, I felt like I was all alone. So, I said 'Let me say a few more prayers.' And I said a couple of Hail Mary's."

"Then we heard, 'Are we ready?' All the troopers shouted all at once, 'Yeah. Let's go.' With the roar of the engines in my ears, I was out the door and into the silence of the night. I realized I had made the jump into darkness. . . . Looking up at the chute and then down at my feet, I had the shock of my life. I plunged into water. My heart was pounding and my thoughts were running a mile a minute. 'How deep is this water? Can I get free of my chute? Am I too heavy? Will the weight keep me in the bottom?'; all this in a split second. I hit the water in a standing position and when my feet touched the bottom, I was leaning forward. I managed to straighten myself and realized that the water was over my head and I had to jump up for air. . . . So, I held my breath and tried to stand. The water was just above my nose. Quickly I stood on my toes and I was gasping for another breath of air. My heart was beating so rapidly that I thought it would burst. I pleaded, 'Oh God. Please don't let me drown in this damn water in the middle of nowhere.'"[26]

Some would tragically not overcome this first battle in Normandy. The struggle and challenge would be arduous. President Roosevelt did not fail to grasp the intensity and gravity of what was at stake that morning in a broadcast radio address: "Last night, when I spoke with you about the fall of Rome, I knew at that moment that troops of the United States and our Allies were crossing the Channel in another and greater operation. It has come to pass with success thus far. And so, in this poignant hour, I ask you to join with me in prayer: Almighty God: our sons, pride of our Nation, this day have set upon a mighty endeavor, a struggle to preserve our Republic, our religion, and our civilization, and to set free a suffering humanity. Lead them straight and true; give strength to their arms, stoutness to their hearts, steadfastness to their faith. They will need Thy blessings. Their road will be long and hard. For the enemy is strong. He may hurl back our forces. Success may not come with rushing speed, but we shall return again and again; and we know that by Thy grace, and by the righteousness of our cause, our sons will triumph."[27]

Bob Slaughter of the B Company 116th Regiment, 29th Division, recounted the first assault force on Omaha Beach in which soldiers from small mid-Atlantic towns in Virginia who had never seen combat would land and die heroically: "I crouched down chin deep in the water as shells fell at the water's edge. Small-arms fire kicked up the sand. I noticed a GI running, trying to get across the beach. He was weighed down with equipment and had difficulty moving. An enemy gunner shot him. He screamed for a medic. An aid man moved quickly to help him and he was also shot. I will never forget seeing that medic lying next to that wounded soldier, both of them screaming. They died in minutes. Boys were turned into men. Some would be very brave men; others would soon be dead men, but any who survived would soon be frightened men. Some wet their pants, others cried unashamedly. Many just had to find within themselves the strength to get the job done. Discipline and training took over."[28]

Felix Branham of K Company who had climbed into a landing craft at 4:20am recalled upon landing how many of his comrades drowned; how the boats stopped at the sandbar were demolished, and how "seasick men who had stayed on board were blasted to smithereens." His testimony attested to the horrific violence: "I got out in water up to the top of my boots. People were yelling, screaming, dying, running on the beach, equipment was flying everywhere, men were bleeding to death, crawling, lying everywhere, firing coming from all directions. . . . Col. Canham, Lt. Cooper, and Sgt. Crawford were screaming at us to get off the beach. I turned to say to Gino Ferrari, 'Let's move up, Gino', but before I could finish the sentence, he had been hit in the face and his brain splattered all over my face. I moved forward and the tide came on so fast it covered him and I no longer could see him."[29]

Remarkably, these heroic acts in the midst of the brutality of war encapsulated a moment in which the story of France and America merged to become one, as both people shouted in one voice the piercing cry of a suffering humanity engaged in a struggle for liberty. That morning of June 6, a few miles away from the Normandy shores, members of the "Alliance" underground network were executed at gunpoint range in the prison of Caen. They included husbands and fathers like Désiré Lumière, Robert Boulard, Albert Anne and Georges Thomine. Since the beginning of the war, the organization had been providing the Allies with vital information about the German troops and their strategy. Backed by the members of the Free-French Paratroops battalions who had landed on the night of June 5 in the region of Britanny, the underground of St. Marcel began the following day to fight with fury to keep several German divisions pinned down during the Normandy campaign. And on June 10, following a regional uprising in the Massif Central region, a group of 6,000 underground were fighting two German divisions at the Mont Mouchet and delaying the junction of German troops from the south to the north.

The attempt through France to slow the advance of German divisions toward Normandy and the ceaseless harassing activities and ambushes of the Resistance had devastating effects on the civilian population. On June 9, 1944, when groups of the SS Das Reich Armored Division entered the small city of Tulle, then held momentarily by a partisan group, they shot and hanged ninety-nine of its members on the town's balcony and street lamps and deported over a hundred others to concentration camps. A day later, the same units burned Oradour sur Glane to the ground along with its inhabitants. The destruction of communication, bridges and railroads continued. The *maquis* of Vercors pursued in June the struggle initiated by hundreds of underground members at Les Glières in February 1944. These actions led to further horrific retaliations, the burning of villages and the killing of civilians. Through the war, the executions of members of the Resistance had been conducted in places like the Mont Valérien near Paris and Souges near Bordeaux.

Like millions of their American counterparts working in factories and living in constant fear of their brother's, friend's or husband's death, thousands of French women played a decisive role in the Resistance to the Nazi occupation. Just in the surrounding region of the small town of Châteaubriant in Western France, Berthe Besnard, who hid American pilots, was arrested and deported on December 24, 1943; Marcelle Baron was deported to Ravensbrück; Annie

Gautier was tortured by Klauss Barbie and gunned down August 19, 1944; Esther Mousson and Anna Roul sheltered Jewish children; after the execution of her husband in February 1943, Anna Viaud took his place in the Resistance; Geneviève Letertre, mother of six, housed the Buckmaster network after the deportation of her husband and son; and Angèle Miseriaux, widowed with also six children, was arrested and died in deportation after sheltering allied pilots.

These women were part of the thousands of French "citizen soldiers" who could not accept the capitulation of France and its occupation by the Nazi regime. Among those who were not killed, an estimated 56,000 French Resistance fighters were captured and deported to concentration camps from which only half would return. Like the American soldiers, they returned home in silence forever marked by the folly and aberration of war. From Africa to the Pacific, the Russian front to the sites of the Holocaust, millions would die a violent death in the most horrific conflict that the world had ever seen. WWII resulted in the deaths of 60 million people, half of which were Russians and 11 million political, social and racial minorities, of which 6 million were Jews.

In this context, the success of D-Day and the Normandy campaign found its origin in the greatness of America, and the nobility, integrity and decency of its citizens. Their sacrifices exemplified the highest calling in human life, which makes us reflect to this day on the mystery of humankind. Active in the underground movement, French authors like Albert Camus wrote during these years that the absurdity of existence required us to rebel, in solidarity with our fellow human beings, against our condition. Arrested by the Gestapo in 1944, André Malraux had contended in his earlier writings that humanity was engaged in a permanent struggle with itself whose purpose was to counter and transform its destiny. Killed in action the same year, Antoine de Saint-Exupéry had explored what this fate and new world for humanity ought to be. The French and American experience also shared and responded to a common calling when the head of the National Council of Resistance fell in 1943 into the hands of the Nazis' Gestapo. André Malraux concluded in his homage during the ceremony of transfer of the ashes of Jean Moulin to Paris' Pantheon in 1964, that on the day of his death, Moulin's deformed face that had refused to speak under torture was the visage of France.

The struggle against the violence and racism of the Nazi Party had begun before the war in its birthplace when German-Jewish author and dramatist, Erich Mühsam, was transferred to the Oranienburg concentration camp where he was tortured and murdered on July 9, 1934. Motivated by moral considerations and patriotism, Carl von Ossietzky, recipient of the Nobel Peace price in 1935, was detained until his death on May 4, 1938 at the Esterwegen Concentration camp. Later, Dietrich Bonhoeffer, founding leader and member of the Confessing Church who had opposed Hitler's anti-Semitic policies was arrested and hanged in March 1943. The "White Rose" group of students and their professor from the University of Munich were executed for their anti-Nazi activities in 1943. Ernst Thälmann was arrested in 1933 before being shot after eleven years of isolated confinement in Buchenwald; and Claus von Stauffenberg, leading figure of the failed plot to kill Hitler on July 20, 1944 was executed the day after.

The Fall of France in 1940 had "transformed the international balance of power, sucking other powers into the conflict until by the end of 1941 the war had become a truly global one. De Gaulle had been right to proclaim [on June 18, 1940] from London that the Battle of France was only the first round in what would turn out to be a world war. The Fall of France was the end of the beginning, not the beginning of the end."[30] On the plane from Bordeaux the day before, De Gaulle recalled flying over La Rochelle and Rochefort where ships had been set on fire by German planes and over the town where his very sick mother was living. As he reached London, having been sent by members of the French government, he saw himself as alone and wholly un-provided for, like a man on the shore of an immense ocean who maintains that he will cross it by swimming through it.

The radio address he made to his compatriots marked the beginning of the Resistance: "The leaders who have been at the head of the French armies for many years have formed a government. This government alleging the defeat of our armies has entered into communication with the enemy to stop the fighting. To be sure, we have been submerged, we are submerged by the enemy's mechanized forces, on land and in the air. . . . It is the German tanks, planes and tactics that have so taken our leaders by surprise as to bring them to the point they have reached today. But has the last word been said? Must hope vanish? Is the defeat final? No! Believe me for I know what I am talking about and I tell you that noting is lost for France. The same means that beat us may one day bring victory. France is not alone. This world is not confined to the unhappy territory of our country. This war has not been decided by the Battle of France. This war is a worldwide war. Today we are stuck down by mechanized force; in the future, we can conquer by greater mechanized force. The fate of the world lies there. . . . Whatever happens, the flame of French Resistance must not and shall not go out."[31]

Committed to the principles of democracy in its struggle, Jean Lacouture observed that "what made Gaullism a 'moving force' was not only the dynamism of its leaders, the clear mindedness of its Resistance fighters . . . it was also that its legitimacy arose from a proper relation between action and ethics."[32] Exhorting the living to continue the struggle, De Gaulle's Free-French soldiers met the danger face to face and choosing to die resisting rather than to live subjugated, they honored the sacrifice of their compatriots. Men and women of different ethnic, political, moral and religious views united for the resurgence of their country in military campaigns in North Africa, the Near East and Europe. They numbered more than 400,000 by the time of the landing in Normandy, of which many would land in Southern France in August 1944, and 1,250,000 in May of 1945, with several infantry and armored divisions among them fighting in Germany.

Yet, the GIs' landing in Normandy had played a significant role in the liberation of France and Europe. Jacques Chirac remarked during the commemoration ceremonies on June 6, 2005 that France would not forget the day hope was reborn "when men made the supreme sacrifice to liberate our soil, our native land, our continent, from the yoke of Nazi barbarity and its murderous folly. Nor will it ever forget its debt to America, its everlasting friend, and to its Allies, all of them, thanks to whom Europe reunited at last, now lives in peace, freedom, and democracy." The French president concluded his homage with these words: "Today, as we stand in respectful silence, our emotion is undimmed at the spectacle of these rows of crosses, where your companions, your brothers in arms fallen on the field of honor now rest for all eternity. Our hearts are heavy as we contemplate their courage, their abnegation and their generosity. Our spirit is uplifted by the supreme abnegation of these young men who offered up their lives to save the world."[33]

In a moving tribute on June 6, 1984, Ronald Reagan recounted the story of Peter Robert Zanatta of the first assault wave to hit Omaha Beach as told by his daughter: "I don't know how or why I can feel this emptiness, this fear, or this determination. . . . I know that my father saw so many of his friends killed. I know that he must have died a little inside each time. But his explanation to me was, 'you did what you had to do, and you kept on going.'" She made a promise to her father who had died eight years earlier of cancer and who had not returned: "I am going there Dad, and I'll see the beaches, the barricades and the monuments. I'll see the graves and I'll put flowers there just like you wanted to." In the same oration, he reminded the audience about "the [Resistance who] will be a timeless inspiration to all who are free and to all who would be free. Today, in their memory, and for all who fought here, we celebrate the triumph of democracy. We reaffirm the unity of democratic peoples who fought a war and then joined with the vanquished in a firm resolve to keep the peace."

Faced with the forces of obscurantism, President Reagan underlined the uncommon aim of the American mission in Normandy and beyond, and the mutual purpose of all the nations who partook in this undertaking: "When these troops swept across the French countryside and into the forests of Belgium and Luxembourg, they came not to take, but to return what had been wrongly seized. When our forces marched into Germany they came not to prey on a brave and defeated people, but to nurture the seeds of democracy among those who yearned to be free again. . . . From a terrible war we learned that unity made us invincible: now, in peace, the same unity makes us secure. We sought to bring all freedom-loving nations together in a community dedicated to the defense and preservation of our sacred values."[34]

In the context of a post-September 11 world, Dominique de Villepin, the French Minister of Foreign Affairs, reaffirmed twenty years later this unity in a speech given at the United Nations Security Council in New York, in February 14, 2003: "We all share the same priority, that of fighting terrorism mercilessly. This fight requires total determination. Since the tragedy of September 11 this has been one of the highest priorities facing our peoples. And France, which was struck hard by this terrible scourge several times, is wholly mobilized in this fight which concerns us all and which we must pursue together." At the same time however, he expressed the concerns of his government regarding the risks of a military intervention in Iraq that would possibly decrease the effectiveness of the Western alliance, and "increase tensions and risk paving the way to other conflicts."

Not excluding the use of force, he raised a series of questions about the impact the use of military action would have: "Would not such intervention be liable to exacerbate the divisions between societies, cultures and peoples, divisions that nurture terrorism? . . . To what extent do the nature and extent of the threat justify the immediate recourse to force? How do we ensure that the considerable risks of such intervention can actually be kept under control?" His conclusion alluded again to the shared French-American experience: "In this temple of the United Nations, we are the guardians of an ideal, the guardians of a conscience. The onerous responsibility and immense honor we have must lead us to give priority to disarmament in peace. . . . This message comes to you today from an old country, France, from a continent like mine, Europe, that has known wars, occupation and barbarity. A country that does not forget and knows everything it owes to the freedom-fighters who came from America and elsewhere; and yet has never ceased to stand upright in the face of history and before mankind. Faithful to its values, it wishes resolutely to act with all the members of the international community. It believes in our ability to build together a better world."[35]

As President Clinton contended in a television interview, the murder on September 11 of over 3,000 people represented an act that negated our humanity; and it resonated with the crimes of the Nazi Regime in World War II, or any extremist group in all times of history. The mood in the streets of Paris was grim on that occasion as it was all over France. The day after, the headlines of *Le Monde* newspaper ("We are all Americans") summed up the solidarity of the French nation with the people of New York and the United States. After the attempted suicide attack in December 1994 by the Algerian Armed Islamic Group that planned to crash a fully fuelled plane into the heart of Paris, the French had experienced terrorist activities at home. It was not surprising to learn that its secret services had in 2000 and 2001 produced reports and informed the CIA about the Al-Qaeda threats to the United States.

4. Return to the Future: Homage, Dialogue and Reflection

How can we honor the memory of those who died in Normandy? Answering this question is in many ways the purpose of this book. In his Gettysburg address, Abraham Lincoln declared that the dead of battle spoke more eloquently than the living ever could: "In a larger sense, we can not dedicate, we can not consecrate, we can not hallow, this ground. The brave men, living and dead, who struggled here, have consecrated it, far above our poor power to add or detract. The world will little note, nor long remember what we say here, but it can never forget what they did here. It is for us the living, rather, to be dedicated here to the unfinished work which they who fought here have thus far so nobly advanced. It is rather for us to be here dedicated to the great task remaining before us; that from these honored dead we take increased devotion to that cause for which they gave the last full measure of devotion."

The above inquiry, which one can never fully answer, offers us the occasion to revisit the character of French-American relations. More than disagreements, what emerged from the tête-à-têtes conducted with veterans on both sides of the Atlantic is a strong commitment to their alliance and democratic values. But what also became apparent is the complex and paradoxical nature of the issues the world faces today. Following the events of September 11, it was believed that removing Saddam Hussein was an essential step to take in the war against terrorism and to pave the way to peace in the Middle East. When the French government expressed its opposition to what it considered to be a premature military intervention, a few members of Congress suggested that the cafeteria at the House of Representatives should serve "freedom fries" and "freedom toast." Others rallied against France's "appeasement of terror," and one member went as far as expressing his desire to go to France to disinter his relative.

The facts demonstrate today that the French government's position had its merits and that the questions it raised were legitimate. The Congressman who joked that nobody knew how many Frenchmen it took to defend Paris, because it had never been tried, should have known that one and a half million of them had died from 1914–1918 doing exactly what he was describing. This is as if at least 15 million American men had died in war from 2003–2007. Considering however that we have a common enemy, international terrorism, and apart from how one felt about the false allegations and the real motives for the war, meeting Brenton Smith, age 21 from Colorado, at the Annual 82nd Airborne Division Convention in Milwaukee, made me consider that the American sacrifice in Iraq was as worthy as the one in Normandy. Having spent time in Mosul and Baghdad, he linked his mission to bringing liberty and democracy to that country.

This series of conversations across the United States and France gave the WWII veterans of both countries the opportunity to reflect on the role played by their respective nations in the world today. How we adequately respond to September 11 is a question that leads to a broad range of possible answers and to intricate outcomes. The commentaries on the subject revealed that what is anchored in the French and American consciousness is the necessity to distinguish people from governments when making judgments on foreign policy. It is not the Iraqis or any other nationality that are responsible for the ills caused by terrorism but extremist groups and leaders around the world. Just as there were several anti-Nazi movements in WWII Germany, there are many groups of people in Iraq, Iran and other parts of the Middle East who aspire to democracy. Hence, to be faithful to one's values must also mean not to simplify and generalize, and to be engaged in critical thinking. The divergences over Iraq have not broadened the gap between France and the United States on issues such as peace in the world and international terrorism.

The discussions also addressed and shed light on a series of paradoxes characteristic of our modern times. One of them pertained to the notion that the United States is the sole country responsible for the ills of the world while many countries have benefited from the American security umbrella during the Cold War. To the skeptics who "mock the United States invested in a kind of universal mission," Jean-François Revel replied that "thousands of equally grotesque statements have issued from French mouths, celebrating, over the course of the centuries, the 'universal radiance' of France, the 'country of human rights' burdened with the responsibility of spreading liberty, equality and fraternity throughout the world." It was American leadership, the French critic argued, that, through Woodrow Wilson, Franklin Roosevelt and Harry Truman, "replaced the concept of *realpolitik*, indifferent alike to morality and the interests of others . . . and brought to Europe from the United States the principle of collective security."[36]

Affirming that the war in Iraq and WWII would share a similar outcome was also contradictory. The facts have thus far revealed that winning the war does not mean winning the peace in all circumstances; democracy cannot emerge overnight, freedom cannot be imposed by force and it does not necessarily bring justice for all. If one considers the alternative to taking action in Iraq, each side has measured the limits of its vision and ambitions. Facing this reality, the exchange with the veterans centered on the belief that, in order to face the complexity of today's world, both France and America need to remain faithful to the pursuit of their original and universal ideals: liberty, equality, and the pursuit of happiness.

In spite of their geographic and geopolitical differences, the two countries have in their inception common values and each has played and is playing a significant role in the history of Western Civilization. Their diversity can also be a source of enrichment for the world community. They represent, as Tocqueville suggested, two distinct socio-economic systems in a democracy: one that is leaning toward equality and the other liberty. If the 20th Century has witnessed the limits (and even the evils as practiced in the Soviet Union) of communism, the 21st Century might reveal the transgressions of a form of capitalism solely preoccupied with the accumulation of materials and deprived of any humanism. In a recent book questioning the morality of capitalism, André Comte-Sponville pondered whether as a system left on its own like meteorology and physics, capitalism in fact existed and functioned outside or in the absence of any moral consideration.[37]

Today, these inconsistencies require more than ever the forethought and critical thinking of a Montaigne or Montesquieu who celebrated the ideals and aspirations of the West but also questioned its achievements. They also demand that a constructive dialogue between people of different cultures and religions exist in order to understand their tradition, lives and hopes and go beyond what Samuel Huntington described as "the clash of civilizations."[38] The combined efforts of France and the United States are essential from this standpoint and the exchange with the WWII veterans in this book takes place in a spirit of friendship. The eminence of their actions did not stem from a belligerent victory that none of them would seek to claim, but from the dignity and righteousness of the mission they were asked to fulfill, and that characterizes the exceptional nature of the American experience in Normandy.

The return to the future advocated here, whereby the knowledge of the past allows us to reinvent the present and create what is to come, is of great importance in our post-September 11 era. In the context of post-modernity, Francis Fukuyama's prediction in *The End of History and the Last Man* that the fall of

Communism and the end of the Cold War has brought forth a teleological vision of history in which the "universalization" of democracy and peace among nations would take effect, did not fully grasp the challenges to come in the 21st Century: not only the struggle among peoples of diverse cultural and religious backgrounds, but also, from an environmental standpoint, the conflict between planet Earth and Civilization, which no human being is assured to survive.

The legacy of D-Day and of the American and French veterans who changed the world through their actions and sacrifices finds its meaning today in the preservation of our liberty and the betterment of humanity. How does true democracy take root and not fall into an oligarchic and despotic form of authority? How do we put an end to the death of 18 million people a year in the world from hunger and preventable diseases? How do we address the root causes of the conflict in the Middle East, confront terrorism, and give back to politics its *lettres de noblesse* by making it the realm of the possible?

America's institutions had become for Tocqueville a model from which one could study the functioning of a democratic form of government. In an 1850 prefatory note to the 12th Edition of *Democracy in America*, he contended that the fundamental principles of the American Constitution (order, balance of powers, true liberty, and the sincere respect for the law), were indispensable to all Republics. They had to be known to all, and where they would not be met, the Republic would soon cease to exist. To admire and fully support democracy did not mean the end of its criticism: "Since I am firmly of the opinion that the democratic revolution to which we are witness is an irresistible fact, and one that it would be neither desirable nor wise to oppose, some readers may be surprised to discover how often I find occasion in the book to be quite severely critical of the democratic societies created by this revolution. My answer is simple: it is because I am not an enemy of democracy that I sought to deal with it in a sincere manner."[39]

The difference between Hitler's Nazism and the terrorist organizations such as Al Qaeda is only a historical one. Yet, it is not enough for a regime to call itself a democracy or a parliamentary monarchy to ensure that it stands straight in view of its presumed principles. Tocqueville asserted that democracy could be put in peril with the renunciation of liberty and the tyranny of the majority. In 1840, he strongly condemned the outcomes of colonialism in North Africa and when its proponents put forth the civilizing mission of France, he pleaded not to force the indigenous to come to French schools, but to help them rebuild their own and form the men of law and faith without whom Muslim civilization could not achieve anymore than France's could.

Tocqueville was no less critical of the Americans who went to the Temple where they heard a priest repeat each day that all men are brothers and the Eternal God who has created them all gave them the commandment to love and rescue one another. In a chapter of *Democracy in America*, he denounced the deportation and depravation of Native Americans in the following terms: "If by chance an Indian nation can no longer live within its territory, the Americans offer a fraternal hand and lead the natives off to die somewhere other than in the land of their fathers." This process was achieved "without violating a single one principle of morality in the eyes of the world. To destroy human beings with greater respect for the humane laws would be impossible."[40] Similarly, as "an old and sincere friend of America," he made clear that slavery delayed the progress of the "freest nation" on Earth: "There is one evil that makes its way into the world surreptitiously: at first it is barely noticed among the ordinary abuses of power. It begins with an individual whose name history does not bother to record. Like an accursed seed it is planted somewhere in the soil. Thereafter, it feeds on itself, spreads easily, and grows naturally with the society that accepted it: that evil is slavery."[41]

Looking boldly into history does not take away the nobility of the soldiers who on June 6, 1944 during WWII gave their lives for the cause of liberty. Their actions and sacrifices deserve our eternal gratitude. We needed them. Through the valor of their deeds, they offer a unique example to follow, a light that guides us through the shadows and the darkness of the night, and inspires us to be engaged and vigilant in a world that threatens or continues to deny the most fundamental precepts of human dignity. Tocqueville alluded to the fate of the human condition caught between grandeur and misery. Similarly, to the great shame and dishonor of the Vichy Regime who collaborated with the Nazis, De Gaulle and the Resistance opposed an unyielding contradiction.

The spirit of Tocqueville's writing extended also to the farewell speech given from the White House by the Normandy Campaign Commander-in-Chief, Dwight Eisenhower, which addressed how the abuse of power could endanger the survival of American democracy: "In the councils of government, we must guard against the acquisition of unwarranted influence, whether sought or unsought, by the military-industrial complex. The potential for the disastrous rise of misplaced power exists and will persist. We must never let the weight of this combination endanger our liberties or democratic processes. We should take nothing for granted. Only an alert and knowledgeable citizenry [can ensure] that security and liberty may prosper together. . . . As we peer into society's future, we—you and I, and our government—must avoid the impulse to live only for today, plundering for our own ease and convenience the precious resources of tomorrow. We cannot mortgage the material assets of our grandchildren without risking the loss also of their political and spiritual heritage. We want democracy to survive for all generations to come, not to become the insolvent phantom of tomorrow."[42]

President Eisenhower also maintained that the world needed to avoid becoming "a community of dreadful fear and hate, and be, instead, a proud confederation of nations [bound by] mutual trust and respect." His message resonated in his country and abroad. Published in 1919, Paul Valéry's "The Crisis of the Mind" underlined the mortality of later civilizations in the aftermath of the massive death and destruction caused by WWI: "We see now that the abyss of history is deep enough to hold us all. We are aware that a civilization has the same fragility as a life. It was not enough for our generation to learn from its own experience how the most beautiful things and the most ancient, the most formidable and the best ordered, can perish." The results of the conflict put in question all forms of knowledge and systems of values: "So many horrors could not have been possible without so many virtues. Doubtless, much science was needed to kill so many, to waste so much property, and annihilate so many cities in so short a time; but moral qualities in like number were also needed."[43]

The military crisis of WWI set in motion an intellectual crisis: "Thousands of young writers and artists have died; the illusion of a European culture has been lost, and knowledge has been proved impotent to save anything whatsoever; science is mortally wounded in its mortal ambitions and, as it were, put to shame by the cruelty of its applications." The void left by science was filled by the humanities and spirituality: "Never has so much been read, nor with such passion, as during the war: ask the booksellers. . . . Never have people prayed so much and so deeply: ask the priests. All the saviors, founders, protectors, martyrs, heroes, all the fathers of their country, the sacred heroines, the national poets, were invoked."[44] The outcome of the war demonstrated that the fate of a civilization could not rest solely on military power and scientific and technological achievement, but more importantly, on the promotion of dialogue and understanding.

Learning the lessons of history honors the sacrifice of the veterans of Normandy because they enable us to foresee and transform the future. In the same way, the account of the French-American experience through the story of its soldiers who defeated an ideology of hatred in the name of democracy and civilization, compels us to think about larger questions today: To what extent are we civilized and what makes us so? What is the barbarity that we must confront today? How do we make democracy desirable for all? Following John F. Kennedy's speech of 1960 about the worldwide aspiration of people to be free, what do we do with our liberty, and for what purpose? It is through these queries that we share a common destiny. And in the fight against terrorism, we should not forget our shortcomings and responsibilities.

Faced with these larger questions, differences disappear and we are again one: "In Pluribus Unum." Both America and France must realize their humanistic ideals in accordance with their current roles in the world. Religious principles must be reconciled with secular ones and Ben Laden refuted when he insists that the West must be defeated because it is in conflict with Islam. One ought not to underestimate the common values of tolerance, justice and liberty that are shared globally in every culture, religion and country. In the post-September 11 world, the ensuing dialogues and reflections that follow both celebrate the French-American experience and the accomplishments of the greatest generation, and explore the challenges of today and tomorrow that we must face together. After over two centuries of shared history, the veterans recognize their differences but also their common ultimate hopes that the path to peace and the pursuit of happiness for all mankind will be followed.

Notes

1. Jean de Crèvecoeur. "What is an American?" *Letters from an American Farmer.* New York: E. P. Dutton and Co., 1912, p. 43–44.

2. Joseph H. Schlarman. *From Québec to New Orleans. The Story of the French in America.* Belleville: Buechler Publishing Company, 1929, p. 61.

3. *Ibid.*, p. 62–64.

4. The term "liberal" refers here to having political or social views favoring reform, progress, and the attainment of civil liberties.

5. François René de Chateaubriand. *Travels in America.* Translated by Richard Switzer. Lexington: The University Press of Kentucky, 1969, p. 42–43.

6. Alexis de Tocqueville. *Democracy in America.* Translated by Arthur Goldhammer. New York: The Library of America, 2004, p. 633–634.

7. Ernest Duvergier de Hauranne. *A Frenchman in Lincoln America.* Huit mois en Amérique, Lettres et notes de voyage, translation and introduction by Ralph H. Bowen and Albert Krebs. Chicago: R.R. Donnelley and Sons Company, 1974, p. 346–347.

8. *Ibid.,* p. 349.

9. *Ibid.,* p. 349–352.

10. *Ibid.,* p. XLVII–XLVIII.

11. *Ibid.,* p. XLIX, L.

12. *Ibid.,* p. LIII.

13. *Ibid.,* p. LIV.

14. On the subject of the construction of meaning in societies, Cf. Clifford Geertz. *The Interpretation of Cultures.* New York: Basic Books Inc., 1973.

15. The most recent of these studies is by Bernard Henri Lévy, *American Vertigo: Traveling America in the footsteps of Tocqueville.* New York: Random House, 2006.

16. Michael Lind. *The Next American Nation. The New Nationalism and the Fourth American Revolution.* New York: Fee Press, 1995, p. 19–20.

17. Emmanuel Todd. *After the Empire. The Breakdown of the American Order.* New York: Columbia University Press, 2006, p. XVIII.

18. *Ibid.,* p. XXIII, 11, 21

19. Jean-François Revel. *Anti-Americanism.* Translated by Diarmid Cammell. San Francisco: Encounter Books, 2003, p. 62.

20. Michael Brenner, Guillaume Parmentier. *Reconcilable Differences. US-French Relations in the New Era.* Washington D.C.: Brookings Institution Press, 2002, p. 2.

21. *Ibid.*, p. 116.

22. Joseph S. Nye. *The Paradox of American Power: Why the World's Only Superpower Can't Go It Alone.* New York: Oxford University Press, 2003.

23. Robert Kagan. *Of Paradise and Power. America and Europe in the New World Order.* New York: Alfred A. Knopf, 2003, p. 95.

24. Jean-François Revel, *Op. Cit.*, p. 53–54.

25. Stephen Ambrose. *D-Day June 6, 1944: The Climatic Battle of World War II.* New York: Simon and Schuster, 1994, p. 10.

26. Phil Nordyke. *All American All the Way. The Combat History of the 82nd Airborne Division in World War II.* St. Paul: Zenith Press, 2005. p, 213–214.

27. *Ibid.*, p. 221.

28. Gerald Astor. June 6, 1944. *The Voices of D-Day.* New York: St. Martin's Press, 1994, p. 188.

29. *Ibid.*, p. 190–191.

30. Julian Jackson. *The Fall of France. The Nazi Invasion of 1940.* Oxford: Oxford University Press, 2003, p. 235–236.

31. This passage is taken from Charles de Gaulle's Radio Address made on June 18, 1940 to call for the continuation of Resistance against the German occupation of France.

32. Jean Lacouture. *De Gaulle. The Rebel 1890–1944.* New York: Harper Collins Publishers, 1990, p. 413.

33. Jacques Chirac. Address made during the Commemoration Ceremony of the landing in Normandy at Omaha Beach in Colleville-sur-Mer on June 6, 2005.

34. Ronald Reagan. Address made during the Commemoration Ceremony of the landing in Normandy at Omaha Beach in Colleville-sur-Mer on June 6, 1984.

35. Dominique de Villepin. Address made at the United Nations Security Council in New York on February 14, 2003.

36. Jean-François Revel, *Op. Cit.*, p. 30.

37. André Comte-Sponville. *Le capitalisme est-il moral?* Paris: Albin Michel, 2004.

38. Samuel P. Huntington. *The Clash of Civilizations and the Remaking of World Order.* New York: Simon & Schuster, 1998.

39. Alexis de Tocqueville. *Democracy in America.* Translated by Arthur Goldhammer. New York: The Library of America, 2004, pp. 479–480.

40. *Ibid.*, p. 389–391.

41. *Ibid.*, p. 393–394.

42. Dwight Eisenhower. Farewell Speech given as President of the United States on January 17, 1961.

43. Paul Valéry: "The Crisis of the Mind", *Complete Works*. New York: Pantheon Books, 1962, p. 24.

44. *Ibid.*, p. 25.

Chapter 1
Landing on D-Day and Beyond

All the interviews transcribed in this book were made from August 2005 to May 2007. In the first chapter, I examine the relation between France and the United States from the perspective of the veterans who landed in Normandy on June 6, 1944. The first four interviews were held in the Blue Ridge Mountain region of Virginia, in the city of Roanoke, at the annual reunion of the D Company 116th Regiment, 29th Division. Bob Slaughter and Bill Simms depict the life in the 1930s in this city from where a number of young men would be part of the initial assault wave at Omaha Beach in the early morning of D-Day. Along the lines of Bob Slaughter, Charles Neighbor from E Company discusses his landing at Omaha and his return to Normandy. David Silva evokes D-Day through his personal spiritual calling, the prism of the changes that have taken place in America since WWII, and the dialogues among cultures in a post-September 11 world.

The following interviews were conducted at the 59th Annual Convention of the 82nd Airborne Division Association in Milwaukee, Wisconsin. The four veterans recount their landings in the early morning of June 6, 1944 near the city of Sainte Mère Église and the fierce battles that followed. Frank Bilich narrates his upbringing in Chicago and his friendship with the mayor of the French town he helped liberate. He also recalls the first month of combat after D-Day and the death of Bob Niland, with whom he fought and whose brother is portrayed in the film *Saving Private Ryan*. Wesley Ko describes his experience as a platoon leader on D-Day as well as the different battlegrounds of Europe from a Chinese-American perspective. Both he and Matt Wojtaszek discuss the purpose of their involvement in Normandy and the current presence of the American military in Iraq. Bill Tucker pursues this reflection in the context of his witnessing of past and present French-American relations since 1944 through his participation in the John F. Kennedy administration and his frequent visits to Normandy over the past decades.

Robert Slaughter

ETM: You landed at Omaha Beach in the early hours of June 6, 1944. There is a D-Day memorial in Bedford, Virginia, a few miles from where we are, and you were one of the founders of that memorial, one of the few people who made it happen. Could you tell us a little bit about this memorial? Many of the veterans of the 116th Regiment, 29th Division, of which you were part who landed in the first waves and died on D-Day, came like you from the Roanoke and Bedford region.

RS: The Memorial was built in 2001. As the years and decades passed, after we got back from the war, I felt that people were beginning to forget about World War II and since we lost 20 men from Roanoke and 19 from Bedford on D-Day, I didn't think it was fair for people to just ignore what these heroes had done in 1944. So, I started thinking about some way to commemorate the event, and talking to one another, we decided that maybe some kind of memorial in downtown Roanoke, some statue, might be the proper thing to have. We got into it, and some of the men that we selected to be on the committee felt that D-Day was the largest air and sea battle ever fought and that we could not just build a statue. It had to be something with more grandeur. So then we started thinking about something large, and eventually we hired an architect who came up with a plan for a monument, a huge monument. This was after Bedford had offered us the land, you know the 88 acres.

ETM: This monument, I understand, is built just right next to a school so the students can visit the area at any time, and many school children come from the state and perhaps out of state. I even heard that students have come from Normandy.

RS: O sure, yes. The purpose of this memorial is to remember. It's something that they will take with them. It's part of the heritage of this country.

ETM: Alex Kershaw who wrote the forward to your book *Omaha Beach and Beyond* said that the morning of June 6, 1944 was America's finest hour.

RS: Yes, we the people who sacrificed over there think that it is. We didn't do it for ourselves or for glory or anything like that; we did it mainly for each other and also because it was something that had to be done. It was for our country, but it was also to fight and defeat a regime. I remember when we first went to the service, I was by myself. I didn't enlist to go to war. I didn't realize we were going. I knew that Europe was at war but I didn't think that we were going to get involved; after I joined the National Guard, we were inducted into the federal service for one year of intense training and I thought that we would return home and resume our lives. Instead, Pearl Harbor and December 7, 1941 happened, which threw us into a global conflict.

ETM: The 116th Regiment lost from 800 to 1000 men on D-Day. You knew many of the people in the company. What was it like to grow up with some in Roanoke, Virginia?

RS: Well, I knew all of them. They were people I grew up with and joined the army with. With the Great Depression of the 20's and 30's, everybody suffered, even the people who were used to being wealthy. Jobs became scarce and people were going hungry. There were children that couldn't have the things that we have today and we didn't have much more than just an existence. My father had a very good job in Bristol, Tennessee, but when the Depression hit, he lost it. He was in the lumber business which was hit hard. I was only twelve when I moved to Roanoke. We played sports. I was the pitcher on the baseball team. We also worked cutting somebody's lawn or doing some odd jobs for neighbors. The other folks with me in Normandy were just like we were, just ordinary boys who grew up in an impoverished neighborhood. Jack Ingram, George Johnson and some others I grew up with ran around together and joined the National Guard together. Medron Patterson was the fellow who talked to me into joining the National Guard, which I joined in August 1940.

ETM: But you were fifteen?

RS: I was fifteen years old and I turned 16 on February 3, 1941, the day that we were inducted into federal service. I fibbed a little bit because I was supposed to be eighteen. But, I was tall. I was 6 feet 2. We would get a dollar for each drill and in the summer time we would go to Virginia Beach and we would drill, getting a couple hours off everyday to go swimming in the ocean or fishing or whatever. We were sent to England in October of 1942. We learned much later that we were going to land on D-Day in the first wave when we were being briefed at the embarkation area. They kept us in the dark about our mission. When we were finally briefed, we were in this great big tent and they had these sand table models of Omaha Beach, and it looked just like what we saw on D-Day.

ETM: But it was not like what you would expect?

RS: No, we didn't; the storm came up and that changed everything. But with those troops that we faced, and the terrain the way it was, we were going to catch hell anyway.

ETM: You also learned about your father's death in Normandy. It must have been a terrible loss and you must have wondered about your mother also.

RS: That was my biggest concern but, you know, I had seen so much death and destruction and it really didn't sink in too much that I was losing my father forever and I would never see him again. It just didn't register. I had gotten myself into a mode, I guess, that death didn't mean that much.

ETM: What was the feeling about the day, about being there? Eisenhower had talked about a crusade, what was to be done. There is an episode which really touched me when you talked about Stanley Koryciak.

RS: Stanley was a good soldier. He was a tough little guy. He was probably about 5'7", weighed about 140 pounds; he was built, he had broad shoulders, a good athlete and a very likeable guy; everybody liked him. But we got into tough fighting; he began to act funny, you know. He cried, you know, just anything would make him cry. I wasn't with him all the time so I didn't know all this, but people came to me and said: "Stan is not doing well; you need to send him back and give him a rest." So I told the lieutenant, we need to let him go back and get himself together. And so, Stan went behind our line and there, he shot himself; he took off his shoes and just blew the top of his head off.

ETM: For you, he is an American hero; it was said that he had died in action.

RS: You see, that was a court martial offense to shoot yourself, you know.

ETM: But you consider him a hero because of the struggle, the pain, and because he had reached his limits.

RS: That's all. And we didn't see it. It's our fault not his.

ETM: This is what makes this generation great: you pushed yourself to the brink of rupture for a cause that was noble.

RS: Yea, that's right. We all ended up in bad shape, but you just got to keep going because you know, you have to.

ETM: There is a picture of you walking down the Champs-Elysées in Paris with the veterans thirteen years ago in 1994. What does D-Day represent for you 63 years later?

RS: June 6, 1944 was the beginning of the end for the Germans, and for World War II, because everything changed after D-Day. It was a great honor to walk down the largest avenue in Paris. In 1940, the Germans had marched this way toward France and we were marching the other way four years later, to wash the slate clean of the Nazis. Instead of them coming and taking over Europe, we liberated Europe.

ETM: And I saw another picture where you are walking for a ceremony with school children.

RS: Yes, that was in St. Lô. That was done in a symbol of friendship for Americans who liberated Europe, a friendship with the new generation of children, you know, and it was a great honor for us. Retuning to France after all these years has been a wonderful experience. Right after the war, I wasn't quite sure whether the people of France or the people of Europe appreciated what we did. I just didn't know. I didn't see any sign from them of wanting to thank us for it. But then when we finally got a chance to go to France, oh my, it changed. It was so much different because the people wanted to show their friendship and they wanted to express their thanks. And I for one really appreciated it; and everybody did.

ETM: So, given your Normandy experience and return, how do you feel about French-American relations today?

RS: Well I was a little disappointed by Chirac, you know; but now, looking back, he was right and we were wrong. That's my opinion. I think we should have stayed out of the thing as long as we possibly could and we definitely needed to have a coalition of all the allies before we went there and try to do something like that alone. Chirac could see that and we couldn't. George Bush wanted to go into that war and he wanted to be a hero, be a war time leader and be in the history books. And Chirac wanted to save his country and his life and soldiers.

ETM: They saw it from a different perspective.

RS: Well, you know, Chirac knows what war is like. He has lived in a country that had been in war several times and Bush has never seen anything like that. And he didn't know what he was getting into. This country is a much different country. We weren't a superpower back before the war. In World War

II, I think, we changed into a world leader. Our country led the world in a lot of ways. I could remember when downtown Roanoke was not the beautiful city that we have now. There was a lot of poverty. You could tell the stores were empty; the buildings were in bad shape, but after World War II, people started building and reconstructing, the infrastructure, you know the roads, the interstate highways and things like that, that brought more commerce.

ETM: And power brings responsibility.

RS: Yes, that's right, it does. After September 11, we should have gone to Afghanistan and gone after Osama Bin Laden instead of getting into Iraq. Iraq wasn't the right war for us. George Bush wants to change Iraq into a democracy thinking that it would spread over the Middle East. That has not happened. Those people have been the way they are for a long time; they're not going to change and I don't think we can do anything about it and we're just making a lot of enemies in the world by doing what we're doing. If someone or a country blew up buildings like they did with airplanes or if they were to drop an atomic bomb, a dirty bomb, in one of the big cities, that would be a reason to go to war. I think we need to keep the coalition alive. England, France, you know Germany, even Russia if we can. I don't know about Russia, but I think we need to keep the coalition and try to make it so that the world is safer instead of being ready to blow up.

ETM: What are your hopes for humanity in the future?

RS: We have to be strong, we have to stay strong; a peaceful world, peace at all costs, almost; and freedom for everybody. It may not happen in certain parts of the world but that would be a goal. But you do it diplomatically, not with a rifle, and I think also that we need to work with the other European countries and our friends. I don't know whether global warming is a fact or not but why take a chance? I think that if we could all get together, it wouldn't hurt to clean the air and the dirty water in our lakes and rivers. It can only happen with everybody doing their part. If we do our part and nobody else does, it doesn't do any good. It has to be everybody. The best thing we can do is to make sure that we don't have another war. I think that would honor the dead more than anything, you know, if we have a peaceful, happy world. We also should remember these men and women who died through the ceremonies and memorials, like the one we have in Bedford, and through teaching in schools. We need to teach children what caused this thing and how we can prevent it from happening again.

Bill Simms

BS: I taught a lot of these guys from the 116th Regiment, 29th Division, in basic training. I don't want any credit for the win; the hardship, ok. I remember when Bob came into the D Company in 1942. I had joined the company in 1939 and I was sergeant at the time. I was born right here in this city, Roanoke, Virginia, on March 11, 1922. Then in 1939, I joined the National Guard. Things were getting rough in Europe, and in about 1938–1939, Hitler was going around in a rampage. President Roosevelt in 1941 mobilized all the National Guards into federal service for a year of compulsory military training. We left Roanoke, Virginia and went to Fort Meade, Maryland. The 29th Division was made up of units from Virginia, Maryland, and parts of the District of Columbia. In 1942, when I graduated, I was transferred to train people in the 98th Division.

ETM: You tell me that you are not the one who should get the credit. But you have known each other now for over seventy years.

BS: I tell you, I get overwhelmed to think about it, but these are my dear friends. I was in a lot of units in the military, but this is the only unit that I took part in, in any manner. The rest of them had no desire to meet after the war. But we have known each other since we were teenagers and are dear friends. I don't know whether you know it but my brother Jack Simms talked to me into joining this D Company and he lost his life with them on D-Day. It's just a special group; there is unity, a bond between us.

ETM: Could you tell us about your brother Jack Simms? How did he lose his life on D-Day?

BS: My brother was seven years older than I. He was already a member of D Company and he got hit on the beach June 6, 1944 along with a lot of other guys. Richard Atkins said that he was right there next to my brother when he got hit. I learned of his passing three or four weeks later. First you get a notice that they're missing in action and then you get the details later on. Both of my parents were deceased. When I was eleven months old my father passed away and six years later my mother followed. My brother was buried in France and my older brother at that time had his remains brought to Roanoke after the war, in one of the local cemeteries. We all grew up during the Depression; times were tough, no money. All these gentlemen that we are talking about were growing up under the same circumstances as I was. So, we had something in common in that respect and I found that they were great guys. I'm proud of all of them and to me, they're heroes. I remember well when Bob came the first time to a drill at the armory here in Roanoke. He was one of the tallest guys in the company and some of us said that he might be a target being that tall, but he just turned out to be a great individual and we love him.

ETM: What does it mean to be from Virginia? Is it different than coming from New York or other places in the country?

BS: There's a lot differences between New York and Virginia, and California, and Texas. What it boils down to is upbringing and morals and love of family. There was a Depression going on at that time, but we did not know it; we were already poor. The Depression was a great lesson, but we got along. We grew up and we were jolly and we greeted our neighbors, shook hands, joked and made life pleasant. Now life's moving a lot faster and I assume that's a necessity. But we talked to each other and it seems like the pace has increased considerably today. They don't have time, the pace is too fast. That's my opinion, but when you're eighty-five years old, you sort of sit back and watch. You think, but you don't express yourself as you did before. You don't get on a soap box because it's too hard to get on a soap box.

ETM: Are you optimistic about this country, about the youth of this country?

BS: When it comes to this response, the youth will respond in an advantageous manner if they're put to the test. I think that will be the outcome. I think that you should never forget what the veterans have done and what they mean to this country. It should maybe not be the uppermost but at least in the back of each person's mind. Words cannot express what I think about the role the veterans have played in this country.

ETM: How do we live a life that is worth their sacrifice?

BS: When a person gets up in the morning, and spends the day thinking not of what he can do for his own gain but what he can do for his country itself and be unselfish, I think we will be better off.

ETM: This reminds me of what John F. Kennedy said: "Ask not what your country can do for you; ask what you can do for your country."

BS: That is a good expression. He gave a lot. He gave his life too for what he believed in; not what he could do for himself, but what he could do for his country. Somebody out there took issue with that. Now who would take issue with that statement?

ETM: What do you think makes a good leader?

BS: Unselfishness, resourcefulness, firm belief, compassion for other people's feelings, personality. That's what makes a good leader.

ETM: Did Eisenhower and FDR exemplify these values, these qualities?

BS: I think so. FDR was the savior of this country. Both turned the country around and were great leaders.

ETM: Your brother, Jack Simms, died on D-Day at Omaha Beach in Normandy. He gave his life for his country and other people around the world for them to be free. Do you have a message to convey to the youth of France?

BS: There are reunions and commemorations every year in France whose government thanked the veterans on many occasions. There are thousands of veterans who go to Normandy to commemorate D-Day. This is today the 20th reunion of the 116th Regiment veterans of WWII and I am having a wonderful time and I'm also happy to take part in your program here. Well, we were in a bind when France came to our assistance and when France was in a bind, we came to their assistance. That showed friendship, and I hope it continues, and may God bless America and God bless France!

Charles Neighbor

CN: There was a storm right before the D-Day landing and when our boat left, we drifted to the East quite a bit. So, we were about two miles East of where we should have landed, in the vicinity of where elements of the 1st Division landed. I was born and raised in Iola, Kansas, in the southeast part of the state, about 40 miles from the Missouri line and 50 miles from Oklahoma. It was primarily a rural community. We grew corn in the area, small grain crops, oats and wheat. I graduated from high school and was going to college when the war broke out. I was drafted and had basic training in Texas. As a general draftee, I did basic training before we went to Europe. Well, we didn't know where we were going.

ETM: Was D-Day the first theater of operation in which you were involved?

CN: Oh yes. I joined the 116th Regiment, 29th Division in February 1944 so I was enlisted with the company for about four months before the landing. It was also my first experience outside of the Kansas, Missouri, Oklahoma area and my introduction to the world. And during the campaign, we didn't have much time to get around. On D-Day, we landed at about 6:30am. We were fortunate to land much further East, because the concentration of Germans wasn't quite as intense, and we landed with elements of the 1st Division. So it helped us out in a way. When we landed, there was a bunker up on the cliff in front of us and we got arms and mortar fire from the pill box. We joined the elements of the 1st Division with mortars and so forth until we were able to neutralize it.

I was the assistant to the flame thrower and not long after we landed the guy that I was with got hit and I took over for him. I also had my rifle, so finally I got permission to take off the flame thrower after we captured some Germans.

ETM: How soon were you able to get off the beach?

CN: We had two officers with us and they couldn't tell where we were but they decided that the best thing to do was to go forward and we went across the fields on the other side where there were mines, arriving at a big villa, or a chateau. It was under attack by another group on our side. We went in that area and, shortly after, we reached an important crossroad. One of our guys who was walking down the road with a radio said that we were outside of Colleville and that they were expecting an air strike at about 10 o'clock. It was about 10 o'clock. We stayed outside the city, which I think was liberated the same day by other units, and decided just to go forward. We messed up ahead with the Germans and then drew back some place else. After we returned to our company, we went into battle at Saint Clair. That's when we realized that D-Day wasn't the end of this and we had a rather bitter battle there. Actually, for me, it was worse. We had several days of really intense activity with frequent mortar bombardment. I also remember being in Couvains about ten days after the landing where we took a defense position.

ETM: Did you return to Normandy?

CN: The first time I returned was in 1983, a year before the 40th anniversary. I returned there as a tourist with my wife. And I guess it was this trip that rekindled my interest in the war experience and I was able to hook up with the association. The first reunion of the 116th Regiment veterans was around 1984.

ETM: How do you feel about having been part of D-Day? Do you have a sense of appreciation for what you did for this country?

CN: I don't think so really. You know, right when I came back after the war and I went to college, we had all these fly boys talking about all their air raids and all their glory. But, we did our job. I went back to college after the war and became a mechanical engineer. I started my work in Kansas and ended up on the east coast in Baltimore, Maryland, and then I was transferred to Roanoke. Right after D-Day we were aware that the A Company of our regiment had been disseminated; some members of our E Company were sent to refurbish the A

Company. When we got to the battle of Saint Lô, I think kind of got a real feel for what the significance of all this was. We knew we had to take Saint Lô and I didn't make it there because I got wounded. I was hit I think on July 13 by a mortar shell. I got this scar on my face and so forth. I was out until November. I had a diaphragm puncture too and I was out for four months.

ETM: So, you came back in November before the Battle of the Bulge?

CN: Well, the 29th had some very difficult battles just before I got back to the company. So, by the time I got there, the company was not more than two platoons. So, when the Battle of the Bulge came they left us there on a defense position to the north by the Roer River. One day, we learned that there was a farm house where two or three families were hiding in the basement that had been destroyed. We spent a day to bring the families back to a place where they could be safe. That was about the only time that we saw civilians in the area. They were very close to the front line. The men had gone to look for food, so women and children were there, one about twelve years old and the rest of them very small. It was a nice relief for them. We waited for the men to return and we took them out.

ETM: What was your experience when you returned to Normandy?

CN: We went back in 1994 and then in 2004 and that made all the difference in the world because it put an entirely different cast on the whole experience. It made it feel a lot better to have made that landing. The people in Saint Lô and in Normandy in general welcomed us with open arms. And the last time we went back in 2004, we stayed with a French family, which was a great experience. The first time I went, we stayed in a hotel and we really didn't get to communicate or mingle with the people. The second time was so much better. We developed a sister city relationship between Saint Lô and Roanoke and we also had groups of people coming from Saint Lô to Roanoke stay in their homes. That was after 1994, so it just opened the groundwork for doing this in 2004. And then children from Roanoke went to Normandy as well. During our last visit, we stayed for three or four days and my son and sister were with me. My sister stayed with one family and my son and I stayed with another family. They were close together; they communicated, and we cooperated about going to the meetings and for what we would do each day. We took our hosts to dinner because they had to tell us where to go and they had dinners for us while we there. So it was just great. The people who hosted us were born shortly after the war. One day they took us to a place where we had crepes with ham and cheese, and some with cider. That was a great experience.

ETM: This close relation has lasted for a long time, but you have a question.

CN: Well, I'm 82 and I'm one of the younger ones. The French Revolution came shortly after the American Revolution. You are from the Southwest. Is that feeling of friendship still continuing to grow? We felt since the Iraq war that things were uneasy between France and the U.S.

ETM: Yes, I think that it is still there; there is a reciprocal respect and awareness that we need to work together. The GIs from the region from Roanoke and Bedford played a very important role on D-Day, and this is why I wanted to be here and met them. With respect to Iraq, there was perhaps the ability to win the war, but the Administration did not seem prepared to win the peace.

CN: That never even entered the equation. They had not done their homework properly to get ready for this war.

ETM: And the French officials said when you talk to your friends, you have to tell them how you see things. You have to be honest. When they were debating in the parliament about this, Prime Minister Raffarin said that it was hard to say no to our American friends, but they felt that they had to do it because when you talk to your friends, you have to say what you think; you have to be able to say what you believe. The French had this experience in the Muslim world that the Americans did not have and they had a different understanding of the complexity of the issues with the Sunnis, the Shiites, and the parties involved.

CN: Basically, we had no understanding.

ETM: I think that there was a different understanding. They did not measure the difficulty that it would bring in the same way. It is very complex because many people say we should not have been there and leave, but many others believe that we should not leave. I understand the American administration's position and how the American people think. The new French president said several times during his campaign that he had great admiration for this country and that both countries agreed today on a broad range of issues. He said that we had much in common in terms of how we think and what we do. And he was elected so it shows that France is not anti-American.

CN: I knew that the people never were.

ETM: There are differences, but the two countries are very close not only diplomatically but in terms of security. Even four years ago when they disagreed, the agencies continued to work closely together. So, it has been a friendship that has evolved a long time and will continue.

CN: I'll always have a real close feeling for French people. I also have met people in Paris when we were there in 2004. We stayed at a hotel near the airport. And one night, my sister and I went to a French restaurant, not a tourist place. We had supper, and I realized that there wasn't much difference there from the people in Normandy. I had a good feeling from this experience.

ETM: When you travel in France, in most places, people are very friendly. So I'm very happy to have had this conversation.

CN: I am glad too. I feel warm about the whole situation. I hope you got some good information. When one man cuts an elephant's nose and gives it to a blind man, the blind man has the impression that he is given a hose. And when this blind man gets the leg of the elephant, he has another impression of the elephant. So from a very narrow form of knowledge, he has a vast array of impressions and ideas about what an elephant is like.

ETM: Television and technology provide information but it is always limited information. We need to keep this in mind. There is nothing better, in order to know people, than to visit the place where they live and know them personally.

CN: We live here in the United States, separated by an ocean; we don't have a close interrelationship and interconnectedness with European and other countries. Incidentally, I have a son who lives in Scotland. He is married to a Scottish woman. So, they visit from time to time.

David Silva

DS: I landed on D-Day at Omaha Beach around 7am. I don't know how the boats held on the water to tell you the truth. We were about thirty men on that boat and there were about four boats for each company. We were loaded on one and we didn't see the rest of them after that. We didn't quite know what to expect because it was the first time for all of us. We probably had the same feeling when the boat came to the point where the rafts came down and we all had to move out. We hoped and prayed that we were in knee deep water. And fortunately for us, when we landed, we were able to at least get off and start walking. The first thing that happened was that the machine gun fire was coming our way because you could see the ripples in the water. It was very heavy fire too. I just said to myself, well there's only one thing I can do. I'll have to crawl through the water so they don't see me, you know, standing up. So, I started crawling and that's what I was doing so that I wouldn't be hit too badly. After I reached the shore, I saw a sea wall, maybe four to five feet high, and it was only then that I realized I had been hit. But the salt water has a healing effect; I didn't have any serious wounds. I had to take care of my own wounds because there was nobody available to do that.

ETM: What was the wound that you received?

DS: The wound was received in the leg. Bullets came down through the pack in the back, and they were deflected down through the water I was carrying and clipped the side of that container. They didn't go through, so the water didn't come out, but all the bullets went through my pack, and didn't touch me until they got down to the calf since the calf is soft because there are no bones there. So fortunately, there was nothing but bleeding. It was a small injury. From the time I put my foot on the ground to the shore I had gone about 100 feet. I think the tide was moving in, if I'm not mistaken, but I was able to move in and I fortunately found a sea wall which was the only one around. A number of us just stayed behind that sea wall for most of the day, because the casualties among our officers were very heavy; we didn't know that until afterwards when we learned that the number of casualties on Omaha Beach were pretty serious.

ETM: It was a safe place.

DS: It was safe, yes, it was solid. Only mortars could have reached it but it's very difficult to hit somebody with a mortar because one sees them fire up in the air. There were already dead bodies in the water. They had come a few minutes earlier. They were the rifle men from our company. There were three units of rifle men in every battalion. We were the heavy weapons people, so our object was to defend if a serious counter attack came. But the casualties were so high that we could see the bodies when we got off the boat. You could see the bodies floating in the water.

ETM: That came as a shock.

DS: It did, and it almost spelled a disaster. The casualties were heavy.

ETM: You didn't know whether you could make it at all, or whether the landing had been successful.

DS: Well that's true and it almost seems like a miracle that we were able to get there. Other units in different areas didn't have the same problem. We stayed there behind that wall until late afternoon. By that time tanks had been able to come on the sand, and they were kind of running up and down, actually pin pointing where they were firing from, and they made the Germans decide to move back. This was after about five, six, seven hours that we had been there. So by the middle of the afternoon, things were looking better. Tanks played a role but it was not at the time of the landing. Many of them drowned because it was rough water and the imbalance of the tank could not overcome that.

ETM: But when you saw these casualties, there must have been despair and discouragement.

DS: A lot of it. It was terrible because they were up, scattered up on the beach when the tide came in.

ETM: How did the campaign go after that? Were you involved at Saint Lô?

DS: Not directly into the city itself, but the approach triggered probably one of the heaviest amount of casualties that we had, a lot of casualties. I didn't myself experience any casualties. We were really pinned down. Some must have found some holes in the hedge rows; they offered protection too when you ran through the area and got into combat situation. We had to go along and therefore, we did have casualties, though not as many as we had on the beach.

ETM: Did you meet any French people during the course of the campaign in Normandy and then later on?

DS: People would come out, you know, and offer us cider because they knew we were there, and I think that they were pleased that we weren't Germans. They treated us like, you know, we were their own people and we enjoyed that too, but we didn't make many friends among them because we were pitching and moving at that time. Some of them had probably fled, but there were some who stayed. And then after that, we had to go to Brest. There were maybe forty, fifty thousand Germans up there and that was a second battle for us. There were German Panzers with U-Boat in the area, so it had to be all cleaned up and I think there was more than one division there beside us. I think there was some street fighting, but because of our heavy weapons we didn't get into it unless we were defending some troops, because they had to retreat and we would use our fire power when necessary. But we used it very seldom because of the great danger of hitting some of our own people in the back, you know. So you could not have used the weapons when they were making progress. We could only fire in the flanks of the offensive. Their problem was that the Germans, in the next hedge rows, could see them coming. It was greatly difficult for them to head on because they would be in danger of getting killed.

ETM: They counted on your support.

DS: Yes, they did. In the beginning, there were so many casualties from the landings at Omaha Beach that it took a few days to get replacements from the casualties and the wounded. That was difficult, but that was in the earlier part; once we had the beach secured and there were other areas of the country, of Normandy where they could come safely bring replacements, it was better.

ETM: What was the most horrific battle in which you were engaged?

DS: I think the progress that we were trying to make through Vire, Normandy, was a tough one. It was not too far from the coast, a little bit to the West I think from where we landed. It was difficult because the Germans were able to pin us down to the point where we couldn't advance. We had to have air power to support us and it was very difficult to carry our heavy weapons and use them at that time. There was a lot of fire power during this battle. The Germans were really hanging on to Vire. They didn't want to let it go. We didn't see civilians there at all. They must have left and I don't really know what happened to them. Much later, I remember going through the Siegfried line, but there was no problem there. The Germans had retreated.

ETM: I note that your original full name is Silva Gaspar.

DS: That was a name my grandfather came up with when he came to the U.S. because he came in hiding on a boat. My grandfather originally came from Portugal. I knew him fairly well. He lived not too far from where we lived. He immigrated to America in the 19th Century. I think that he and my grandmother could speak Portuguese but she was not full Portuguese; she was a mixture of nationalities. Unfortunately, I did not grow up in the Portuguese tradition because I didn't see my grandfather often, but I knew him really well. They lived with us for a while.

ETM: I learned from another veteran attending the reunion that you are a man of faith. What was the ultimate purpose of June 6, 1944 and how does it compare to September 11? What should be our answer to September 11?

DS: I think that Normandy was a turning point in the war because the Germans had taken so much of the beating. It was foolish for them to continue. I thought the war would then end. When we landed on the beach, the Germans were desperate. They had sent old men on the line and even children of sixteen and seventeen years of age, youngsters. I saw that very soon after we landed. There are all their troops standing close to Britanny, a hundred and some thousand, waiting, waiting and waiting. Hitler would not release them. They didn't have enough forces and we had a lot of forces. You mentioned September 11 and I think the only response to it is that it is something that we could never have possibly known would happen. It was the first time in the history of America that we ever had people in airplanes used as weapons dying for what they must have thought was a cause. That was the excuse for us going to war. I don't think we would have gone to war without this event, casualties caused by airplanes loaded with gasoline. They wanted to hit the U.S. and even maybe the White House and some of the buildings there. It is what made war possible, the terrible war that we're in now, because the same weapons they used to fly the airplanes are now used individually as weapons of terror, destroying their own lives in the process. That's what they are doing. All casualties for Americans now are mostly invisible ones, on the roadside. Our greatest enemies are the ones that are supplying this. They're not even called soldiers as in WWII. They wear no uniforms. They're not even individual citizens either.

ETM: Does it mean that our approach should be different?

DS: I don't know, the protest is I think what really makes it terrible. The fact now is that Americans want the end of the war. If we do end it, the Iraqi people will be fighting against each other and there will almost certainly be civil war. I don't know how that's going to work out. It's a very difficult thing. I would hope that September 11 offered opportunities for our people to understand that we have to protect our own country because we feel that, with the war that is going on over there, terrorists would take every effort to come and do the same thing in our country that they're doing to our soldiers who are in a foreign land. I think so. But I am not too sure about the young people. There has been a cultural change in America. When I was a young, everything was relatively safe, families were strong, and people had a sense of good over evil. Today, you see some of these fancy people, the way they are acting up, ruining their own lives; they don't know what they are doing. They are in their 20s, early 20s, but it seems like they publicize themselves just to give themselves away and then their lives are ruined. I mean it's really difficult to deal with, but the girls are the bigger problem, the young women out of high school. There's no respect in the world, in our country. There are a lot of wonderful people, but the culture has changed. You never felt any danger before to be attacked in your own city by somebody. I don't know what's wrong with them; they snatch people and sometimes rape women, and it's just not a good era for young people today unless they have had good parenting and they have a good education. But there are too many others that don't make much money and cause trouble and there's gang fighting and things like that. The culture has made society unsafe.

ETM: Yet this country has been seen as a land of promise.

DS: I think that people have to become more and more aware of the evils being done and of the responsibilities that all parents have to their children. That has to change; if you could change it, it would be the best thing in the world, but how to do so is another question. The children that are in the schools now, especially in the higher grades, could learn how to take care of children; you have to raise those children properly. I guess we took for granted when we were small you know, that what dad said, mom said had weight and that you did not challenge your parents. But it's a different time in which we're living. I can't put my finger on it; it just seems that morality has disappeared. To try to teach children, it just seems like, the culture just doesn't fit in at all, for some reason. Our culture has changed. I don't know if you ever read about this, but we had in one town not too far from here thirty-two children and a few teachers who were killed at a university. This has happened before and it's usually a student that's very upset because people weren't fair with him or he had a problem at home or whatever it might be. He comes in, just literally by himself to murder, kill, and that's not uncommon.

ETM: Could this climate of violence, could this void, this loss of morality, endanger the fabric of our democracy?

DS: Well, it's a danger because it's a very difficult to deal with. You know. If you take these kids that are seventeen and eighteen, maybe they're younger and sometimes they just go crazy and, you deal a little differently with kids than you would with an adult person, but they cannot be let completely free on their own. They need guidance.

ETM: How do you think America should conduct itself internationally? There is a tradition of generosity in American democracy, for example, the GI Bill and the Marshall Plan after World War II. In that light, how do you see the role of this country with respect to other countries in the world?

DS: Well, I think at that time it seemed like Americans were very willing to help, to do anything to bring about peace among nations. A lot of money was spent bringing Europe back to life. But when our forces went into Iraq, it looked like that was the time for peace to settle down and then rebuild; all of a sudden we had the terrorists moving and the Iraqis fighting among themselves. So, it's very difficult. There is hope to achieve peace. The only thing the President is trying to do is say, we didn't run out and leave the country to itself and its own doing because it would be hell on earth. About whether we should have gone in, there's a lot of questions about that too, which we didn't know ahead of time. If you look at the Germans they had all rebuilt and peace was achieved.

They built back and cleared things up quickly. I am sure it took some time.

ETM: There is the importance of freedom on D-Day. But do you think that liberty has limits, that it cannot be imposed or become a license to do whatever one wants to do? The right of the individual also exists within the necessity of the common good.

DS: Sure. And I think peace is something that we would like to see in the world. But it seems that everybody has their own mind about it. Well, I'm sure my hopes would be for something better. It would be peace really and the peace would come about because people would see how foolish it is to be, not just at war, but to be in a culture that is so contradictory to what would be best not just for Americans, but for the whole world. That's what I say. That's broad. Today we're all concerned about our security, about those who are just coming in to do evil, not good.

ETM: And for someone who has known the atrocity of war, you would hope for peace for the next generations.

DS: I would certainly hope that there's something better than what we currently experience in general and I would hope that the Iraqi problem won't hurt an awful lot of people. There is war in many places and it just seems like they are wars of doctrinaires who just go ahead as much as they can because they're in power. It's not the right kind of power. But you have to find somebody who is going to be the boss I guess.

ETM: Ultimately then, is the U.S. intervention done in the spirit of making peace? It may appear contradictory to some people in the Middle East. Was the intention in Iraq to build democracy and provide what was provided during World War II?

DS: Oh I would hope. It would be an ideal to achieve peace. I think in Europe, after the war, it was peaceful for quite a number of years. Even a lot of the nations in Eastern Europe that are now together like Slovakia, it seems that things are working out pretty good for them. Personally, the French people got along with Americans pretty well in past history; French people gave us the Statue of Liberty, if I'm not mistaken. And I think this had a great influence in our relationship with France over many years. Maybe I'm too hopeful for peace, but I would like to see peace around the world, including the poor ones. So many people have come to America in large numbers with this in mind, and they are happy, in general. There was peace and there were no problems with Poles and the Germans. I don't think there were a lot of French people for some reason in terms of numbers. But I respect the French people very much. People in Normandy treated Americans just like they were their own children; they lived under German occupation for five years and when we went in it was a liberation for them.

ETM: How did you decide to become a priest at the end of the war? Was this decision linked to your war experience?

DS: Not exactly, no, not for the war experience. I had thoughts of it in the sense of, I'd like to be a priest, but I didn't talk to anybody about it, you know; that is in the seminary. I didn't have any friends in the seminary. So, the only way I approached this, and this was in my own mind, was that if I lived through this war, I would enter the seminary if they accepted me. And the soldiers that I was with all knew that I had wanted to be a priest. And it worked out fine. In fact, they were in awe of that, and they would ask: would you have a smoke, after the war is over if we're all still together, I'll have a smoke. But I didn't smoke at all. I was nineteen; I just turned nineteen in March of 1944.

ETM: Did you think about the commandment of not to kill?

DS: Well, circumstances probably prevented me from getting into much opportunity to shoot and kill enemy combatants. We fought about 1000 to 1500 feet away; so you would never know if you'd hit anybody. And of course it was the same way with the mortars. I didn't fire mortars at all. I was a machine gun person, but that didn't affect me too much because they were doing the same things to us. Because of being Catholic, some of us went to what we call confession. I'm sure that there's a need very definitely for a more spiritual world today. I would say that when this occurs people seem to have more of a handle on what is the right thing to do especially in avoiding conflicts in general or just arguing with people, to keep peace. The only way you keep peace is not to be one who pushes it too heavily; if they want to talk about it, that's different.

ETM: It's not something you can impose?

DS: No, that would be wrong in the sense that you don't need to impose something like that. The way this war has gone in the Middle East, it seems to me that they don't want to discuss anything that would bring peace. They have never once approached to say that we have a peaceful plan, that we would prefer a peaceful solution to this rather than to kill. I think there are also mainstream people in the Middle East who also want peace, and from what I've gathered, it is said that there's nothing in the Quran that associates the right to kill with the right to go to heaven.

ETM: Could you say that in some ways, what is taking place among these extremist groups relates to the abuses of the Inquisition?

DS: Well, it could go back to those days, but you know, that's another thing that prevents peace because people are hanging on to something that happened hundreds of years ago as if it happened today.

ETM: Yes, but the Inquisition was itself in contradiction with Christian principles.

DS: A lot of it was.

ETM: Would you like to share with us one last recollection from your experience on D-Day?

DS: Though I was wounded on D-Day in Omaha Beach, June 6, 1944, and again the next morning above the beach from artillery fire power from the retreating Germans, I never again was wounded. The pain of those wounds was nothing to the incident of the killing of my best buddy who shared a fox hole with me as we moved from one battle to another. John and I were responsible for two machine guns. Before we moved to capture Saint Lô in late July, we had to dig in for the night. John chose a position on my left; as we were digging in, a stray artillery shell struck John's position. He never knew what happened; he was killed instantly. The pain of a lost friendship is far beyond the pain of battle scars. After the war, I regret that I never was able to find my friend's parents to comfort them. I know that John is in heaven and shares God's love with his parents. Only God knows if I will share a divine friendship with him for all eternity. I always said to my friend that if I lived, I would enter the seminary to become a priest. *Oremus pro invicem!* Let us pray for each other!

Frank Bilich

FB: My father came in 1919 from Dalmatia, Croatia, and my mother came from a place called Ravna Gora which is close to the Italian border. She came in 1922. In those days, marriages were arranged by fathers. My grandfather came here after the war to make a better life for his family. He only had one daughter which was my mother. Unfortunately my grandmother died when my mother was only seventeen. So, immediately he brought her to a little town outside of Chicago called Joliet. He arranged my parents' marriage, and they got married. Then, my father being in construction, my mother had to go everyplace he went. He worked in Iowa on the railroad where my brother John was born. They moved back to Chicago where I was born and two years later my younger brother was born. Basically my first eight or ten years, we lived in a Croatian neighborhood, went to Croatian Church, Croatian schools, and spoke very little English. But when we moved out of the neighborhood, my brothers and I caught on pretty quickly. It was very difficult for my mother because she only spoke Italian and Croatian.

ETM: She had come to this country at age seventeen.

FB: Yes. What made it even worse was that my father died when I was only nine years old. It was the middle of the Depression and my mother had three boys she had to raise. It was pretty rough. She did not work much, but she did crocheting and sewing and she used to sell bedspreads and sheets. She did housework for others, scrubbing floors, doing drapes, house cleaning and maid service. She would send all three of us off to school and do her work, always making sure to be home when we got out of school. It was very hard, very difficult. I've seen times when we didn't have much to eat but she always seemed to put things together.

ETM: Moving forward, could you share with us your D-Day experience? How did it begin?

FB: I enlisted. I didn't wait for the draft. I graduated in high school on January 29, 1943. I went to the Marine Corps and they turned me down. They said I had flat feet and an irregular heart beat. Three days later, I went to the Army and was told again that I had flat feet. I told the officer: "You got a sign outside that says 'Men Wanted'," so he let me go and I left for air corps training. I was in Scott Field about three weeks and they shipped a whole bunch of us to California. I didn't understand what was happening. When I got there I asked to see the company commander. I said: "Somebody made a mistake." He said: "Why?" I said: "I don't belong in the Infantry, I joined the Air Force." He said: "No, the Air Force is a branch of the US Army. You joined the Army and the Army needs you more here." I was pretty disgusted. But, after we were in training about ten weeks, a recruiting group came through and showed us pictures of paratroopers. A couple of us were listening and a friend of mind Benjamin said: "What do you think Frank?" I said: "Let's join." It looked exciting. From there they sent me to Fort Benning for jump school, then Camp McCall and overseas. I joined the 505 in Northern Ireland in December 1943. Then from Ireland we moved to England to prepare for D-Day. The preparation was intense and we were very ready.

ETM: What was your experience flying over the Channel and the coast of France?

FB: I really did not have any apprehension about the jump because we went through the procedure in training: stand up, hook up; stand at the door. I wasn't worried about the jump itself. I had a lot of equipment on me, a little over 100 pounds. But it was my first combat experience so I didn't know what was going to happen on the ground. When I talked to the soldiers who had been through Africa and Sicily, they never really discussed combat. They didn't really talk about it. Their favorite saying was: "You'll know soon enough." Perhaps it was better that we didn't know. In our company, we had a lot of comedians, playing tricks on each other. That was the core of everything I remember. We had a lot of older men too who were 28, 30 and 32 years old who were in the Army before Pearl Harbor.

ETM: There was no fear, just expectation. Did you get any shelling, could you hear anything?

FB: I could hear the bullets and bombing. The company commander was the jumpmaster, then the radio operator, Floyd West, then the first sergeant. I was number four. It was pretty easy when you are in the front of the line to get out. Outside of the noise I heard, I was mainly concentrating to make sure that my chute would open. We jumped around 1am and landed right on the edge of

Sainte Mère Église. There was a two story building there that we used for the battalion aid station. Across the road was an old cow pasture and we landed right on that field where the cows were. We could hear the fighting going on in the town which was just a short way up the road; but our object was to assemble all our equipment and to meet up at a point with the first sergeant. Within 20 minutes, our D Company had its equipment, we were together and right away the order was to move on to Neuville-au Plain. That was the town outside Sainte Mère. We were asked to block the road there and hold that position, and that's what we did.

ETM: So you were not scattered, you were pretty much together. It worked out for you.

FB: D Company was very good. The only company in the second battalion that suffered initially was F Company. The wind drifted them right into the square and a lot of them got killed right in the square.

ETM: That's what we see in *The Longest Day*.

FB: That is correct. We could hear a lot of the fighting going on. In an airborne outfit, they drum this into your head from day one: what the other unit is doing is not important; you have a job to do. If you have three platoons, fine; if you don't have three platoons, you go out with two. Immediately that's what you go out and do. I think we probably jumped from around 400–500 feet because I remember looking to see if my chute was open; I only swung a couple of times and I landed right on the ground. I didn't have a bad landing. The only one of the bunch who got hurt was a guy by the name of Don Ellis. He hurt his ankle pretty bad. He turned to the sergeant and said: "I can't walk." Sergeant Rabig replied: "We're going up to position. I don't care how you get there, if you crawl or not. If you stay here, you're dead." We moved out to that position. By daylight around 5 in the morning, D Company was in position and ready for the Germans.

ETM: That was when you saw the Germans for the first time?

FB: That was the first time. We moved in a position and by daybreak, I heard action behind me and nothing in front of me; so naturally, it was nice and calm and I thought: "This ain't so bad." Then in about fifteen minutes, all hell broke loose. First came the artillery, then came the mortar rounds and we were under attack. It just seemed like it would be one attack, we would repulse them, then another one, and another one. It went on like that all day. We were on our way from Sainte Mère Église to Neuville au Plain, and the Germans chopped up the third platoon. They just about wiped out the whole platoon. That's where Bob Niland died in the rear guard action. They portrayed his brother's life in *Saving Private Ryan*. He was one of the Niland brothers and a mortar sergeant killed in action.

ETM: What was his name?

FB: Robert Niland. The Germans thought we were going to be overrun. Turnbull came down from Neuville and he said "I need all the men I can get." The company commander turned around to us; there were about eight of us dug in there. He said "all you people take your rifles and go with Lieutenant Turnbull, all but the radio operator." So, we all got up and there is a slope that comes down from the field and we got into that field and we started going down that slope and the German artillery opened fire on us. They threw in a couple of rounds. Everybody hit the ground and finally there was a lull for about two or three minutes and John Rabig said that we better got out of there because we were out in the open. The Germans threw some more artillery at us. As we got up to go back to the hedgerows, we started running back and we made it to the ditch and another big barrage hit us. One of the fellows said: "Where is Lieutenant Turnbull?" John Rabig said: "He is dead." He said that when he went past him an artillery shell had taken off the side of his head. We couldn't go forward, so we went back to company headquarters. The company commander asked us to get back in our foxholes; there was another attack coming. What was left of the third platoon tried to withdraw and to pull back. The second platoon and first platoon filled in the gap and they repulsed them. Then the Germans pushed again, that was on D-Day plus 1. They had to overrun us to get to the beach. The only thing that saved us was a forward observer with the Navy. He jumped with us. He had never made a jump in his life. He had a radio pack and he called in artillery support from the USS Nevada and they fired a heavy barrage, a ferocious barrage, and that stopped the German attack.

ETM: That was from the sea.

FB: Yes from the sea. The Germans never hit us again in strength because by that time the beach forces were coming in; actually, they did not reach us until D-Day plus two. By that time, D Company had lost almost the whole third platoon. We had big casualties in the first and second platoons. Normandy really hit us hard. We went in with 161 people and came out with 41. The others died. We had some wounded that we were able to get to the beach, but basically the first couple of days if you got hit bad, it was a sure thing, you were dead, because there was no way they could help you.

ETM: You were on your own for those two days. Were you able to contact some French farmers or civilians or had everyone left?

FB: No. I heard later that some of the other companies had contact with the French. I know that the company commander asked 2nd Lieutenant McLean who was the first platoon leader to try to contact somebody from the beach. He sent two or three people, but the Germans were on the beach, between the beach and us. They were everywhere. They all came back with the same report. Of course, the longer D-Day lasted, the worse it got. The landing troops were supposed to meet us by noon. On that night at midnight, they had barely gotten off the beach.

ETM: You mentioned *Saving Private Ryan* earlier and the brother of the soldier who was portrayed in the film was next to you essentially.

FB: I knew Bob pretty well. He was killed there. In the movie, they go to find his brother Fritz. It was Fritz, Bob, Pete and I don't know who the other one was. Somebody realized that out of the four brothers, three of them had been killed. So they tried to contact Fritz. It is based on a true story. Bob Niland was at the rear guard. He said: "You guys try to get out and I'll try to hold them back." When we came back up through that road on D-Day plus 2 he was laying next to the road, riddled with bullets.

ETM: You had known him before this?

FB: Yes. John Rabig who was first sergeant was my neighbor in Chicago, two doors away. When I joined the company, it was like being with a member of the family. Of course, he was ten years older than me and John and Bob Niland were like this, like two brothers. Of course, when we came up there and John saw him, he broke out in tears, but we couldn't do anything. We had to move to the position to push the Germans out.

ETM: We see in the movie hand-to-hand combat with the Germans. Did you witness this?

FB: That was true. There was some hand-to-hand combat. Normandy was repetitious. You would fight, take a piece of land, the Germans would counter attack. Then you would repulse the attack. Then you would stock up the ammunition. Usually in a firefight, we produced a lot of fire power in front of us to discourage them from breaking through. Sometimes they broke through the platoon's perimeter and we closed the gap. We did not have tanks but we had bazookas. However, most of them could not fully destroy the German armored vehicles, the Tiger tanks. What we did do was that we had a couple of bazooka teams and they did knock out self-propelled guns and the ones situated on half tracks. On that road from Neuville au Plain to Sainte Mère Église, our job was to hold our position and prevent the Germans from moving forward.

ETM: We have not talked about heroes. It is said they are the ones who died fighting.

FB: That is true. We went back to England and the process started all over again. You trained and you knew there was another mission coming up. You know you are going to lose some more friends. You say to yourself: "When is my turn coming? Am I going to be next?" Then, you put it out of your head. Someone gets shot or wounded next to you and you say to yourself: "Well it was him and not me." I am lucky again. It is always in the back of your head; but paratroopers are tough and the most important thing is that you have to take your position and hold it. You have a job to do and that is what you do. That is what you are trained for. When we went back to England, the people met us and were very good to us. When we landed in Liverpool, the civilians came out to help us carry our bags and brought tea out. The sad part was when we came back to Quorn where our base was located. A lot of the fellows dated English girls and they would later come to the pub looking for their boyfriends.

ETM: You held your position in Normandy and what was your feeling when the night came after the first day?

FB: When the night came, we knew that we beat them off quite a few times. I was very fortunate. I was in a company with older men and good officers. We had one officer named Waverly Wray from Mississippi would run up and down the lines. If two men got killed and the position was vacant, we would stretch out, move out and cover that area and make sure we had enough ammunition. That was our biggest problem. We were running out of ammunition. Another couple of hours and if the landing troops hadn't reached us, we would have been overrun. That was D-Day plus 1; we were already scattering up ammunitions from those who had fallen. You reached over and got his ammunition and grenades. That night, they hit us again and of course they weren't sure how many we were. We repulsed a couple of attacks. That went from night to night and the next day was the same thing again. It started with the artillery, then the mortars, and you knew what was coming. Nothing was definite, even the possibility that the Germans could push us back into the sea.

ETM: How long did you stay there in Normandy?

FB: I stayed the full length. I spent the whole 28 days there. We were released on July 8 and they took us to the beach. We didn't have a hot meal, nor did we shave or clean. We did the whole campaign with the same clothes and shoes. When we got to the beach, we had a chance to clean up and wash up before we got on a boat. I am going to tell you something. The Germans were prepared for war. They had the equipment, machine guns, bazookas, artillery, and they were professionally trained. By comparison, I was a civilian, I wasn't a soldier. It made a difference.

ETM: And yet you prevailed. Was it your spirit?

FB: I think so. Our way of thinking was different from the Germans. I had already been exposed to what Germany under Adolph Hitler was like as a young man. I experienced that in high school. I could understand the French people and everybody being subjugated by the Nazis. The American way of life is not that way. We believe in free living. What they stood for was evil. All of us who were in the military, whether in Japan or in Germany, had the same idea; what Hitler was doing was wrong and we had to get rid of him. We were on the right side. And when you have a free mind, you have the advantage no matter what the equipment is. In your head, if you are fighting for something that is more than what the other stands for, the mind beats the machine. In all our training, I never had a doubt about my officers or the men with me. I just knew that if something hit us real bad, the guy next to me was like my brother. He would be right with me. There was a bond there with the paratroopers. It lasts until this day.

ETM: What else should we remember from your experience of D-Day?

FB: Well, the destruction to buildings, the damage that was done to the civilians. You don't see that as you are fighting through an area, but when you come back. You see the devastation. It really has an impact on you. You knew that maybe you weren't the cause of it, but a lot of the suffering of the civilians and of the damage was because of the war. It is not a nice thing to see.

ETM: Have you since returned to Normandy?

FB: Well, Sainte Mère Église adopted us. I went back the first time for the 25th anniversary and I was amazed. The whole area around Sainte Mère Église has been the same ever since. Madame Renaud came to the United States a couple of times. I met her personally and I became good friends with Henri Renaud, who was the mayor of Sainte Mère Église. I really went there for two reasons. First, I thought that if I did not go, I would forget. It wouldn't stay with me. And second, I thought I had a duty to go because we have some friends buried in that cemetery. When I got there I realized I didn't forget, the French people didn't forget, and it was going to be a part of my life forever. Then I went back again. I waited another twenty years and of course, by this time, we were down to eight buses. I returned for the 55th anniversary because I had had heart surgery and I didn't think I had many more years left. So I thought, I would bring my son and daughter with me. So I took them. Then the 60th rolled around and I went again. You don't forget. I go there and I see that field. The only thing that changed is that gate that we went through. Now, there are houses, and where the cow pasture used to be, there are new buildings. When I walk up that road to Neuville au Plain, I see the same intersection where Bob Niland was laying and I could see him to this day. You don't forget.

ETM: It remains with you. People do not die, they stay with us. Places do not die, they stay in our memory. These white crosses in these cemeteries are living crosses.

FB: I go to the cemetery every time when I am there. We have eight men buried there. They are at peace. I don't think any of us liked it. I think war is terrible; a man trying to kill another man. After the war is over and you see what is going on in the rest of the world. You say to yourself, "is this going to happen again?" That is how he started out. Making little speeches and threats; look all over the world today, it is happening in other countries. I am wondering if America is going to be the police force of the world. I think about some of these young guys. I met with some of them yesterday. It is nice that they have this gung-ho spirit, but war is a terrible thing.

ETM: What was it like to return to Normandy with your son and daughter?

FB: They did not study much the culture and the wars of different countries in their class. For some reason, I don't know why they don't teach it. So I thought maybe if I took my son and my daughter there and they met the French people, and they saw what took place, this would make a difference. Up until then really, I never talked to my kids about the war. I never discussed it. So when the trip came up, my daughter said: "Dad, you never said anything." I said "Why, what was I supposed to say?" She said: "It would have been nice if we had known these things." I said: "Well, I'll tell you what, when you talk about killing people and people getting killed, it is not a very good subject. I thought I don't have that many years left, I wanted you to see some of the things that happened." So I took them to where I landed. I showed them. I showed them where we fought the Battle of Neuville and we traveled all through France to that part of Normandy. I showed them, and we met the Renaud family. I am in good rapport with both of the boys, all of the time. We met some of the civilians and so my daughter and my son probably got the first lesson in history, a real lesson, something that wasn't in the books.

ETM: What is in the books doesn't tell the whole story.

FB: See my medals and decorations when I got discharged. I had a uniform and when I got discharged, my mother asked me: "What do you want me to do with this?" It wasn't important, I was a civilian again. She took everything that was on my uniform and wrapped it up in plastic and the same with my brother John. My mother had a hard life. It wasn't easy and she died at the age of 72. When she was sick, she told me that there was a suitcase up in the attic. Some of it is your stuff and some of it belonged to your brother John. I went up into that attic after she died and got that suitcase down. My mother had taken a picture of me when I was two years old, one when I am four with my brother and my father, one when I made my Holy Communion, my Graduation picture, pictures that I didn't even know existed, then the pictures that I took in the Army. She had put the date on the back of each of them. So I have all those pictures now. My daughter is working with me and I am going to put them all in a book. I never got to take a picture with my uniform on after the war. I was just like everyone else. I came back home to look for a job, you know. I was very fortunate. I got into the construction industry. I became a construction superintendent on big buildings, 40 stories and more. I did that for thirty some years. I had a pretty good life, not much to complain about.

ETM: They now know about the story of your life in Normandy and beyond, and that is something that will remain with them. Thank you very much.

Wesley Ko

WK: I was born and raised in Philadelphia. My father was brought to this country from Canton, China, by a physician and missionary. He educated him at Princeton and Temple University. My father received his degree in Theology and became an ordained Methodist minister. He served in the Chinese Methodist Church in Philadelphia for many years. The idea was for him to help the people who emigrated from China to learn the language and at the same time teach them a little religion. My mother was also part Chinese and part German. Her Chinese father had been brought to the U.S. as one of the workers who built the first railroad. I believe she met my dad at Temple.

ETM: Looking back at your youth and childhood what can you say about this country when you look at it today? In what sense is this country different from others?

WK: I can remember as a child when Hoover was president. I believe at that time he turned down aid to China. I think that this caused them to go communistic. Being a minister, my dad was poor. There never was any money in religion. He made very little. In fact he had to supplement his income by managing a hand laundry. We grew up poor and when the crash of 1929 came, he lost all his money in the bank, his business and property, and the only thing he was able to save was our home; so we knew what a depression was. That's how we grew up and how I guess I compare things today. The cost of things today compared to those days is tremendous. For instance, we decided that after we left New York, we would rent the rest of our lives. We owned homes up until that point. We sold our last home in New York. When we moved to Cape Cod, where we now live, we decided to rent. I remarked to my wife the other day, do you realize that what we pay in rent in one year is three times the cost of what our first home was, and it took us 30 years to pay that off.

ETM: How did you become involved in the war?

WK: I was working for a small printing company. I had worked from my sophomore year in high school after school. The war came along and I found that the fellow who owned the business got me an exemption. It was a neighborhood thing and he had influence I guess with the draft board and so forth. He did this without my knowledge to get this deferment to help his business because he didn't want to lose me as an employee. As time went on, all my friends were being taken into the service and I just had to volunteer. So, I just volunteered. I got my basic training and was sent to an infantry division. We were on maneuvers in Louisiana. There was a chance for me too; there was a notice posted for officer candidates; so I applied for it, passed the interview, the requirements and was sent to OCS when I graduated. I guess it was January of 1943. Originally, when the time came to go into the service, I wanted to join the Air Corps and the Flying Tigers. It was my ambition as a kid. But I couldn't pass the physical with my eyesight; so I was turned down. I volunteered and wanted to get into the service and do what everybody else was doing. When I became an officer, I was sent to the 82nd Airborne.

ETM: What was your rank and responsibilities?

WK: I began as a second lieutenant. Being Chinese at that time, there were many prejudices, although it wasn't evident. I never experienced any problems. In retrospect, I've looked back at the things I have done. I was with the 82nd for one month as a platoon leader. Then I was assigned F Company 325th guarder infantry and after another month to the battalion S-1. Now I see, looking back, that it had something to do with prejudice. They took me out of troop command and put me with the staff because they weren't sure about my role with the combat troops. I guess it wasn't until Italy when they needed somebody to handle machine guns platoon that I was transferred as a platoon leader to handle heavy weapons machine guns. I spent a couple of weeks in Mount Saint Angelo di Cava as a platoon leader where we had relieved the rangers. I received a promotion to 1st Lieutenant after the Italian Campaign. I was assigned to head up the 81 mm motor platoon when we went to Ireland and England. From that time, I had troop command. I went through Normandy in that capacity, as well as Holland, the Battle of the Bulge and then, when the regiment was reorganized, we became a three battalion regiment. H Company was formed. I was assigned as a company commander, and promoted to the rank of captain.

ETM: In Normandy you were in a glider. How was the landing?

WK: The problem with Normandy was misinterpretation of information on the aerial photographs. We were informed that there were only hedgerows in the fields we were to land. But when we arrived there, there were trees, some 100 feet high. So, in order to land, because the fields were small, we had to go through the trees. Of course, we severely damaged the wings on our glider. Fortunately in our case, there were no injuries and we landed safely. Many gliders were overturned or shot down when they were airborne. We landed in Sainte Mère Église, south and west of it, about a mile outside. There were two types of gliders that were used: a WACO CG 4A which was the US glider originally made by Ford. That held 13 men plus the pilot and co-pilot. We were also equipped with the British Horsa glider. That held 26 men. We flew over the beachhead. I happened to be designated as co-pilot because the Air Corp couldn't provide a pilot and co-pilot, so they took the ranking member of the glider load and made that person co-pilot. With that, I had a view of everything. I could see the machine gun placements and the tracers weaving back and forth and, on occasional rounds, snapping through the fabric of our glider. I don't know of anybody who wasn't afraid. As a leader, I could not outwardly display any fears. We were young and adventurous and threw danger to the wind. In fact, it wasn't until a few years ago when I saw on the History Channel a series of programs called "Suicide Missions" (one of them was on glider operations), that I realized how dangerous it was.

ETM: Throughout the campaign, from Normandy to Berlin, did you think about your mission and the impact it would have on history?

WK: I don't know that I thought so much of the big picture. The only thing that I really noticed in the fighting when we were in Germany, towards the end of the war, was the fear the German people had of the Russians. They could sense a Russian soldier 50 miles away. They had so much fear of them because of what they did to the Soviet Union. They knew that. At the end of the war, the 21st German Army surrendered to us, over 150,000 men, rather than the Russians who were pushing them towards us, and they just gave up. What a sight that was. Ludwiglust, Germany, was our final engagement of the war.

ETM: Could you tell us about experiencing the death of a friend during the war?

WK: When it comes to death in the service, I think I became hardened in Italy. We were to relieve Darby's Ranger Battalion on Mount St. Angelo di Cava. On our way up to that mountainside, which we ascended from the sea coast village of Miori, just north of Salerno, at about 3,000 feet altitude, we saw the dead Rangers along the trail. They had been defending the mountain for two weeks. It was the highest point in the area and it overlooked the plain below. The Germans wanted this observation point and fought desperately to regain control of it. I think the closest person that I was standing next to and speaking with when he was killed was my first company commander. His name was Captain Porter. At the time, he was our Battalion S-3. We were going on the offensive in Normandy. He got caught in an artillery motor barrage and he was killed instantly. I'll never forget how I was panic-stricken, being next to a fellow officer who was killed and still alive in my mind. One does not realize the full brunt of the experience, and how it would be felt later on. He was from South Carolina. He was a career officer.

ETM: How would you characterize D-Day from your own perspective?

WK: It was a good war in the sense that we accomplished our mission which was proving freedom, and the fact that Europeans, generations later, are thankful for the liberty they now have. The thing that pains me about today's situation is that the personnel that was called into war and ordered overseas seems to object to the length of time they must serve, and yet they volunteered. In our day, it was not a volunteer army. We were drafted. We didn't have a choice. We never had the feeling they have today. We were only too glad to achieve our part. You did what you were ordered to do. You felt it was your duty to accomplish it before you got home.

ETM: Have you been to China? Do you have relatives there?

WK: I have never been to China. It has always been an ambition. My wife and daughter visited Asia for three weeks about thirty five years ago. At that time China was not open and they were only able to reach the border. Two years ago, two of our granddaughters attended the Pacific Rim Charter School in Boston where Mandarin is taught. They spent two weeks in China two years ago. Now, my oldest granddaughter, a student at the University of Massachusetts is spending her junior year in Beijing. She reads, speaks and writes Mandarin. It's hard for me to believe because I don't speak the language. It was never spoken in my home. It seems that there is the same battle to open up China. There is a wealth of natural resources in that country that are not being put to use. I think once they open it up it will be one of the biggest successful countries in the world.

ETM: What do you think are the challenges globally for the next generations?

WK: September 11 is one of the reasons we are involved abroad. It is something that everyone has forgotten about in wanting to end the war and pull out the troops. I don't think we have accomplished our mission until it is resolved and terrorism is eliminated. I think people look at the deaths and think that what is occurring is tremendous; but losing a couple of thousands men in all of this war today is nothing by comparison to losing two thousand men in a day during WWII. We must rid ourselves of terrorism regardless of who our enemy is. I just feel very strongly that we have a mission to complete and it should be done. I think that is what we are trying to do but it is very difficult because of the importance of religion in their culture. We must help the democratic government we helped to establish, and resolve the problem. Look how old those countries are compared to this country. If we can accomplish this, it will end our involvement.

Matthew Wojtaszek

ETM: Could you tell us about your uniform?

MW: This is an overseas cap. The wings and stars represent the Normandy landing and the Market-Garden operation. These are my glider rings, this is occupation duty in Berlin Germany and these are the six bronze battle stars from the different locations where I served, from Casablanca to Germany. This is the Polish Paratroopers. I am an honorary member of the Polish Paratroopers. We were kind of associated with them. And I got the Belgian *Fourragère*, the French *Fourragère* and the Military Willems Order. We fought in Salerno up to Naples. We were looking forward to going to Rome but the generals had other plans. We went to England; we trained and were set for the D-Day landing. We stayed in Normandy a little over a month, about thirty-three days.

ETM: When did you land in Normandy?

MW: I landed on June 6, 1944, early in the morning. We left at about 3am in the morning. First the pathfinders left, then, the paratroopers, and we glider men followed. I was kind of excited because I liked flying. A C-47 airplane towed the glider by a rope, a nylon rope. When we got to the landing zone, they broke the tow and it just took seconds for us to hit the ground. There is no engine in a glider, so we depend on the glider pilot. If he gets shot, fourteen men go down with him. Coming across the English Channel from England, everything was fine; you could look down and see all the ships in the water. Everything was fine but once we got to the coast of France across Omaha and Utah Beaches everything started to fly up at us: machine guns, anti-aircraft, puffs of smoke all over the place; it was kind of scary. It looked as if these tracer bullets were coming right at us. There were some pieces that blew through there but luckily nobody got hit.

ETM: You said earlier that there was a sense of excitement.

MW: Well, we were looking forward to fighting into the war yes. When we hit the ground with the gilder, the first thing we did was pile out of there with our rifles, and we were ready for action. I was in the artillery anyway; so, the infantrymen were the ones who caught much of the action. There was also a sense of camaraderie. And as we flew, it was silent for a while and it was as if we were all for one and one for all. We looked after each other.

ETM: Tell me about your life growing up in Chicago.

MW: Well, my father's name was Michael and my mother's name was Seweryna. They came from Poland. At first, they went to West Virginia because that's where the work was. They were working in the mines. Eventually they came to Chicago and that's where we were born, my brother, my sister and I. I was the last one to be born. My parents got married in this country. They met in West Virginia. When the people were migrating to this country they were going where the work was. As a matter of fact, the neighborhood in which I grew up was kind of mixed up. I lived in what they called Lakeview. The parish that I belonged to, St. Josaphat, was a Polish parish and down the road, about a mile away was a German parish, St. Alphonsus. On the other side, there was an Irish parish, St. Vincent de Paul. So, it was kind of a mixture. Today, there still is a strong Polish community in Chicago around St. Hyacinth Church. At the time, the migrant groups stayed together. Germans stayed together, Poles stayed together, and the Irish kept to themselves. But today it is like the League of Nations, almost.

ETM: What was your reaction when you heard that Poland had been invaded in 1939?

MW: It was kind of a shock. I was looking for other countries to help them. They said they would and they almost didn't. Finally, England and France declared war on Germany. I think the war lasted three weeks in Poland. They had all that good equipment that they had been saving for years. My dad had relatives, brothers and sisters in Poland. They used to write back and forth. He used to tell us what was in the letters. He let us read them.

ETM: I looked at the picture you gave me yesterday and you are smiling. To have a positive outlook was probably essential to survive in these circumstances. When I talked about the hardship, the drama and anxiety that caused the war and earlier the invasion of Poland, you did not talk too much about it, but it was real. How did you become involved and how did you enroll in the 82nd Airborne?

MW: I did not enlist in the Army. I was drafted. I graduated out of high school in 1940. Then I went to work during the summer, trying to make some money so I could go to college. I actually went to the Art Institute of Chicago. I thought I would be an artist of some sort. Well, that didn't go very far. So they gave me orientation classes at Ft. Sheridan, and then sent me to Ft. Bragg, North Carolina for my initial training into the service. Here was something that was new for the US Army. It was called Airborne and they wanted to get us in the know how and send us overseas. It was pretty nice although I found England kind of backwards in comparison to our country. They also seemed to be quieter. The Americans, we're in a rush all the time and the Europeans seem to take their time, perhaps because they had experienced the war for three years. I was kind of lucky that Uncle Sam took me into the service there. I went to overseas duty and I got to see many countries in Africa, then, Italy, France, Holland, Belgium, and Germany. As a matter of fact the last place I got to was in Berlin, Germany where I served in occupation duty.

ETM: When you landed in France on D-Day, did you have a sense of the big picture, of what your actions meant at the time?

MW: It was to restore the freedom they once had, get the Germans and Hitler out of there and let the people live the way they wanted to live. That is the meaning of this country. They want everyone to be free. The people in France were very good. I met them during the war; they were very helpful to us, they showed us where the Germans were and all that. When I went back there in 1999 for the fifty-fifth anniversary of D-Day they were even finer. They appreciated what we did.

ETM: Going to Germany in 1945, were you angry at what the Germans had done to Poland and the misery they had caused?

MW: Not really, not really. As a matter of fact, I almost felt as sorry for a German soldier as I did for an American soldier. He was doing what he was told to do and we were doing the same thing. Although he had the wrong idea and what Hitler was telling them was madness.

ETM: What you felt perhaps was compassion because Germany was in pretty bad shape.

MW: I remember flying over Berlin in a C-47 plane and I looked down there and all you could see in the middle of Berlin was four walls would be standing and the incendiary bombs had burned the heck out of all the insides of the buildings. All you could see was the four walls standing. There were a lot of them, a lot of destruction, all over the place. When I was there, as a matter of fact, you had to have a pass to get into the British zone, a pass to get into the French zone, a pass to get into the Russian zone; we had to have a pass for each one of those places to go to. When we were in Berlin, the paratroopers were all tough guys or they thought they were tough. They would be drinking in some of those places that they opened up or pubs. They would get drunk and start fighting with these Russians. I am better than you sort of things. There wasn't too much love at first with either of them. As a matter of fact, General Patton wanted to go right to Russia. He didn't want to stop with Germany. He wanted to kick the heck out of Russia too. But they said no, wait awhile.

ETM: What was and still is today the role of America, as you see it, in the world?

MW: I think that what we are looking for is freedom for all; especially women's rights. Women in some countries cannot do anything and we want women to be as free as men to decide and vote. I recall training with a fellow from Wisconsin who died on D-Day. He was married, just had a child, and he was telling me this whole story. During one of my trips to Normandy, I began to talk about him; we were walking through the crosses and I always wondered what happened to him. And out of all those thousands and thousands of crosses, we found his grave. His name was Norton Feirday. We went through basic training in Ft. Bragg but we later separated. Once in awhile, we would see each other and get together to talk. He was from Milwaukee as a matter of fact. He had one daughter that he never saw and a boy. He could not wait until the war was over so he could go back and see his daughter. He never got back to see her.

ETM: There may have been an element of faith through your achievements. Your daughter was just telling me that you lost your mother when you were seven years of age.

MW: I was in the first grade. My father never remarried and he raised the three of us kids on his own. He died when he was 85, my brother died when he was 85; I am 83 but I am not going to die at 85. The loss of my mother was a sorrowful thing. You need a mother to bring you along in your life. A father is a lot different than a mother. A mother is someone that you respect a little more than your father. In combat we had chaplains from every type of religion there is. We had a Rabbi, a Catholic chaplain and a Protestant chaplain. If you were Catholic, you could go to the Rabbi or the Protestant or whatever. They were equally helpful with whatever your problem was. They would write to your home if you needed it. They were very good. Chaplains and Rabbis were people I very much respected.

ETM: In what way would they provide support?

MW: Before we went into combat, the Catholic chaplain would always have a mass. On the jeep, he would put up an altar with candles, a cross, and everything. Before we went into battle, he would give us a general absolution. He would forgive us for all our sins that we had committed in all our lives. It was a general absolution, so we felt good about that. We felt we were clean so if we got killed we would go up to heaven.

ETM: There was thus a spiritual dimension to your actions during that time, a sense that you were possibly going to give your life for your brother and sister. Was there such a dimension in your daily experience?

MW: Yes, you would think in those terms. You were helping people in the country you were fighting for and for the people back home. You were helping them also end this terrible war that was supposed to end all wars. But it didn't. You had others, Korea, Vietnam, Iraq whatever. I don't think there is an answer. As long as you can remember, there has always been war. I think, I won't be around to see any more. That is one good thing.

ETM: This war was a good war. Your actions take on a greater dimension when you consider the calamity of war: the millions of people who suffered extraordinarily, the Holocaust, then the atomic bomb, and so much destruction.

MW: That Holocaust was really something. As a matter of fact, one experience I had before we met the Russians at the Elbe River is that we liberated the Wobelin concentration camp near Ludwigslust, Germany, and those people were just lying dead all over the place. In some of the buildings, bodies were stacked like cord wood, bodies on top of bodies. People were just dying while we were there. I felt very sorrowful. You didn't believe that something like that could happen, that one human being could do something like this to another human being. You kind of feel sorry for anyone who goes through war. It's a sorrowful thing. If you can avoid it, you should. All things considered, the American achievements in WWII are something to behold.

Bill Tucker

ETM: Thank you for inviting me to your home. The first thing you mentioned to me was this painting by Renoir, *Le Moulin de la Galette*.

BT: Yes, I have a passion for Renoir. My favorite really is the one with the two girls at the piano. I remember when I saw it in Paris at the *Musée d'Orsay*.

ETM: Did you have a chance to visit Paris in 1944–1945?

BT: In 1944 after we got back from Holland, we had a two-day pass and we visited Paris and it was a nice experience, but it was in the winter. We just went to a few night clubs. That's about it. Right after that, we were ordered to 'load up' and went to the Battle of the Bulge. They said that the Germans had broken through. But I enjoyed even that short visit in Paris.

ETM: Could you tell us about your experience growing up?

BT: I was born in 1923 and I grew up in this area, not far from Quincy, Massachusetts. In fact, there was nothing here at that time except two beautiful quarries. It was in a little suburb of Boston called Roslindale about five miles from Quincy. We are in an apartment that I use during the week. I was doing some legal work, but I am stopping it. My home in Cape Cod is an hour if you drive; so I just came up from there now. My father was from Kentucky. He had run away from home and joined the Marine Corps and he was wounded in 1916. Then he was placed in a hospital in Boston and he met my mother who worked at the hospital. Her family came from Wales. They got married and I guess you would call us a poor family. He got a job, but during that time, he worked only two or three days a week. It was a tough time, but I have no regrets, and it was a good time. My father's family had come to Kentucky in the early 1800s. I have assumed they came from England, from the British Isles.

ETM: What did they grow in Kentucky?

BT: They grew many things except tobacco. My great uncle could have made a fortune, but he didn't want to grow tobacco as it was against his religion.

ETM: And how did you enroll in the US army?

BT: It was 1942. I was a pretty good football player and I got a scholarship to play football for the University of Miami the previous year. But I still needed a little more money; we didn't have any money at all. I needed money just for the bus fare to get down there. I was working, and then on Sunday December 7' we were kicking a football back and forth in the park, when somebody came and told us about Pearl Harbor. I was in Roslindale at the time, a little town right near here. I was eighteen years old. We all wanted to join the Army. My mother and father told me: "You have a scholarship and you have to go to college even for one year." There was a lot of arguing. My brother joined. He was five years older and went into the Air Corps. Then I went in one day on my own to join the Navy. I was turned down because of a vision problem and I was really upset. Later in June, I was walking by and there was a sign showing paratroopers. I joined and went into the service in August. I was shipped to Toccoa, Georgia, in the 506 Regiment, which was the first to take volunteers from civilian life for direct basic training. Before that time, paratroopers had come from different training areas. We were kind of famous in that regard. That was the regiment that later became associated with the movie *Band of Brothers*, later in the 101st. I was with them for eight months. We went to North Carolina to train there.

ETM: Was your first military experience in North Africa?

BT: Yes, I was transported with the 82nd on the USS George Washington in a big convoy. This was in the South Atlantic in April 1943. We arrived in Casablanca and trained in a desert with scorpions and a lack of food and water. There was still fighting in Tunisia but I was not picked to go. There were two guys I got to know who were picked and jumped in Sicily; one was killed. His name was Kissel, a fellow of German descent from Minnesota. He was killed in action during the second day. Later on I kept asking, "What happened to Kissel?" When I went to Italy in 1985 I found his grave near Rome. After my jump in Italy, I lost 50 pounds. I had malaria and other ailments. I landed at a beach and the medic said to me, "Hey, your temperature is 103. You should not be here." I fell into the water; I was so weak that the first sergeant grabbed me by the neck; otherwise I would have drowned. Then the next thing I know I was in a church and after that I didn't remember anything for two days. When I woke up, I was in a hospital ship, going back to Constantine in Africa. Later on, I nearly died. I was there for four to eight weeks. It was agony.

ETM: How did you learn later that you would be engaged in the D-Day operation?

BT: We first went to Ireland and we were supposed to rest for four weeks because the regiment had done hard fighting. I was in the hospital most of the time. We didn't have much training there, just a few lectures. Then we took a boat to Scotland and the train down to what they call the midlands of England. There was a little town called Quorn where they had set up eight men tents for us. That's where we lived from January to D-Day. We trained mostly at night; two nights a week we would go out. We made jumps. Some of them were pretty scary because the weather was so terrible. It was hard training.

ETM: There was also optimism about the war?

BT: That's a good point. Not many people ask that. I think none of us had the attitude that we could lose. But I don't think anybody ever thought that we would do anything other than knock the crap out of the Germans. We were like a machine, this giant machine that could do anything. We were paratroopers too. The Japanese knew that unless they won at Pearl Harbor, we would crush them. And they were right. They did not get to carry us. We just knew what we had, which was tremendous leadership. Roosevelt was a God to us, and we would sit in the pub and drink one beer with an English family and nobody ever thought of doing anything other than winning the war. The spirit was one of complete unified optimism.

ETM: Tell me about the few days, few hours that preceded the landing.

BT: We were told we were going, but they didn't tell us where we were going. We had to go to the airport, take our equipment and get ready. That probably took a few hours. Then we couldn't have gotten out of the truck even if we wanted to. We were then locked in with two other airborne battalions, and my battalion was in a big hangar, which was about five days before the invasion. We went to get our meals and there were MPs (the Military police), with us everywhere, so that nobody could talk to us. That was for security reasons and we accepted it. The day before the jump, we were taken one platoon at a time into the briefing tent. We used to guess where we were going. My guess was Norway and I was pretty far off. We were just kids, you know. We were not informed and somebody said Yugoslavia and I said: "No," and I added "It can't be France because there are so many Germans there." In the briefing tent, there was a table twice the size of this one, and there was a mock up on an area photo on it. In the middle of the photo it said "Sainte Mère Église." The commander put his finger on the photo and said, "This battalion will seize and take Sainte Mère Église tomorrow night. So let's get ready for it." We studied to see what we would need to do. It never works out anyway. Ours was the 3rd Battalion, 505th Parachute Infantry Regiment. We had the main mission of the airborne troops in all of Normandy. It was to seize and hold the town of Sainte Mère Église because they had tanks across the river and Hitler had an intuition. At the last minute, he sent in the 91st German Air Landing Division, which was a damn good division. Jesus, they were tough. So our mission was to jump and seize the town. The other battalion that was equally important was the one that held Neuville-au-Plain. They had a big fight there with the Germans coming all the way from Cherbourg. We had to hold Route 13, from Paris to Cherbourg that came to Sainte Mère Église, from the south, to prevent the Germans from taking it. That is where most of the 91st Division was. The next day we got all our equipment ready and headed for the briefings; General Gavin and General Ridgeway talked to us. The day before, Colonel Krouse, who commanded the 3rd Battalion, had held up the flag he had in Naples and said, "This is the flag that flew over Naples when we took that city in Southern Italy." And he added, "Do you see this flag? Tomorrow morning it will be flying over the town hall of Sainte Mère Église."

ETM: And it happened that day. How many were you in a plane to jump?

BT: It varied. Usually it was about 19, sometimes 20. I was number 5 on that jump. The equipment had to weigh one hundred pounds. At the last minute they made us carry a mine. We didn't like that. We also got extra stuff like cigarettes, and other things. Then we had the mine down there, and we set the fuses inside of our helmets since the mine wouldn't go up without the fuse.

ETM: What was the atmosphere in the plane?

BT: I'll tell you something. I swore to myself and at the world. To me, that was the only jump I ever made that I had no fear at all. Everything had been built up inside of me. I wasn't brave. I never was a brave fighter. I just did my job. But that jump was so tremendous and it built up, and, above all, I couldn't forget General Ridgeway's words. We were doing something that would be unparallel in History. I was young, but I was a pretty smart kid and those words stuck with me always. When I was in that plane, I was a cold cucumber and I just did not sweat. I knew the guy across from me, Harry Bufford, who later received two silver stars. His problem had been that he got turned down by every service because of motion sickness. He had even been thrown out of the Coast Guard, but somehow he got in the paratroopers. The minute the plane got off the ground his face was in his helmet; but listen, it was worth it having him because he was a hell of a soldier. The thing I remember most before taking off is that I looked out of the windows of the plane, right where you are, and my God there were all these people lined up along the side of the runway, and it was one tremendous moment in a lifetime, believe me. I felt the engine roaring, ready to go . . . and that will be with me forever.

ETM: Where was the base located? Was it Leicester?

BT: Yes.

ETM: This moment remains with you because of its intensity; all the people were getting together to salute you, fully aware of the nature of your mission and not knowing whether you would return.

BT: Yes. The scene also was extraordinarily moving: all the planes all over and I'm looking at these people standing there as if they were saluting us and praying for us. You could feel it. Then our own planes started their engines; three battalions were leaving. We had I think at least three airports or more for the whole division.

ETM: How much time was there from take off to the jump?

BT: It was about three hours. The beach landings came from the east. We came in from the west to the east. Then when we hit the coast, there were a lot of clouds; it was really scary. When we hit that coast, I could see tracer bullets and that turned my coolness into concerns and then we only had five minutes so the jump master yelled and we had to hook up right away; so we stood up. It was very awkward you know. It is hard to describe. You just don't just stand up; you have to make sure that everything is buttoned. The plane was shaking and I didn't want to be on board a burning plane. I just wanted a chance to get out. In front of me was Larry Leonard and behind me was Ray Krupinski, who was a great combat fighter; he was an automatic rifle man. Larry and I were machine gunners. Larry turned to me and he said: "Jesus Christ, Tucker, we don't get paid enough for this job."

ETM: It is said of course that many of the people who jumped did not jump at the right place. How was your personal experience?

BT: Mine was good as well as the rest of our regiment. We were right on target and we only lost one plane. They were killed or captured. I landed on a field an eighth of a mile from the town, and I took out my rifle and a few of us formed a group. It turned out that we had a pretty good unit, and Captain Swingler was there. He was killed that day. Then we went into the town where there was scattered fighting. We had to take out a machine gun, which was firing on us. It was still dark. This was about 3am or so. It must have taken us an hour to group and get into the town. As we got closer we could see the village and we saw a Frenchman coming along. I said to him "Vive la France!" and he gave me a scared look and kept going. Then we, Leonard and I, came to this wall and we went inside. That is when I saw the soldier in the tree who had been in the same squad as I was, in Georgia. It was the 506 (as I later learned). They had jumped a little before we did. Among that same 506 company that I was in, half of them landed on the edge of Sainte Mère Église. As shown in *The Longest Day*, some of the GIs jumped on the main plaza and some of ours, probably from the 506, had been hung up on big trees.

ETM: What do you remember on that day and that morning when daylight broke?

BT: Of course, I remember the soldier in the tree right over me. That was a shock to see somebody hanged like that. It was a terrible sight. The German 91st Division had 800 reinforcement soldiers in the area; we know that now; we didn't know it then. G Company had a road block on the South side. We had to come from that other side of the town crossing these hedge rows with the equipment. It was a son of a bitch, and we went to attack the flank of the German battalion there, 90 of us and 800 of them. They let us come and then opened fire. I was on the road there and the Germans started throwing grenades and firing machine guns, and they had us. Captain Swingler was up there and was killed in the middle of the road. This was between 10am and 4pm in the afternoon. It took us a lot of time to cross south of the town because it was like a jungle. There was a lot of firing. The aim was to hold the town and to gain control of Route 13 which was the key road from Cherbourg. But the Germans were all around us. We got pushed back and then they came after us. So we turned around and figured there was a defensive position. But they came across where the hotel is now. We had to get out of there as we were overwhelmed. There were just eight to ten of us. It is right across from Henri's house. We all moved back. Our captain had been killed and we no longer knew who was in command, so the sergeant led us back to *Rue de l'Ecole*. We took some bad pounding from the artillery because they had somebody who could see us every time we moved and we lost a lot of men. We probably would have been better off if we had been out on the perimeter with G or H Company. We probably lost between ten and twenty: among them two of my best friends which were right near me. They were hit by an air burst. I was going to go in their hole but the sergeant said, "Hey, I don't want more than two men in one hole." That saved my life.

ETM: Who were these two friends who died that day?

BT: We put up a little memorial because I think they were the first I Company guys killed that we knew of. It was Jack Leonard and Bill Laws. Bill is buried here. I see his grave every year at Omaha Beach. Jack came from the state of Washington, and he went home. But they were killed only ten yards from where I had my own hole. I went up and Jack was just lying there. His face was pressed into the side of the wall. I knew he was dead. Bill was pulled out but in five minutes he was dead.

ETM: What did you feel when you experienced these deaths of your two close friends?

BT: Do you know something; I think that it's blankness. You just go blank.

ETM: It is part of what is happening at the moment, and you cope with it, you continue.

BT: Yes. You don't have time for the luxury of emotion.

ETM: When did the troops from the beach reach Sainte Mère Église?

BT: The day after, on the 7th, what happened was that we were down to the CP. General Ridgeway had arrived and we were taking prisoners, a lot of prisoners; and we asked somebody: "Any word?" "No," was the answer. We had started patrols and then when we got back, somebody said "Hey, we saw tanks coming." They were Sherman tanks and that was hours after Laws and Leonard were killed; it was around 7pm or 8pm.

ETM: Bill, what was your experience returning after the war?

BT: The thing in the war that was biggest to me was Normandy. I always had the feeling I might return. I was determined to get back and in 1959 I received an appointment to the International Aeronautic Commission. I went to Paris and I took a train up to Normandy. It was winter time. I hadn't been back there and I took one of those steam engine trains. It was beautiful. Later on, I became a big shot in the US Railroad but we didn't have a train like that. There was a nice buffet car. It was fun. I got off near Sainte Mère and I got a ride from there to the Renaud pharmacy. We all knew the pharmacy that was owned by Mayor Renaud. I went there at about 2 o'clock in the afternoon and I talked to the mayor. I said, "I just want to look around a little bit." I spoke a little French. I had studied it for seven years. He also knew some English. We walked around the town and it was really nice. He took me back to Chef du Point. It was dark when I came back and I got the 5 o'clock train back to Paris. It was about a three hour visit. Then, I went back again in 1961, and then in 1962 and 1964. This is a picture of John Steele. I got to know him in later years.

ETM: He is the one who was hanging with his parachute on the top of the church. When you came back for the fist time that afternoon, were you wearing your uniform?

BT: Yes, in fact I got a good deal. I was in Washington DC. John F. Kennedy had made me a commissioner of transportation. I went to the commanding general and I said: "We have a 20th anniversary coming up and it would be an honor if I could make an inspection in Heidelberg." He replied, "Don't go to Heidelberg; go to Normandy!" I had worked for Kennedy since 1946. He was a dear friend. Here are some pictures on the wall. That's Jackie Kennedy and those are my children in 1958. We were waiting for the Senator.

ETM: How did you come to know John F. Kennedy?

A. I had started a law practice in Western Massachusetts and I received a call from a guy I was in high school with about Jack Kennedy. We had all heard about him and his father, and I was told that he was going to make a run for the Senate. I was chairman of the testimonial for General Gavin in Boston. So I invited Kennedy to speak. This was in 1951. I had Kennedy and General Gavin there, and that is the first time they met, and of course Kennedy would later appoint Gavin Ambassador to France. I worked later for Kennedy in the campaigns of West Virginia, Minnesota and Wisconsin.

ETM: What do you remember about Kennedy? What was his greatest quality?

BT: His greatest quality was that he knew how to step back away from himself and laugh at himself; something I always wanted to be able to do. But he had extraordinary qualities. I thought he was born to face the Cuban Missile Crisis. I was involved in it at the time, and he was the most extraordinary leader that I had ever seen and was connected with in my life, including Ridgeway. He could radiate confidence, and he had the ability, if you were part of the staff, with just a movement of his head or a smile, you knew whether you should just stop speaking or move ahead. He also made the decision that potentially kept us out of nuclear warfare. The last time I saw him, I was at the White House; it was at the swearing in of a mutual friend who he appointed ambassador to Australia. It was in August of the year he was killed. We were at the Rose Garden after the ceremony. There were not many people there, just close friends. We went in and he sat at the end of a sofa and I noticed he was holding his arms, and I asked him: "How are you doing Mr. President?" "Jesus, he said, my back is killing me. This is the only place where I can sit where I do not have any pain." I remember that.

ETM: Considering WWII and today's American experience in Iraq, what is the difference between America in the 1960s under Kennedy and America today?

BT: Well, of course it is easy to say black and white, but there is no comparison at all. During WWII, we had real spirit, and we knew what we were fighting for; it was a broad word called freedom. We were fighting to protect our institutions, our neighborhoods, the ability to do the things we wanted to do. There was also discipline, family discipline. Those were the things that made up our lives. Now, in this damn war, we have a President who was stupid enough to launch an attack just for the sake of conquering another country. There was no excuse whatsoever for us to attack Iraq, anymore than it would be to attack any country where there is a dictator who persecuted people. We are in a quagmire, and then what happened? We had one friend, France, and boy I stood up for France, and the people were saying: "France did not do this and that." I thought de Villepin, the French foreign minister, was magnificent. Some of my French friends don't like him as a politician, but I think that he maintained a sense of order and dignity about the whole thing.

ETM: What is it then that this country and France can bring to the world, in this complex world in which we live?

BT: Well in the first place, they can bring a new leadership. I don't think Chirac was the man for the situation, this is just my opinion; and the prime minister in England put his foot in his mouth on this whole thing. These countries in the West need to pull together for leadership, and I think NATO is the only institution that has been trustworthy to the West to do positive things like in Kosovo. We need to elect new leaders who will work together to make order out of the situation.

ETM: Are you optimistic about the future of this country? We are as we speak in Boston, in one of the birthplaces of major founders and authors of this nation who have imagined and conceived a better future for this country and the world.

BT: We have the heritage of John Adams who lived right down the street and so many others during the time of the American Revolution. When I speak to veterans at times, I ask them, "Who do you think helped us win the Revolution and our war of independence? The French fleet; you forgot that, didn't you?" But anyway, what we are talking about is the nature of the history of America. The question is: will that nature and history, we will call it the Emerson/Adams spirit, will the spirit of great letters overcome the computer age in America? I don't know. We have television, a vast waste land; we have people who do nothing but fiddle with computers; we don't have people writing letters anymore; I don't see any Emerson around; but on the other hand, they are proud of our history, and this can't go away. So we have goodness here to preserve if we want to do it. The only way to do it is to put the right people in office that are bold and honest and willing to sacrifice political philosophy, and do what is good for all the people.

ETM: What should be in these letters since you mentioned Emerson? Could it mean that by writing and keeping our distance from technologies and computers, we would own our history and future, and control our destiny?

BT: I think that we do not teach enough History in school about people and cultures. We don't emphasize this enough in our country today.

ETM: Who could be, who should be, the next leader of this country, and what qualities should this leader have?

BT: I don't see anybody right now or point to anyone as we speak. But we have a year or two, and hopefully the recent change in Congress will be beneficial.

ETM: You are part of a generation who won a just war and who was on the right side of history. Could one of the essential questions be today: What does it mean to be on the right side of history?

BT: We won a war that was just unlike the stupidity and the politicization of the Vietnam War, which we fought because of the so-called Dulles "Domino theory". The assumption was that if we left Indochina alone, it would fall under communism; but you know, what is the risk, communism or Russian capitalism? When I look at Russia, it seems to me that more people were better off when they had communism; now all they have is rich capitalists in a society that widens the bridge between the very poor and the very rich. I do not say this to promote communism but, what I say certainly promotes the philosophical aspects of the Nordic people and their viewpoint on social democracy.

ETM: Did the people of France, in your view, thank you enough for the sacrifice of your generation on D-Day and during WWII?

BT: Yes, profusely with symbolisms, testimonials and decorations; we received the military decoration of the *Fourragère* of France. I will be in Normandy again, I hope, if my health holds on, in March, and also in the Ardennes in Belgium. I just had word from Francine Duchemin that the mayor of Sainte Mère Église, who is a good friend, wants us to come over there in February and they will welcome us as always. They take us in every year and it has been over sixty-two years now. You hear that the cab drivers in Paris are a pain in the ass; well, I say to them, ask any Frenchman who needs to take a cab, he will tell you the same thing.

Chapter 2
The Free-French and America

The series of interviews included in this chapter were conducted in France with the exception of Francine Duchemin's who was a guest at the 82nd Airborne Convention in Milwaukee. During our conversation, she recounted the significance of D-Day in her upbringing and her witnessing of the festivities that took place in honor of the veterans in her home town of Neuville-au-Plain in Normandy. Because her father was mayor of the town, her family became over the years very close with General Gavin's family. She describes how Normandy itself has become part of America and the American experience. I also met Emile Chaline at the *Fondation de la France Libre*, the Free France Foundation, in Paris. In our conversation, he depicted his decision to continue the struggle after the defeat of France in 1940 and his role as an officer in the French Navy in the Battle of the Atlantic. Engaged in battle at Omaha Beach on D-Day, Emile Chaline was later promoted to the rank of Admiral and was involved through his career with high ranking American officials with whom he became friends. From the South-West of France, Joseph Hourçourigary shares his experience in joining the Free-French, first in the Battle of the Atlantic, and from 1943, as a member of a French commando which trained in Scotland, conducted operations in France before D-Day, and landed on the morning of June 6, 1944 at Sword Beach, under the leadership of Commandant Philippe Kieffer.

In line with Emile Chaline's reminiscence and reflection, the following conversations touched on current issues related to French-American relations, in the context of the post-September 11 world, the war in Iraq, and the challenges that both France and the United States face in the 21st Century, both domestically and internationally. At the Museum of Resistance and Deportation in the city of Lyon, Jean Nallit gives an account of his role in the underground, his deportation to Buchenwald and his assistance to the Allies in defeating the Nazi Regime. He was recognized as "righteous among the nations" by the *Yad Vashem* Memorial to the victims of the Holocaust for the work he achieved in his network. I met with Rosette Peschaud and Raymonde Jeanmougin at the *Fondation Leclerc* in Paris. Rosette Peshaud spoke about the climate in France before the war, how she joined the Free-French forces in North Africa, worked as a nurse in a unit created by Florence Conrad, a Francophile American woman, and partook with Leclerc's 2nd Armored Division in the liberation of Paris. Raymonde Jeanmougin recounts how she saved the life of an American soldier while in the same unit. Formerly De Gaulle's cabinet member, Pierre Lefranc explores the past, present and future relations between France and the United States. Also a member of the 2nd French Armored Division, Maurice Cordier evokes life in France before the war, chronicles his journey from occupied France to Berchtesgaden via North Africa, and shares his vision of France and America's future.

Francine Duchemin

FD: I speak English because I used to live in England for a while and my brother lived in the United States for 22 years. He used to live in Charlotte, North Carolina. My father was the mayor of Neuville-au-Plain, just north of Sainte Mère Église in Normandy, where major battles took place during D-Day and the aftermath. I was born after the war but my parents kept a friendship for many years with General Gavin and his family. I was surprised to see a French person here because we were in Milwaukee attending the convention of the 82nd Airborne Division Association. I am pleased to see you and to have this conversation as well. Growing up in Normandy, I heard what my parents said about D-Day. I was involved in the war because everybody spoke about it for many years afterward; so I was really involved in it and when I was a child, I dreamt about it. I did not know it but I had dreams about it during the night. It was rather strange because everybody was talking about it.

ETM: It was part of your imaginary world.

FD: Yes completely. My parents became friends with many veterans who came back later and so I had met them since I was an infant. The dreams I had were scenes of combat and things like that. Sometimes I would wake up frightened in my bed. I experienced and re-enacted the war without being there. It was a physical and psychological experience.

ETM: Mr. Billich, whom I interviewed, told me that your parents helped injured American soldiers where they landed. They could have been shot many times but they took the risk. Your parents stayed there whereas many were fleeing understandably because there was bombing all over the area. What made them stay there and how did they know it was D-Day?

FD: Well, my parents knew because they were supposed to marry in June here, and my father was in the Resistance so he knew a lot of things but he never spoke to me about the Resistance. It is a funny thing but I know now through different people who speak about my father that he was active in the movement though he did not want to speak about it. He knew D-Day was coming and my parents did not get married right away because of it. They married later in October. My father's name was Camille Duchemin. My father was not with my mother on the night of D-Day. He was a few kilometers from here and he took parachutists and showed them how to find their way because they were very close when they parachuted. My mother was with my grandfather in her house in Neuville-au-Plain. It is funny because we have an association in Sainte Mère Église and they interview people about their memories of D-Day and it appears that a lot of people did not see the parachutists because it was night time and everybody was in their house. My mother, who lived in the countryside, saw them as they dropped and she knew right away. In the early morning, she went to the woods behind the house; a lot of parachutes that had been cut were hanging in the trees and she began to look for the injured.

ETM: Your father did not talk about the Resistance in the same way perhaps as the American veterans do not talk about combat.

FD: The underground was involved locally a few days before D-Day. Most of what they did was before and when the Allies arrived on the coast their work had been completed. They had done intelligence work and gathered information. They had also paralyzed communication systems and bombed the railroad; this was also done elsewhere, not only in Normandy. On June 6, 1944, the house where my mother lived became an American hospital. On June 6, the town of Montebourg, nearby, was completely destroyed. It is about 5 miles from Neuville-au-Plain, and a lot of civilians came to my parents' house because it is a large place and they also stayed there for quite a long time because everything was destroyed.

ETM: How do you situate D-Day and the liberation of Normandy and France with respect to the history of the relation between France and America?

FD: Well for myself, I was born and grew up with that relationship and it is a part of me, really. It is not just to say thank you, I think it is a part of me. I think I am half French, half American in my heart, and this is also true with the American friends I meet through my children who live in Saint Louis. The first time I met one of them, she just looked at me and said, oh that is funny you are more American than French and she saw it just by looking at me. I think this episode of D-Day and the French American relation is something within me. This relationship has continued over the years, and there is something special about the relation between the GIs and Sainte Mère Église. The first thing really is that when they came back a few years after the war, veterans like Bill Tucker and John Steel tried to meet people from our region and they looked around through the area. It was about ten years after D-Day. They all wanted to know where they jumped, to find the place again and it had not changed a lot during those first years. I remember we went around the area with my parents and tried to find where the injured soldiers had stayed and where there was a hospital and we visited the farms. We were always received very kindly. The Americans came back more often and we created a private association in Sainte Mère Église through which we organized travels between the United States and France. I remember that for the 25th Anniversary, a train came from Paris with something like 200 or 300 veterans and so they all stayed with the families. We organized big lunches for three or four days and the whole population participated and welcomed them. I have a very good memory of that big 25th Anniversary. But it was private. I remember at my parents' home, we had a barbecue for 300 people and everybody in the area came and asked if they could help with the cooking. Everybody was involved in receiving the Americans and everybody became friends. I remember that when the veterans came back we used to go to school to visit the children and everybody would welcome them. They were all well known in Sainte Mère Église; as soon as they saw the veterans, they would say hello and begin a conversation with them.

ETM: The relation is genuine and the friendship has endured. The veterans have returned year after year and all of the veterans I met here have said that they were welcomed warmly and were delighted to go back to Normandy, and that has not changed a bit.

FD: No, it has not changed. Last year, we had nine buses take them and they could not all stay with families because some of the older ones have difficulty moving and we found different hotels around and we picked them up for the commemoration in Sainte Mère Église. We placed an English translator in every bus, and we took them all around the country to see what they wanted to see. I try to convey to my children the same memory and I think they get it. Our admiration for the GIs will always remain. It is part of our genes, it is in our hearts; and words alone cannot express the feeling of gratitude we have for the veterans.

ETM: Thank you very much for your time. I look forward to visiting you in Normandy.

Emile Chaline

ETM: What influenced your choice to join De Gaulle during the War?

EC: First and foremost, I am from Brest. I was born there in a well-renowned maritime town. Just before the war the Atlantic squadron came into Brest followed by the colonial infantry regiment. In other words, people in Brest lived in an atmosphere of empire builders. The greater part of the "*brestois*" (inhabitants of Brest) had parents or friends who served in the navy, or in the regiment. As a result, the ambition which the men in Brest shared was to enter the navy while the women wished to marry seamen. I was not an exception to this rule. I shared the vocation of my family. To me, being a seaman meant going out in the open sea in the search of distant countries, to live the life of my imagination and dreams and to taste the intoxication of the unknown. It was a bit of all of this plus a feeling of patriotism. The national flag was important because my dad used to fill my childhood with incredible stories in which braveness was only equal to the courage of warriors. My dad was a former soldier in the navy (1914–1918). My strong faith also made me decide to pursue a maritime career. In 1940, I was accepted in the Navy of Brest, something like a preparatory class for the navy school. I was a high school graduate. I was eighteen years old. I just passed the written exams when all of a sudden the defeat came, and we had to retreat.

ETM: What happened during the years before the defeat of France was a considerable debate? Everyone was asking himself about the possibility of the war. What were your impressions as an adolescent during that time?

EC: Personally, I thought only about my education. Since 1936 everyone could well see Hitler's policy of conquest; that was the real conquest of Europe from the Atlantic to the Ural Mountains. Let us remember that in 1934, the Sarre territory was reintegrated into Germany by plebiscite. Then, in 1936 the Rhineland territory was remilitarized; in 1938 Austria was annexed; and finally in 1939, Czechoslovakia was dismembered when Hitler annexed the Sudetenland. In other words, we all lived in an atmosphere where everyone knew that war was coming. That's why nobody was astonished when war was declared. But our governments were actually optimistic. They assured us that everything would go well, and that with our arms we would forge a solid victory.

ETM: How can one explain this optimism? Was it due to a denial of reality?

EC: Yes, that's a good explanation. It was like brainwashing and this aspect has not changed.

ETM: Was this due to the trauma of the First World War?

EC: No, I think that was just a common feature of all the governments. That is a constant of international politics as a whole. All governments are alike, and they believe they are right in their points of view. In the US, for example, President Bush deems his invasion of Iraq as right. As a result, the majority of Americans are persuaded that it is a good thing. That's why everyone is somehow a prisoner of brainwashing.

ETM: What was your image of the US in the 30s and 40s?

EC: The US was associated with El Dorado where the streets were paved with gold. Everyone hoped to have an uncle who had escaped to America, had made a fortune, and who would die childless, leaving him his fortune.

ETM: In his message of June 18, 1940, General de Gaulle alluded to the mechanical force of the US that would permit us to win the war. Did something change after the debacle of 1940? Did America become a hope for you?

EC: We must not forget that, I believe it was in 1937, the US government voted on an embargo. They refused to sell us war materials or munitions. Great Britain and France had to enter the war, so this law was annulled in 1939 and replaced by the law of Cash and Carry.

ETM: But from another more emotional point of view, what was the relationship between France and America in your opinion?

EC: At the age of eighteen, I held great admiration for the US without really knowing anything about it. During those years no one traveled as they do nowadays when everyone can move about at will. The US was quite far away.

ETM: Where did this admiration stem from?

EC: America had an enormous economic power. It was however an unrealistic estimation, since when WWII was declared in 1939, the capacity of the newly-constructed American shipyards was only 400,000 tons. Let's not forget, however, that at that time the English navy had a construction capacity of 20 million tons and that when we started suffering losses to German submarines, it was terrifying. The Americans made a considerable effort during the war when in July, 1943 the capacity of the American shipyards reached 12 million tons, a thirty-fold increase.

ETM: America had gone through difficult years during the Depression, but maintained its capacity for reconstruction.

EC: The image of the Depression was passé because everyone knew that the country had recovered. However, at the time, most Frenchmen did not see further than the blue line of the Vosges region. My dad was a soldier in WWI. As of 1939, he put small flags representing the front line on a wall-map. He could not understand this collapse. It is he who actually told me, "Go to England, do your duty and know victory. Come back as a successful midshipman." I left home on June 18, 1940 without having heard the call of General de Gaulle, but obeying my dad, who, like other patriots, anticipated the General's call. It was the eve of the capitulation when Marshal Pétain asked for armistice. I left with the troops on the Meknes with the Béthouart Division with a group of mountain hunters and legionaries who were coming back from Norway. This was the Division that committed all the operations in Norway. We arrived in England the next day. We set off for a camp we heard about, and we were asked on June 29. If we wanted to join General de Gaulle (who was already recognized by the British as the leader of Free-France), and fight alongside the English in an English uniform or would we rather be repatriated? To my surprise, the majority of the guys there chose repatriation. Many insisted that their attitude was an act of discipline. Marshall Pétain would now be the chief of the Armed Forces and although he asked them to return to France, the impression I had was that these guys did not want to fight anymore.

ETM: Even though the Free-French would be considered traitors and their family subject to threat, you saw war as a necessary act of disobedience. Everyone had to disobey the orders sent from Vichy France.

EC: Yes, my dad told me to leave home and my youth told me that I had the right to follow my own rules. But one must admit that those who fought under the French flag, and who had been mobilized, were also part of a constituted unit that was also under the command of the Béthouart Division. I was not the only one taken over by a warlike spirit. Actually, for my dad, defending one's country meant defending family and territory. While defending our country, we defended ourselves.

ETM: When one thinks of your experience and the fact that you decided to stay with the French Resistance from the very beginning, what lessons do you think the French youth should draw from your experience?

EC: I do give conferences now and then, in particular to youngsters in high school. Youth is the time when we are ready to give our all. I believe the youngsters understand my attitude, and given the same circumstances, would do the same as I. I do not say that this is the right thing to do now when there is no motherland; because now, we follow European rules. I am not sure whether the youth would be ready to defend Europe the same way we were ready to fight for France.

ETM: Do you think that the birth of Europe has brought the end of patriotism or a certain type of patriotism?

EC: Yes, a certain type, but I don't think what we see is a 'good' Europe. They should have created a Europe of nations the way General de Gaulle wanted it. In this way, there would be certain sovereignty. Europe as we know it is necessary; this goes without saying. We should not be focused on ourselves alone but we should keep our identity and the pride that comes with it. The Corsicans are proud to be Corsicans, the Bretons are proud to be Bretons, but right now no one is as proud as they used to be of being French.

ETM: What do you think or what would you like to tell the veterans? What would you say about the American soldiers who sacrificed their lives here in France?

EC: I admire those veterans greatly, as they do us. Let me cite as an example the winning over Saint Pierre et Miquelon to Free France. I would like to cite Saint Pierre et Miquelon, an island off the coast of Canada on the Atlantic. That was a terrible moment, a moment when the Americans started to lose respect for De Gaulle. You must remember Cordell Hull, the US State Secretary who insulted us by condemning "these so called Free-French." In other words, the relations between both countries didn't start well after the defeat. But a few months later in July 1942, the French corvette La Roselys, who was with the Free-French, escorted a convoy through the Russian port of Murmansk. On the way back, the convoy of American ships that had just helped the Soviets ran over a mine field in the Atlantic. All the boats were destroyed and La Roselys entered the mine field (you do realize the risks it took) and we rescued the American survivors who escaped from the seven ships in the convoy. The head of the ship, Commandant Bergeret, was the first Allied officer to be nominated as Officer of the Legion of Merit. During the following convoys in the Atlantic, every time we passed by Newfoundland, instead of going to St. John, we went to Argencia, an American base where the Americans wanted to meet us. You can see that we had good relations.

ETM: Where was this mine field situated?

EC: To the north of Iceland. This field was intended to stop the German ships (remember the Bismarck episode) between Greenland and Iceland and to pass through the straits of Denmark. Actually, the weather was so horrible; there was such an extremely dense fog that the chief of the escort was misled and took the wrong route.

ETM: How can we pay tribute to a young American soldier who came here and died for France at eighteen or twenty years old?

EC: During the commemoration ceremonies on the sixtieth anniversary of the debarkation in Normandy, the media followed these events closely. I can honestly say that all the French were really moved by the image of those courageous soldiers who stepped on our land under fire of the German rifles and mortars. All Frenchmen felt deep admiration for those young men who had sacrificed their lives to liberate France. There can be no doubt whatsoever. I believe we all are deeply grateful to those Americans who sacrificed their lives for the sake of France.

ETM: Is there such a thing as anti-Americanism in France?

EC: We will always value and show gratitude to the Americans who saved us. What is going on is a result of the current political situation that finds French and Americans with opposing opinions. If we take Iraq as an example, it's absolutely certain that the majority of the French think that Bush and Rumsfeld are a little arrogant and the French don't agree with their politics regarding Iraq. That's all.

ETM: Can we interpret the American intervention in Iraq as an attempt to liberate it the same way France was liberated from Nazi Germany?

EC: No, we can't. It is very probable that the American intentions were honest, but nobody sees it that way. Do you remember de Villepin's speech at the UN with which the French agreed completely?

ETM: So when we speak of anti-Americanism, we actually refer to an opposition to a specific political position they hold?

EC: Yes, it is a temporary situation. But it is not something having to do with the American people themselves. Americans, per se, are not put into question in anyway. I was an attaché to the US Navy for three years. I made a lot of American friends there. Today, at the age of eighty-four, when I visit the US, my friends there always welcome me. I visited California and Florida where they are spending their retirement days. I always welcome them the same way when they come to Paris. In other words, we still maintain very good contacts. We love the American people.

ETM: So you are rather optimistic about French-American relations?

EC: Yes, I can honestly say that the small conflicts we may have are passing. These conflicts simply mean that we are not in agreement with a particular political position of a government which is momentarily disturbing to us.

ETM: Are you pessimistic about the war in Iraq?

EC: Right now, I just can't see how exactly we have profited from going into Iraq. I just can't.

ETM: Do you see the French-American relations as important? As a Frenchman, you will probably respond positively but why?

EC: The United States is a major power. Nowadays, the entire world depends on their attitude. If they want a war in Iran, the US is the one to decide.

ETM: So what exactly should France's role be?

EC: Its role resembles the one of General de Gaulle. Remember that during the time of the conflicts between the US and the Soviet Union, General de Gaulle took a middle position. He did not want to be a yes man like England. General de Gaulle required a policy that could benefit France. Don't forget that he was the first one to initiate relations with China. I remember when I was in the cabinet of the French president having access to the transcription of the discussion between General de Gaulle and Nixon when he was vice-president. It was evident that General de Gaulle influenced Nixon's decision to open relations with China.

ETM: So how should we look at the relation between France and the United States? Is it a token of friendship or a part of *Realpolitik*?

EC: It can be both of them; we love American people, but we cannot blindly obey what Mr. Bush says.

ETM: Are there any relations or links between both countries? What are the common points that we share?

EC: The common point is that we have both helped each other to become independent. It has been over 200 years since Admiral de Grasse and Lafayette were at the side of the American rebels against the English. That's the first link.

ETM: Was it the idea of liberty they were fighting for?

EC: Yes, I believe so. The motif was to support the country that wanted to gain liberty.

ETM: When we think about history as progress, these are two countries favorable to progress, of humanistic progress, favorable to the development of democracy. Is this what we have in common?

EC: Yes, that's it. I do think that is a general tendency. In the Soviet Union, under the Communists, it was awful. Today, the country opens slowly, maybe not as fast as everyone wishes, but I can certainly see the change as an expanding liberty. I have traveled several times to Russia since the end of the Soviet Union. Russia is a country that is becoming more and more democratic. It is a country that is not absolutely changed, but is on its way to change.

ETM: There is a certain influence coming from both sides; an exchange, sometimes certain disagreements which in the long term can become profitable. We saw such an example with De Gaulle who influenced Nixon in his decision to establish a diplomatic dialogue with China. And, speaking about General de Gaulle, what exactly did America represent to him?

EC: It represented mechanical force.

ETM: From a military point of view, it was the force that France lacked in 1940. Did it mean something else?

EC: He thought that it was the Americans who permitted us to win the war. I can say this without any doubt. For example, England had to survive. Everything she needed or almost everything came by sea, mainly from the US. It was the US that provided the food, the clothes, the munitions, the weapons and the petroleum products. Everything crossed the Atlantic. It was the Americans who helped us win the battle of the Atlantic.

ETM: And beyond the war, toward the end of his life, in his speeches and interviews, did he talk about America? What image did he have of it?

EC: I believe that he had a great gratitude for this country. Think about Eisenhower when they were both generals. It was thanks to their personal conversations that they succeeded in establishing an agreement. The fact that the Leclerc Division could go to Paris was an agreement between them, without Roosevelt being consulted. That was an accord of two military men, between two humans. That was exactly what influenced General de Gaulle and his appreciation for General Eisenhower.

ETM: How exactly can General de Gaulle be an example for France nowadays?

EC: I think that de Gaulle influenced the destiny of 20th century France the same way Churchill influenced England. These are people who marked their time by their deeds and who will always be historical figures. But when it comes down to De Gaulle, it is difficult to say something specific because of the difficulty he had in his relations with Roosevelt. De Gaulle reminded him of Joan of Arc without mentioning all the nicknames he could have given him. This is due to the fact that Roosevelt was surrounded by all the Vichy government representatives, especially Alexis Léger, also called Saint-John Perse. I think Roosevelt was poorly advised and that nobody opened his eyes about the positive aspects of de Gaulle. As a matter of fact, he did not want to recognize Free France.

ETM: Roosevelt wanted to keep in contact with Vichy.

EC: Yes, that is why the interests of French politics do not always coincide with those of American politics. Every country has its own way of viewing the world. History shows it; from that point of view, Roosevelt was wrong.

ETM: Did he progressively change his opinion the same way many French did?

EC: No, not when it comes down to de Gaulle, who was considered as the liberator by the French. De Gaulle had no problem taking control when he arrived in Algeria and then in Paris.

ETM: The people from your generation know that you owe our liberty to the Americans.

EC: Yes, they do. I am not familiar whether now in schools they discuss this and whether in the history books the US is paid the tribute it deserves. But even during this time, during the sixtieth anniversary of the Normandy landings, the way the media (radio, press, and television) talked about the role of the American soldiers was the highlight of the event. Personally, I was irritated at times to see that the media did not pay tribute or purposely ignored the role of the Navy. God knows that the people who landed did not cross the English Channel swimming; they were transported, escorted, covered by the fire from the ships which were present in the debarkation. There were 4,000 landing crafts and 1,500 military ships; there were also 300 escorts who prevented the approach of the submarines and the enemy patrol boats.

ETM: Did you participate in the Normandy landing?

EC: Yes, I did; I was at Omaha Beach. I was in a corvette that escorted the Mulberries. It was those artificial ports in the caissons that were dragged. The convoy, which I escorted, dragged the caissons designed for the artificial ports in Omaha Beach. That was on June 7 in the morning.

ETM: How did you feel? Were your spirits high?

EC: It was amazing; the joy was amazing. The liberation had begun. At Omaha the battle was difficult, but at Sword or Juno for example, it went well because the very first day, the English and Canadians had succeeded in sending 115,000 men there.

ETM: And the outcome of the war could no longer be doubted.

EC: Yes, in that moment everyone sensed the victory. Afterwards, I partici- pated in the reinforcement of the bridgeheads. Every day, there were 8 convoys of 300 ships, barges, cargos, and tramp boats, which were needed to re-supply the bridgeheads. For two months the transport of 39 divisions was provided which equaled 2 million men. And let's not forget that the Normandy landing was the decisive moment of the war. It was then that the German forces were caught in a stranglehold between the united attacks of the allies which had landed in Normandy, the Red Army, and two months later, the French-American troops landing in Southern France. That was the beginning of the end.

ETM: You participated fully in those events and I would like to thank you for sharing your experience.

EC: I am deeply persuaded in one thing: I have a great deal of admiration for the American veterans despite the differences that may exist. From a political point of view, it is a temporary situation since politics fluctuate. In a matter of fifteen days, we can show support and then hatred. But that is politics.

ETM: Do you believe that Europe can be a friend of America?

EC: Oh, yes. It must. Europe is like England, which is turned toward the Atlantic. We have to remember that since 1945 up until the decay of the Soviet Union, we and our security were all dependent on the US. And of this fact, we are all acutely aware.

Joseph Hourçourigaray

JH: I was born March 1921 in a little village called Esquiule in the Basque region. It is located in the South-West of France. I was the first born in the family of six children. My father was tall and strong and he wore an immense moustache. His left arm had been sectioned by shrapnel during WWI in 1916. He also had other bodily injuries that I was very impressed to see. His arm looked terrible and I would ask him questions about the war that was supposed to be "la der des der," the war that was presumed to end all wars. That war was in fact very cruel and inhumane for the soldiers who had suffered much through it. He died in 1943 and I only learned of his death two years later in 1945.

ETM: Could you tell us about your life before the war?

JH: I had a tranquil childhood. As in all villages, the Catholic faith was much practiced and I was an altar boy until the age of fourteen, when I received my first schooling certificate. We played in the open air a lot, rugby and handball *pelota*. When the season came, we also enjoyed picking black cherries in July and mushrooms in September and October. I spent my vacations at my uncles' place. I would go there by a bicycle that my father had offered me at the end of my schooling in 1934 to work at their farm. We were not short of labor. After three years of high school I received my degree. I was still more drawn to rugby and *pelota* games such as *Chistera Joko Garbi*, but I wanted to become a plane pilot. I would go sometimes to the civil aerodrome nearby to see the planes fly. Unfortunately, my father could not afford to pay for the necessary lessons to become a pilot. I later thought that with a certified qualification, I could have been enrolled in the Royal Air Force to fight the Battle of England. In 1938–1939, my father was reading the paper and he thought that there would be war. When the war broke out in 1939, I accompanied my father, who had previously received the Legion of Honor, to Camp *Bernadotte* where the 18th Pyrenean Regiment was based. He firmly intended to enlist but was told that as a wounded of war and father of a large family, it could not be done. I was also disappointed that I could not volunteer because of my young age.

ETM: How did you join Free France?

JH: Right after the fall of France, I was informed that I could enlist in the French Navy in the city of Toulon. We took the train, my father and I, for what was for us an expedition. Members of the military personnel who recognized his rank were saluting him in the train stations that we passed through. We both cried when we embraced to say goodbye. A few days later, I embarked on the Tourville, a French cruiser and we navigated the Mediterranean Sea under the command of Admiral Godfrey. We traveled to Corsica, Malta and Lebanon. We were not well informed about what was happening in occupied France. The thought that the Germans had invaded was unbearable and the capitulation without condition that had precipitated that event was unacceptable. We wanted to save the honor of our country. Some of us felt that we were being betrayed by lies and we had one desire: to kick the Germans out of France. The appeal of June 18, 1944 made by de Gaulle to continue the struggle and the fact the British were still in the war led me and others to volunteer by joining their troops in Alexandria, Egypt. Through this act, we were disobeying the orders of Vichy and became clandestine as Free French fighters.

ETM: What was the nature of your involvement during the war?

JH: We were interviewed by officers of the Intelligence Service and transported on the Bermuda along with soldiers from Australia, India and New Zealand. We passed the Suez Canal and reached Durban in South Africa where we spent two days on board. We arrived in Plymouth after 32 days at sea. From there, we took the train to Glasgow and Northern Scotland where people were coming to join Free France from the four corners of the world. It is during that period that the Battle of the Atlantic began. Hitler was seeking to cut Britain off from American military supplies and life resources. I was engaged in this conflict on board of one of the anti-submarine corvettes, under the command of Admiral Muselier. For 23 months, until March 1943, we escorted convoys coming from the United States, Canada, Iceland and Newfoundland. It was difficult because of the harsh weather conditions, but also because in most convoys, boats were sunk by German U-boats. We managed to sink some of those German U-boats even though they were hard to detect.

ETM: You then volunteered to fight in a French commando that would land on D-Day. How did that happen?

JH: It was during a leave in Camp Greenock in Scotland that I met Commandant Kieffer and volunteered to join his company that had been assembled a few months earlier. There, we trained extremely hard, rain or shine with 70 pounds of equipment on our backs. I can assure you that we needed to be motivated. Some were eliminated and wounded, and after three weeks of training, we received our badges and green berets. I was under the command of Lofi and Hulot, who were later killed in action. We continued our training and by the end of 1943, around Christmas, I participated in several raids made in Belgium and Holland. A few of us partook with a British captain in more raids, notably on the island of Jersey in the English Channel and on the French coast in Falaise not far from the lighthouse. The Germans and their barking dogs came very near us but did not see us. We had several casualties in one of these raids, in Holland, where six friends of mine lost their lives. These operations conducted at night were principally designed to gather information in preparation for the D-Day landing. As June 6 approached, we were transported by trucks to well guarded encampments and we began to be embarked. Our commando was led by Philippe Kieffer, and Lord Lovat was the head of the Commando Units landing at Sword.

ETM: What do you remember from your experience on D-Day?

JH: There were boats on the Channel that day, as far as the eye could see. And we had come to rejoin our France and kick the Germans out of there. There were also incredible massive bombardments coming from the hundreds of cuirassiers, cruisers and torpedo boats. The noise was deafening; a deluge of fire was landing on the coast. In the blink of an eye, we all jumped from the ramps with our arms up in the air to not dampen our weapons, and as Lord Lovat later described, it was the French fury: an indescribable assault with the bayonets joined to our canons, and for some, the dagger in the hand. We had 8 killed and 34 wounded; and in the afternoon, I was wounded while our commando made the junction with the paratroopers at Pegasus Bridge. These are unforgettable memories. Humans are more ferocious than animals.

ETM: What message would you like to send to the men and women who live on the other side of the Atlantic?

JH: Honor and Glory to all the dead. Immense gratitude to the Americans who had already come in 1917! Honor to all the soldiers of the *Pointe du Hoc* and Omaha who gave their lives for countries that were not the United States. For more than 60 years, I think a lot about the war from 1939 to May 1945. I am an Officer of the Legion of Honor and I received other military medals but I never speak about war. I think about the suffering of all people, and more than anything, about all the dead in all countries. I am a pacifist and apolitical. I hope for peace in the world, the suppression of social inequalities, and a more just sharing of wealth.

Jean Nallit

JN: I was born in Lyon in 1923. Therefore, I was a bit too young to be mobilized, but my father was severely wounded in the First World War and I asked him to sign me up in 1939. He did not want to sign. At the time, the parents were the ones who could sign the engagement and he told me that there was already one who was badly damaged, which was him, and that he didn't want another broken body in the family. However, several years later I was in a concentration camp as a consequence of the resistance I had become involved in. My father was injured at the Battle of Ladies' Way (*Le Chemin des Dames*) while covering the retreat of the French troops which were moving back at that moment. He was in charge of a machine gun and from the class of 1917. Moreover, he had entered the army ahead of the appeal.

ETM: What motivated you to want to be engaged in a war at the age of sixteen when its outcome was completely uncertain?

JN: Since I was very young, twelve approximately, I read the newspapers and this regime which was taking power in Germany did not please me much.

Since there was no television at the time, we had read about *Kristallnacht*, the occupation of the Rhineland and the arrival of German troops in Czechoslovakia, which was our ally. If one added what was also happening in Austria, all of that did not please me at all. When it came to France, I was of course against it. My father had never predisposed me against the Germans. In any case, he had been injured, for sure, but it was not my father who influenced me to join the Resistance. Ultimately, I forged my own opinion on the matter. The war in Spain, as well, with the intervention of German and Italian troops, did not really please me; this represented an accumulation of factors which made me join the Resistance.

ETM: So in 1940 you were not mobilized and at what point did you make the decision to get involved? In concrete terms, how did it happen?

JN: Initially, I was studying in a technical school which closed during the war; the teachers had been mobilized for war and thus it was closed. And at that moment, my father asked me: "What do you want to do?" One could find a job easily at the time, not like nowadays; and he helped me to find work at the gas company in Lyon; and I went to an electric power-station, which means I entered into contact with the guys who were already in the Resistance. They were union workers who had measured the gravity of the situation and were taking action. That was in 1940–1941.

ETM: What did their resistance consist of?

JN: Their resistance was to blow up the transformers and the high tension power lines so that the factories could not work at full speed for the Germans. This was their first activity. The day they contacted me, they asked me if I wanted to help them. I automatically said yes because one did not choose at the time to be a *resistant* based on political preference, the right or the left. They confided in me the distribution of underground leaflets and newspapers. This was supposed to be less dangerous than blowing up power lines, so it seemed. I do not completely agree now, but anyways; we received leaflets to be distributed and we used to put them in saddlebags because all this was done by bicycle. We would then throw the leaflets on the street. The newspapers were more precious and we distributed them like the mailmen; but when one had gone around a city block, one went quickly to the other side of town to go through another block without being spotted. That was during the day though sometimes we delivered them at night because I had ID papers from the electric power-station. The papers permitted me to circulate during the day, as well as during the night, in case I was needed to repair the station.

ETM: You were taking care of the destruction and the repair.

JN: The electric power station was necessary and we were not supposed to destroy it. Moreover, we faced a dilemma. The young ones like me wanted to blow it up completely, and the older ones were saying no, arguing that we would need it after the liberation. They were, in fact, right.

ETM: What was the message of the leaflets?

JN: The message on July 14, for instance, was to stage a protest in Place Bellecour, for example. But that was not an official protest. There was a gathering of people that was organized at a specific time; and we were watching the density of the pedestrians passing by at that very moment as a sign of opposition and solidarity. We could not have openly protested because we would have been repressed. However, I do remember singing the Marseillaise in the Hall of the Perrache train station with a group of young people on their way to the *Chantiers de jeunesse*, the youth forced labor camp, on July 14, 1943.

ETM: And the Germans were there.

JN: Yes, of course, but we did it any way. However, we did not sing all the verses.

ETM: Hence, that is already a type of resistance.

JN: That was already resistance. Later, I got in touch with another resistance network of action and information which was directed by the nephew of General de Gaulle, Michel Cailliau. At that moment, we were in charge of gathering information for the Resistance and the allies. It was different than the active military resistance; information is something extensive, and I was given the responsibility to work for the service of identification and document printing in the Lyon region. We made a large number of false identification cards. But that was not the only thing. Doing information work meant we were doing an inventory of the German forces in the area by identifying their badges, in order to know where they were coming from, their weapons, and where they might go next. There were pieces of information coming from all over France, and the allies were making a synthesis of it. They had a better understanding of the enemy. I also partook in the photographing of the German barges which descended the Saône River and which were carrying submarine pieces to be assembled in Toulon. They had previously been passing via the Atlantic and the straights of Gibraltar where they would be bombed; so the Germans could not build them on the Atlantic coast and they had found that path down the Saône and Rhône Rivers to bring the submarines down in detached pieces to Toulon, directly on the Mediterranean coast. We were passing the information to our allies and the barges were bombarded down the Rhône River. We did all kinds of things, such as looking for a terrain for parachute landing, searching for hiding places where we could install transmitting stations to be in communication with the BBC in London; among other things.

ETM: When the Germans invaded France in May 1940, what was the atmosphere in Lyon?

JN: Lyon was declared to be a free town, so it was not bombarded. As for the atmosphere, it was a feeling of dismay and consternation. The people quickly became aware of the situation but the regime of Vichy stalled and played for time. Moreover, the Americans entered belatedly in the war. And we counted on them.

ETM: And when you were thinking about America, you were thinking about what? What did America evoke in your mind in 1940?

JN: Freedom, a strong country capable of helping others.

ETM: When America entered the war, they landed in Algeria, in Northern Africa. That was one of the turning points of the war. Did you interpret this in similar terms?

JN: I deplored the fact that there were troops opposed to their landing. It is difficult to understand but there were these fellows in the army of Vichy who commanded these troops, who did not have strong convictions. They had been in full flight in 1940 and the regime of Vichy influenced the soldiers.

ETM: What made an impression on me when I entered the walls of the Museum of Resistance and Deportation, where we are today, is the plaque at the entrance that reads: "Ici, en 1943–1944, la Gestapo Nazi aidée par des traitres a torturé des milliers de résistants et d'otages avant leur mort ou leur déportation. Leur sacrifice permit la libération de la France. [In this place, between 1943 and 1944, the Gestapo of the Nazis with the collaboration of traitors tortured thousands of French resistant fighters before their death or their deportation to concentration camps. Their sacrifice permitted the liberation of France.]" Could you tell us about the place we are now in today, the Museum of Resistance and Deportation?

JN: This place was a military school where medical doctors, pharmacists and veterinarians were trained. In 1942, the Gestapo occupied the facility; and it became a center of torture. Besides, when I was arrested, I was immediately brought here and I was tortured by Klaus Barbie, later called "the Butcher of Lyon," whose trial is broadcast in this museum. They locked the prisoners up for several days into the basements beneath as they were being tortured. They placed you there and then if you survived they would transfer you to Fort Montluc which was used as a prison for all the people in the Resistance arrested in the region.

ETM: They sought to get information.

JN: We were not supposed to speak.

ETM: When talking about tortures, what kind of tortures were those?

JN: There was the bathtub; they forced us under water on the verge of drowning and death. Afterwards, they restored us to consciousness by beating us with sticks, blows and kicks, and finally by any means necessary. We were not able to move because we had handcuffs.

ETM: When talking about the Resistance in France, one thinks of Jean Moulin. Was Lyon a center of resistance in France?

JN: Yes, because the occupied zone in the North was too difficult, and that was not because of the lack of resistance, but because many movements withdrew to Lyon, and of course, when everything was occupied, it got difficult. But the control center was here in Lyon.

ETM: Jean Moulin, the leader and hero of the French Resistance, came here as well. What can you tell us about Jean Moulin?

JN: I met Jean Moulin. I learned not so long ago that during his stay in Lyon, he used to go to a store in town, and the two people who ran the store were from our network. So I met Jean Moulin there, but I did not know who he was. It was better that way; in fact, when he was arrested, the members of my network designated me to find out who had been arrested that day at the office of Doctor Dugoujon in Caluire in order to eventually cut off endangered networks and mail boxes. A companion and I crossed the square where Jean Moulin (we would later learn) had been arrested, and as soon as we looked toward the windows of Doctor Dugoujon's office, the Gestapo began to chase us. Fortunately, I was able to break away from them in the back streets of Traboule. We regularly organized car "pick up" at specific times in town everyday for the reestablishment of the tracking in our services and I was able to escape. I told my superior that what I had done was not glorious since the only thing I could do was to cross the square and nothing else. He said that we would get to know what had happened precisely afterward, because we had people in the police, who were working with us, someone by the name of Niquet. In fact, he was the head of police who was also from our network and who later became the national director of the DST, the French Intelligence Service.

ETM: What was the name of your network?

JN: Charette, with one "r"; I specify that because that is not a cart (as in "charrette"). Charette was from the Vendée region, in Western France. Michel Cailliau, the head of our network, was a prisoner of war and had escaped. He received the mission to establish this underground organization, which spread all over the national territory.

ETM: You were later arrested and then deported to a concentration camp. Could you tell the story of what happened and the way it happened?

JN: In the Resistance, I was arrested at the end of March, 1944. We were preparing the Allies landing and we did not know the date. So, we were working with our allies and we were arrested at that moment. We had groups of underground resistance movements that we had created in the Beaujolais region. These were passive groups of resistant fighters who were not trained to attack at any moment, but they were created in order to rejoin us when the proper moment came. Thus, we were arming and preparing neuralgic centers in order to stop the Germans in the region. From then on, we had to expose ourselves more than we usually did, because this is the way it was. It is during this time that I was arrested by the Gestapo in the streets of Lyon, and I was immediately transferred here to this center, where I underwent the torture of Barbie. He put me through the bathtub torture many times to make me speak. There were three or four with him. I did not speak. If you watch the trial of Barbie, to know how it happened, listen to Lise Lesèvre's witness account. It is exactly what I would have said. I did not testify in the trial. There were enough witnesses to get him condemned. Afterwards, I was transferred to Fort Montluc; from there to Compiègne, and from Compiègne to Buchenwald.

ETM: What were you about to do or doing when you were arrested?

JN: Normally, I had to help out a friend with fake ID papers, since at the time I was responsible for the printing for the Lyon region in my network. I had a Jewish friend who needed to be helped out, and I was arrested while doing this. But the Gestapo hurried a little too much, because if it had waited a bit more, they would have arrested this friend with us. Seeing that we were being arrested, he contacted members of the network and the material that was at my home was removed. It was diverse equipment such as a typewriter, the fake German stamps used in order to make false documents and passes for the prisoners of war, as well as blank documents to make fake identity cards.

ETM: All this was at your home?

JN: It was at our home and it was evacuated immediately. My parents were separated but my mother and my sister remained there. My mother was the typist for the network and my sister was a liaison agent. I did not need to persuade anyone to enter the Resistance. My father was very handicapped after the first war, and although my parents were separated, he too was in the Resistance.

ETM: What was the nature and significance of your work with respect to fake identity cards?

JN: I was working in cooperation with a broad information network (*Bureau Central de Renseignement et d'Action*) in London, and I have the *Médaille des Justes*. The Israeli services found out that our network produced locally between 25,000 and 30,000 fake documents that were issued to individuals. We sent false papers as far as the camps of the prisoners of war. We sent them German passes so that if and when the prisoners escaped, they could cross Germany almost in complete safety. We had people who were helping out the aviators whose planes had been shot down to pass through Spain and to get to England because a pilot is precious; one cannot train him in five minutes. We issued false documents for these people. We had a service run by an Austrian who had fought on the barricades at the time of the *Anschluss* in Austria. He had been injured and arrested by the Germans. He had managed to escape in 1939 and joined us in the network. He was put in charge of the "German interior front." Its role included making the anti-Nazi German soldier desert. As for us, we would bring these deserters to special resistance centers where they would be watched closely so that the underground would not be infiltrated. In the end, they would fight better than our own men because they knew who they were fighting against. They fought on our side.

ETM: Hence, in the end, they were fighting with the members of the French underground?

JN: Yes. These German soldiers who deserted ended up fighting in the underground. They were deserters because they were anti-Nazis. They had not been able to refuse to be incorporated into their army, but as soon as they could desert, they did. We were very careful. I will tell you right now that they were supervised closely; we paid attention. If it worked out, they were incorporated as everyone else.

ETM: That is not a well-known fact.

JN: No, that is not a really well-known thing.

ETM: You received the *Médaille des Justes* as "righteous among the nations" from the Yad Vashem memorial in Israel on August 3, 1992 at the Israeli Embassy in Paris.

JN: I did not know the fellows I helped out in my network. We had the photo and then we issued the false document. In my network, we had fellows who were Jews and who were able to attest to what I did. I think that anybody who was persecuted, whoever they are, I would have helped. It happens that there were many Jews whom I did not know in fact and who were helped by what we did in producing fake documents.

ETM: You were personally arrested and tortured, imprisoned and then deported. Did this occur over a few weeks?

JN: This all happened quickly. I was arrested at the end of March, 1944, and transferred to Compiègne. I left Lyon on May 1, and we left Compiègne on May 8 arriving in Buchenwald on May 12. It all took place quickly. In Buchenwald, there were people from all backgrounds and origins, resistant fighters and political opponents. There were also prisoners from the Red Army and they angered the Germans because they were marching in the camp as if they were on a military parade. They were walking proudly surrounded by their officers, in cadence and rhythm as if they were free. It was impressive, and if you consider the deplorable conditions in which we found ourselves, it was formidable.

ETM: Did you fear for your life when you arrived at the camp?

JN: Not more than before. When we were transferred, we did not know about concentration camps, even though, before the war, there had been a weekly paper, which had talked about concentration camps, but it had passed a bit unnoticed. We thought those camps were like convict prisons similar to the ones that existed for the criminals in France who were sent to Guyana. All of that passed a bit unnoticed. However, we figured out what it was as soon as we arrived. During a previous visit to the camp by the Red Cross, they had planted flowers around the buildings outside; this is what former inmates told me. I did not see that. They gave clean clothes to the prisoners and they allowed visits to the camp. It appeared to be a "normal" camp.

ETM: But once one entered inside, one entered into a different universe.

JN: Exactly. They did not show them what was going on inside.

ETM: What did you go through there? Starvation?

JN: Starvation, yes. The rations we were given would allow us to survive for six months and then disappear because of the lack of food. I am here and I do not have an explanation. I survived. We were under the control of the Kapos who had the right of life and death over us. We suffered unexpected beatings which weakened us in the long run as well as the lack of food and forced labor. I was assigned to work at the stone-pit at a certain time and to dig stones for twelve hours a day. There was no extermination at the camp. The fellows who died went to the crematorium, but their deaths were not due to the violent and systematic extermination occurring in Auschwitz for instance.

ETM: Were there gas chambers?

JN: I had a discussion with other deportees who told me that there were no gas chambers in that camp. But I think that there was one there which did not serve as a gas chamber. I will tell you why; because when you entered into a shower area and the doors closed in like a submarine, if one injected gas in the space, your fate was sealed. It did not serve but it could have served in my opinion. Now, we are in contradiction on the subject among ourselves, the deportees.

ETM: I just saw earlier this morning high school students enter the center and you welcomed and guided them. You talk to them often though you have a busy schedule?

JN: This is my schedule and all that you see in red after 12 noon are indications of my meetings with groups of students to whom I have spoken or will speak about the history and the significance of this place.

ETM: These young French people visit the center everyday. What lessons do they need to learn and remember from history and from your story?

JN: That a regime like the one the Germans had in the 1930s and 1940s should never be in power again. That is what we wish for them; and if there were resurgences at some point in the future, that they might know how to face them. I have a friend who went to England and did studies to be a parachutist and a saboteur, and who was parachuted in the region of Toulouse with the mission to blow up the Dewoitine factories. When he completed this task, he went to the underground of the Cantal, in Central France, and assisted groups of resistant fighters. These groups of resistance had received a large parachute drop which was organized with another man named Cardozzo, who was a British citizen. They dropped off armor, munitions, even cars and jeeps from air planes. The Americans I met later told me that it was the largest material drops from Norway to Burma during the whole war. Thus, the role and organization of Resistance under similar circumstances is of primary importance.

ETM: Eisenhower recognized the importance of the Resistance and of its role under the occupation and during the campaign of Normandy.

JN: These groups of resistance blockaded several German divisions which were unable to rejoin the front in Normandy as they had wanted during the time of landing. If these armored divisions had arrived, I am afraid that the landing would have been rendered more difficult. In fact, I had a monument erected in their memory at the Pass de Neronne with the fellows from these groups in the Cantal. The parachute drops had been made on the plateau. The Germans were at the bottom and they did not dare to go upward. They believed that it was parachutists who were landing and that were going to attack. But it was the material which would serve greatly during the following days. Hence, there was solidarity between the French Resistance and the American Army. There was an objective in common. I consider the Americans as liberators capable of defending liberty. It may be in fact what they wanted to do in Iraq.

ETM: What do you think when we sometimes speak of anti-Americanism in France?

JN: That exists in certain circles but I think that without the Americans we would not be free; even through our resistance, we would not have been able to liberate our country on our own. We needed all of our allies, including the Americans.

ETM: You were involved in the struggle at a very young age. How did that form your character, values and your ideals for the rest of your life?

JN: I think that my experience in the concentration camp made me age by ten years in maturity; despite our young ages, we now have reflections and judgments about people in front of us that are very precise. We have a way to study people, according to what we have gone through and we make judgments. We are not obliged to express it but in fact we make a judgment, and we judge the value of the person in front of us. The experience made us age by more than ten years because we would have needed those ten years in order to have that judgment.

ETM: How were you liberated?

JN: I was liberated on May 8, 1945 by the Americans. Moreover, I say this to the young people who come here: they had guts because it was an American jeep that arrived with three men on board and machine guns. I did not know the American material despite my work and they told us in their language that we were free. They were thirty kilometers from their line. On May 8, 1945, there were still 150,000 German soldiers in the area that had stopped fighting because of the capitulation but some could still have wanted to fight. Therefore, being thirty kilometers from their front line, these American soldiers had guts. We walked thirty kilometers on foot and we joined the American lines. On one side there were the Americans and on the other, there were Soviet troops. The Germans were surrounded, and not far were the British and Free French forces.

ETM: What did that conflict and your work in the Resistance teach you from the point of view of human experience?

JN: Liberty has no price. This is the main point. When I talk to the young students, I tell them that when one loves one's country, one defends it. This was surely the spirit that animated the American soldiers. For me, it comprises the good and the bad; the good is to have our country liberated, whereas the bad is to have been deported. I could have lived without it but here we are.

ETM: What is your message to pass on to the American veterans today?

JN: That they all have my friendship. We owe them our liberty.

ETM: In this context, why are French-American relations important?

JN: We have had relations for a long time and we share values. There can be some disagreements but it does not mean either that we should break off relations. I tell the young people who come here that without the Allies, no matter who they were (the Russians also accomplished a formidable task), to liberate ourselves on our own would have been difficult. Maybe, we could have managed to do it; it would have taken several more years and much more destruction. That is why we should tip our hats to the Allies.

Rosette Peschaud and Raymonde Jeanmougin

RP: I grew up in Valenciennes in Northern France until I turned sixteen or seventeen. My father fought in World War I and when the economic situation of the family business became very bad, he left for Morocco. I joined him there in 1938 when there was a false war with Munich. My parents brought me there thinking that the war was going to begin but in fact it began a year later. Before this, I was raised by my grandmother, while my parents were living in Morocco. I was present during the mobilization and I saw how men left sorrowfully for the front line in 1938. France was in danger; it was worth it to take the risk to fight and to face the danger of dying. What I never imagined, however, was that I would also take part in the conflict. I arrived in Morocco in 1938 and I studied philosophy in high school. Since I had never lived with my parents before, I really wanted to live with them. I didn't go at that time to study in Algiers, and I remained with them close to Kenitra, Morocco.

ETM: You said that at the time of the first mobilization in 1938 the soldiers were leaving with regret. What was the reason?

RP: Because World War I was very recent, and for them the war was mayhem; so I think that diminished their enthusiasm. They didn't feel like dying. They had already seen the horrific aftermath of the previous war. After all, I was born in 1920 and all the soldiers who were mobilized were about the same age as me, and they didn't leave happily. I don't know if they were asking themselves whether the war was useful or not. I don't know anything about that. I was too young to ask myself those kinds of questions and to find the answers to them. It was scary because they were talking about trenches and killings. What had been the purpose of all those deaths? Or even of winning, if they would start fighting again after twenty years? World War I was thought to be the war to end all wars, but in the end this assumption proved to be wrong.

ETM: What were your personal feelings?

RP: I felt admiration for the First World War generation, and the desire to do the same thing, which was almost impossible for a girl. I never dared to say that I too wanted to do something for the country. They would have laughed at me; they would have thought that I was out of place. We later learned that many women fought in the Resistance when France was under occupation. After the war, they returned to their houses, with modesty, and without making any waves around themselves. There are those whom everybody knows, like Lucie Aubrac, for whom I feel the greatest admiration because of her courage and her intelligence.

ETM: How did you make the decision to get involved?

RP: Well, I knew what defeat was. I was in Morocco, and I remember having listened to Pétain's speeches on the day of the Armistice. I was driving my parents' car. My dad was mobilized thirty kilometers away from the place where we lived, and I was going to stay with him. I listened to Pétain's speech and when I arrived, my father was very upset. He said, "What a disgrace!" In the apartment below there was an acquaintance of my father's, who was a Jew. He rang the bell at the door, entered the living room, sat down without saying anything, and started crying. I must say that the event opened my eyes about something that I used to ignore: the flight from Germany of the Jews who had come to France to seek refuge and who now were living close to the invading Germans. But we just couldn't imagine something like that; that the deportation could have been organized as a massacre. It is something that we didn't believe until we saw Dachau in 1944. That is when we saw it and we could testify to it.

ETM: It is hard to believe that such a crime could actually be committed.

RP: Yes. Starting in 1940, my father was demobilized. He came back to the village and I was living with them. Soon we found out that somebody was talking on the radio from London. Every evening, we listened to Radio London, which was very difficult since there was no electricity. We charged the batteries all day long so we could listen in the evening. It gave daily lessons of patriotism in an unbelievably enthusiastic tone. It was not a radio station that hummed. I was a young girl who mostly listened to what the adults had to say, instead of having my own convictions. But I completely agreed that it was horrible to see the Germans occupying the French land and tracking down the Resistance fighters. For us, especially after listening to London, the Resistance fighters were real heroes. Moreover, my father had joined a movement of the French Resistance in Morocco called the French-American movement, which was a Gaullist movement.

ETM: The landing in North Africa was a turning point.

RP: We witnessed the landing. From where we were living, we could hear the cannons, because they were often drilling, and all of a sudden there were two airplanes flying above us. One of them shot at the other one, and an American jumped. The plane was shot down on our neighbor's property. My father couldn't understand why his movement hadn't been warned. I went with him to Mehdya where the landing was taking place. We were ten kilometers from the sea. I will tell you a story that may seem insane to you. When the Americans saw us, they stuck together around the gas truck. We had no more gas, and they said: "Why did you shoot at us, French people? We learned a song for the landing." So my father said: "Oh really, a song; what song?" They replied: "Marshal [Pétain] here we are! Do you know it?" They had taught this to the landing troops! There was such ignorance. It was incomprehensible. Moreover, my father had been invited by the civil inspector, who was the mayor, the French administrator, with some Americans, so that the French could explain to them what the purpose of De Gaulle's movement was. After an entire night of debates, the Americans left saying: "We also have Democrats and Republicans." It was impossible to explain.

ETM: It was hard for them to understand. And it is true that France is more complex from a political or ideological point of view. However, we also know that Roosevelt was ill advised with respect to De Gaulle by some Vichy representatives in Washington. What was the significance of the landing in North Africa for you?

RP: For me, it involved the Rochambeau group who were a group of ambulance women created by an American woman, Mrs. Florence Conrad. She had already participated in WWI as a nurse, and had volunteered in the 1940 campaign, where she had created dwelling places for the French soldiers. At the moment of the defeat, she was desperate because of what was happening to France, and she wandered from one prison camp to the other to make them sign inter-zonal cards so she could tell their families that they were alive. She was so against the Germans that the ambassador asked her to go back to the United States. He was afraid to find her interred in a camp herself. When she went back to America, after the defeat, she got in touch with the American feminist societies, the American feminist leagues, and she succeeded in obtaining enough money to buy 19 Dodge ambulances. That's not a small feat! She chose Mrs. Suzanne Torres, a young lawyer full of energy, as an assistant; and who later became Mrs. Massu, the wife of General Massu. She also hired a few young women. Coming to North Africa right after the landing, she succeeded in loading the ten ambulances on the boat named Le Pasteur, which took them to

Casablanca; but from there she didn't know which way to go. She looked at what was best; General Leclerc was coming from Chad with his young Free Frenchmen. She was a very wise woman, and since she also knew General Koenig, she told him: "Look, call Leclerc, I have nineteen ambulances, I have women, and I want to join the 2nd Armored Division." Leclerc answered by saying, "I do want ambulances, but I don't want women." She replied, "In that case, you will have neither one nor the other." She then started having secret negotiations with the 5th Armored Division. Since Leclerc really needed the nineteen ambulances, he told Mrs. Conrad that he would take the women, but only up to Paris. In fact, she didn't have enough drivers for the ambulances so they looked for other recruits. This is how I became involved. Ms. Conrad hit the road. She went to the right and to the left, and arrived at my parents' house. I was twenty-two, the ideal profile, and I had been driving a gas vehicle for two years.

ETM: This was in 1943?

RP: Yes, it was in November, 1943, I think and I joined the 2nd Division. At that time I had the intention of leaving my parents and continuing my studies in Algiers. They were scared about sending a young girl into such a learning environment; one never knew who one meets up with. However, they let me leave with a Division of 18,000 men! We had been saying at that time in Rabat that all those young men coming from Chad were the cream of France. I left with them, and I started the big adventure of the 2nd Armored Division on the road from Mers-El-Kebir and Casablanca to England.

ETM: How did the 2nd Armored Division take part in the Normandy campaign?

RP: It was an armored division. It didn't seem to have anything to do there. But we were very mad. We didn't understand why the Americans landed on June 6; but we were there and had to wait until July 31. We were very disconnected from civil life; we didn't have newspapers or radios except for the tank drivers. But we, the ambulance women of the 2nd class, were not informed. There was frustration. We set out on July 8 to join Southampton and General Leclerc landed on August 1. I landed on the 4th. I think the landing continued for twelve days. Immediately, we left for *Mont Saint Michel*. It was a matter of closing the Avranches pocket. At that time, we reached St. James, next to *Mont Saint Michel*. The same night, we were bombed and all that created a lot of damage. A *Rochambelle*, a member of our group, had her legs blown off. I was the one who found her in the field. She told me, "I am hurt, but first take care of the ones that are more hurt than me." I went quickly to look for the doctors and stretchers to take her back. She died ten years later as a result of her wounds. There were very tough fights up until Paris. I really mean it. Being in contact with the enemy on a battle field and knowing how to act is an innate thing.

ETM: The American veterans rarely speak about their experience in battle.

RP: It is not different for us. We gathered young boys who had their intestines hanging out who were politely asking us, "Miss, do you think I am going to die?" We didn't take care of ourselves; usually we worked together with a doctor and a nurse. We followed the armored columns. When there was a battle, we received the shells. We heard the shots of the machine guns, and we were behind the doctor's jeep. At those times we said, "There are wounded people up front." The doctor's jeep got going and followed it. We passed all the columns, and we got upfront so we could take the people from where they were wounded and under fire. I must tell you that I was scared, while waiting in my ambulance and saying to myself, "Where are those bullets going to enter?" Then, from the moment they told me, "Go look for a wounded person," my fear disappeared. It was finished. It was completely gone. I told this to the wife of General Massu, and she told me: "Everybody tells me that I should have been a Rochambelle, but I couldn't have done it; I would have been too scared." And I told her, "Catherine, nothing more than the fact itself of thinking that you could be scared can prove that you already took a small dose of the vaccine against fear." There are people who say, "I know myself, and I have got all the courage in the world." But when it is time to show it, they are frightened. While in action one is no longer afraid. It is when we are inactive that we are scared.

ETM: Was there also a certain pride in being there?

RP: Yes, the fact that we were 36 women among 18,000 men meant that we had to act properly. We women have a certain pride, especially since at the time women were thought to be weak, and unable to control their emotions as well as men do. But I can tell you that we were as able to control them as men were. Our job was to go to the front lines, and usually there we gave first aid to the wounded, and we were in contact with the most awful reality. I remember seeing a truck full of soldiers that was hit by a shell. It was a horrible spectacle, something unbelievable. But in action, we were not thinking about anything anymore. We were only thinking about completing the mission. Of course we had many friends that we lost on our journey. But I was actually asking the question myself: how is it that we accept the death of our friends and we don't let it discourage us? Well, I think that we shared the same dangers, so we didn't have any complex concerning the death of others. Destiny touched them. Tomorrow, it could be one of us. We would have accepted our own death in the same way.

ETM: What did France represent to you?

RP: Well France represented a woman, a country prisoner to the demands of her enemies. I think De Gaulle put France in the feminine genre as well. It was also the land and the soil of France. We were really sure that our fight was worth it, our crusade; I can now say that it was a crusade behind Leclerc. Don't forget one thing: in front of us we had the Germans shooting at us. What they wanted was to kill us. When you are a fighter with a shotgun, and you are shot at, it revives your courage, and I would even say the energy of the fighter that is called hatred.

ETM: The campaign up to Paris was intense.

RP: Very intense, and it was there that we, the *Rochambelles*, started to understand what was expected of us. I am not sure that some of our doctors really knew what to expect from us. It was on the battlefield that things started to move for us and for the soldiers. There were young soldiers that had already been in war, coming from Chad, but that had nothing to do with the battles between armored vehicles.

ETM: You were full of ardor, enthusiasm, and nothing could stop you.

RP: Nothing. This is why nothing stopped us. When we think about those tanks that arrived all by themselves in Paris, in the courtyard of City Hall, I must say that they had a lot of courage. In the area around Paris, the battle began at Sully-Mazarin, Anthony, and Croix de Berny; there were very difficult battles. We entered Paris on August 25, and I remember that, I think it was on the night of the 24th. I was in front of the *Fresne* prison and it was raining. The bombs were falling, and we were taking care of the wounded during the night. There had been an uprising of the population and there were intense battles.

ETM: It is after these fierce combats that De Gaulle, followed by a jubilant crowd, marched up the Champs-Elysées.

RP: Yes, after the fighting had ceased; there were only scattered gunshots. It was August 26. I was in front of Notre Dame Cathedral. I had arrived with the Billotte column, so I was there since about 8am, and my ambulance was in front of the main door of Notre Dame. All the tanks were going around the plaza and from time to time, gunfire broke out. The entire crowd was hugging and embracing us. They threw themselves on the ground, under the wheels of the gunners. I was watching and I didn't even get the feeling that I was being shot at. After that, at the end of August or beginning of September, we reached the region of Lorraine, where we fought battles at Dompierre and Baccarat. These were really tough combats and we spent nights in the forests. Once, we were bombarded without even knowing where we were and I didn't know anymore where the Germans were or the French. Finally, we took Strasbourg and ended our campaign in Berchtesgaden, Germany.

ETM: What lesson can the French youth learn from your commitment? What can they learn from the experience of the occupation and of the Resistance movement?

RP: I will not talk about the Resistance in France. I didn't have anything to do with it. I saw the occupation because I came to France twice during that time. But for me, it was intolerable to see the Germans hissing when I was passing by; it was humiliating. However it was a very brief humiliation, because I had to pass through that area twice for fifteen days, when I came to see a grandmother who was sick. It was unacceptable to be stopped at the frontier, to have to get down off the train. It happened to me when I was with my mother. It was also humiliating to be examined by smug and sinister people.

ETM: While thinking about that American woman who founded the group called the *Rochambelles*, Mrs. Florence Conrad, what message would you like to address to the America of our days?

RP: I remain extremely grateful to America, who gave us everything: our arms, our clothes, our food and the gas. It is incredible. I am still profoundly grateful to America.

ETM: We will always have a common heritage.

RP: You bet!

ETM: Maybe we also have a future in common.

RP: We are all westerners. Between us, there is an undeniable bond of religion and civilization. Americans, Europeans, and Christian nations, have a common bond. I saw the Polish emigrants arriving in the north of France. They were working in the mines, and they were totally out of the ordinary. Then their children became French. There is no difference in our time between someone who has a Polish name and someone who has a French name, just like there is no difference between you and me. None! But I don't know whether in the name of the Muslim religion the assimilation process can be done in the same way. It is a question I cannot answer. But looking at the future as old people do, and saying that the young people are worth even less than we were, that is absolutely absurd. There are circumstances that form humans, and I believe in it with all my heart. If something bad happened to France again, there would be a lot of young Frenchmen to defend it. As a member of the 2nd Armored Division and the Leclerc Foundation, I handle a charity sale and we serve 1,000 meals, and in order to help us, the Division lends us soldiers. I have seen how the young immigrants products of the Muslim immigration, were proudly French. They only show us the bad examples on television, but it is not on the negative that we must dwell. I remember asking a young Algerian, "What is your origin?" He then looked at me in a mean way and answered me, "I am a Frenchman, madam." I excused myself and told him that that was not my question. My question was whether he was an Algerian or a Moroccan at his origin, because I lived for a long period of time in Morocco. My husband met a lot of people in his travels, and I remember an engineer whose father was a Spanish immigrant. He was very grateful to France for the higher education he had received here. When journalists came to ask him questions, and he told them this, they were not interested in it at all. The immigrant child of a worker who was happy to be a Frenchman, didn't interest them.

ETM: Journalists should be educated in that respect?

RP: Most probably.

ETM: I was reflecting upon that last night. I think about France, as everybody else does, and I am here for only five days. I was thinking that one of the keys for the future is in the educational system. You were talking about the children of the immigrants, who had a particular pride in being French, and who blend well into the French society. It is only a minority which does not succeed and rejects French values.

RP: Yes, we say that France is in chaos; that is absurd! I live in Paris and I didn't see anything during the riots. I actually live in Vanves, and I still didn't see anything at all.

ETM: There are problems there; that is for sure.

RP: Listen, I have just come back from a trip to Morocco. I lived in Morocco for thirty years, and I found the country completely changed. I saw many cities being built, and they were a little similar to the suburbs in which people live in France. I started wondering why here in France they are rioting, while there they say they are pleased to live in buildings like this, and that everything seems to be going well. It is a question of having a more authoritarian government that would suppress the slightest riot. Our foundation gave prizes to the sons and grandsons of Algerian soldiers who fought for France during the Algerian War. Some of them were taken back to France and we helped them a little, while the others remained in Algeria where they were massacred. In order to give out the prizes, we questioned many of them, and what amazed me the most was that I've never heard a word of reproach to France. These young people were very well educated; in fact we gave a prize to a young girl who had studied law, and to a boy who went to the *Normale Sup*, the French elite school, while his father was an illiterate metallurgist. We don't talk much about that.

ETM: What is the name of the foundation?

RP: It is the Foundation Marshal Leclerc, which is in charge of the preservation of the memory of Leclerc. There is an association and is a foundation. The association will disappear with the death of its last member. We hope that the foundation will survive because of all the things that we initiated through our events. We already have three perpetual church masses: one on the 25th of August at Notre Dame de Paris, in association with the Foundation of General de Gaulle; a perpetual mass at the dome of the *Invalides* for the anniversary of the death of Leclerc, who is buried there. There is also a perpetual mass in Strasbourg, because every year, on the date which is closest to the arrival of the 2nd Armored Division in Strasbourg, we remember the Oath of Koufra, which is the oath that Leclerc made on March 1, 1941, when he took the oasis of Koufra, in Libya, saying: "I swear that we will not put down our arms until France's flag flies on the cathedral of Strasbourg." So it is all about perpetuating the memory of the liberation of Paris, the liberation of Strasbourg, and the epic of Leclerc. Do you want me to ask my friend, Raymonde Jeanmougin, who was an ambulance woman like me, to come and tell you how she saved the life of an American?

ETM: Yes, of course.

RJ: It was in Chatel-sur-Moselle. There were many wounded people and my teammate gathered all of them in a house, while I was wandering about the area to find other wounded people. There was a soldier who came with me and on the side of the road there was another smaller road, and on each side there were embankments that continued into the fields. There was a half-track that was stopped on one side of that road. The soldier took the left side, and I looked behind the half-track and there was an American soldier who was wounded and who was completely conscious. I tried to pull him but I saw that he had a really damaged leg. I took his neck-tie off and I made a tourniquet knot on his leg. I tried to pull him but he was too heavy, and at that moment we both rolled down in a trench. While we were down there, a shell exploded in the half-track; that saved us. I left the American down in the field. I climbed up and there was an American jeep. I think it was the artillery that saw us, and they helped me bring up the wounded soldier. Then I left again, and the American officer who was in the jeep and his driver must have had a talk. I have a citation for this.

ETM: Were you able to find the American soldier?

RJ: No, I didn't know which American hospital he was in, but I was happy to know that the officer was saved thanks to our rolling-down into the trench.

RP: We maintained a very deep appreciation of the American advanced surgical units. Every time there were wounded people, it was our job to save them. We have the story of Bervialle, who had shrapnel shell in his heart, and every time it beat, a small stream of blood pumped out. His captain, Captain de Boissieu, who later became General de Boissieu, the son-in-law of General de Gaulle, came to salute him as if he was saluting a dead man. He was in the hospital, and he had his heart stitched up, and when the surgeon passed by, that wounded man, named Jacques Bervialle, inquired, and the surgeon was convinced that he was going to die. Next to him there was a woman who was waiting. It was the ambulance woman who saved him. They got married and lived happily together. I will say something else related to this, because we had many severely wounded, like Bervialle, Battistini and Tardieux. They were severely wounded people who lived with horrible handicaps their entire lives. They were the ones who feel closest to the 2nd Armored Division. It was Jacques Bervialle who created the Historical Fund and all the work of putting the documents in order. The gathering of newspapers and photos was made under his direction.

ETM: Thank you for sharing this anecdote with me; I am sure you have many more to tell.

RJ: There are some evacuations which I remember well. There was a wounded soldier, and I saw that his overcoat was going inside his entrails, and he was trying to get it out. I was trying to dissuade him, but the impulse was stronger than him, and he tripped out the coat. I could feel the water, the blood and the body that was emptying. That definitely impressed me. I don't think he was able to be saved.

RP: He had a lung hemorrhage. There is something I didn't tell you and that I want to emphasize now: in our ambulances, we took French wounded, but sometimes we also took German wounded. It is also true the other way around. I myself had a young German who died in my ambulance one night; when we couldn't evacuate. We didn't know what to do. He wanted water and he was hurt in the stomach. He died the next morning.

ETM: In war the best and the worse in a human being comes out.

RP: That is true, and it is also true that we went in as a bunch of innocents, and we came out different. We learned how to control ourselves, and that control that we acquired proved to be useful for our entire lifetimes. It is the same thing for the soldiers. For those who could not control themselves, it was better for them to leave the battle.

RJ: We were not less happy than those young soldiers who joined at the age of seventeen or eighteen.

ETM: I must say that I am surprised by your age, because you really look much younger than you actually are.

RP: You know, I think it is because we go to work every day. We owe everything to the 2nd Armored Division, that second life that we have after our own.

ETM: Thank you very much for welcoming me and for answering my questions.

Pierre Lefranc

PL: I was born in 1922, so I was too young to be mobilized in 1940. After my studies at the Lycée Louis-le-Grand, I became a student at the Free French Officer School. I reacted immediately to the dramatic situation of the defeat and the occupation. One cannot imagine what the defeat of France represented, and the collapse, in a few days, of all the institutions of the Republic. Younger generations had been taken in by the memory of the French victory in 1918, and the French army was now annihilated. The shock and disarray were such that the French people turned toward the glorious personage that was Pétain, and on July 10, 1940, in Vichy, the parliament put an end to the Republican regime and invested Pétain with full power.

ETM: What was your reaction when the Germans arrived in Paris?

PL: The Germans in Paris, the Nazi flag floating on the Eiffel Tower and on the Ministry of the Navy, constituted an unbearable humiliation. We felt that it was our duty to rebel, but what to do? It is in this context that the students' demonstration on the Champs-Elysées was organized on November 11, 1940, on the day that commemorated the victory of 1918. The protest was violently repressed by the Germans. I was myself injured by a grenade, was arrested, and then incarcerated. I remained a prisoner for a month and then was liberated, but kept under control. Crossing later clandestinely in the non-occupied zone, I participated in the creation of a group of resistance, *Liberté*, which was one of the constitutive elements of the larger movement named Combat. Then, I decided to join de Gaulle and I escaped from France through Spain.

ETM: During what period was this?

PL: This was in November of 1942. Arrested by the Spanish, I was imprisoned then placed in a concentration camp. Freed with many others six months later, we met in Gibraltar the General de Gaulle on his way to Algiers and to his accord with General Giraud in 1943. He reviewed us and spoke to us severely: "Everything is left to be done," he said. It was the exhortation of a war leader. When we reached England, we were subjected to a very strict security commission. It was indeed necessary to be very much on guard, German agents having infiltrated the new arrivals. Engaged right away in the ranks of Free France, I was transferred to the Military School of the Cadets, the Saint-Cyr of Free France. As a Cadet officer, I made the choice to be parachuted into France to supervise the underground since they were in need of military leaders. In August of 1944, in the county of Indre, I was given the mission to organize operations in order to slow the German forces that were moving toward the Northern part of France. We also assisted a parachuting American commando who had been put in charge of the Eguzon's dam which supplied the railroad line from Paris to Toulouse. During one of these clandestine operations, one of two Dakota planes which were bringing weapons for us crashed outside the designated landing zone and we had to hide the plane that was damaged, about twenty miles from the important base still under German command in Châteauroux.

ETM: You then pursued your mission after the war along with General de Gaulle.

PL: I was promoted to the rank of lieutenant. I then supervised the forces that came from the underground in the pocket of Saint-Nazaire, and then I volunteered to be appointed to the Headquarter of the 1st French Army of De Lattre de Tassigny, with which I crossed the Rhine and penetrated Germany in 1945. After the war, I accepted a position as a civilian but I placed myself at the disposal of General de Gaulle in 1947 at the moment when he created the *Rassemblement du peuple français*, the Rally of the French People Party, in view of modifying the Fourth Republic which he thought was inadequate. For four years I was an official representative in the party, then responsible at the national level for the youth and students. In 1958, after the so-called period called "*la traversée du désert*," the General was called to power once again and he named me chief of the private staff of the president of the council of ministers. Then, de Gaulle was elected president of the Republic and brought me with him as an advisor at the Elysée Palace. In 1965, during the candidacy of the General for a second term, I was placed in charge of his electoral campaign, the first campaign of a presidential election where the president was elected through universal suffrage.

ETM: What did the experience of working with de Gaulle teach you?

PL: I learned rigor, the ability to say NO. It is not easy to say NO, to refuse what appears to be ineluctable. Each of us meets with his or her "June 18, 1940," that is to say the choice between passivity and ordeal. His defiance was a fundamental example. I also acquired the conviction of the importance of the role of France in the world. Our country is rich with a prestigious past. It addresses a message to humanity through the genius of its thinkers, its scholars and artists. Through this mission, France remains a great power in spite of the effects of globalization. It must, for the sake of its mission, remain free and independent and its power of dissuasion guarantees the security of this independence which allows it to remain faithful to its heritage.

ETM: What did America represent for de Gaulle?

PL: For de Gaulle, America was a great democracy and friend, friend of always, friend for always. During the war, he had been at times disappointed by Roosevelt's positions, as he felt that his struggle and Roosevelt's were the same. Roosevelt's choice of Giraud over him was incomprehensible and cruel to de Gaulle. Later in 1958, de Gaulle sent to the British and American governments a memorandum suggesting that a restoration of balance of responsibilities within NATO was needed. His suggestions were not even discussed, whereas they could have reinforced the alliance. But whatever the misunderstandings that may have existed at times, the France of de Gaulle was without reticence on the side of America as, for example, during the grave Cuban missile crisis. I myself met the Secretary of State of the time, Mr. Dean Rusk, in a salon of the Elysée. He came very early in the morning one day to Paris, to show the pictures of the nuclear launchers' site to the General.

ETM: What would have been de Gaulle's approach with respect to Iraq?

PL: One cannot affirm anything with certainty, but it is likely, knowing him, that he would have been opposed to an intervention vis-à-vis a sovereign state. Certainly, the dictatorial regime of Iraq was condemnable, but it did not present a threat to peace in the world. One cannot want to impose any regime on an independent country if it does not attack anybody.

ETM: Can the links between France and America be as strong today as in the past?

PL: The relation between France and the United States has been forged throughout history for the defense of liberty, during the birth of the United States in 1776, then against German's imperialism in 1917 and 1944. If America were to be threatened at any time, it can count on the solidarity of its allies, but it was not the case in Iraq. This intervention appeared as a certain form of global imperialism under the pretext of an intention that was respectable in appearance, yet one can suspect its motives to have been less so. Certainly, it is necessary to respond to the aggression and the threat of September 11, but the response to it should not appear to be aimed at the petroleum resources. The Americans show an active hostility toward colonialism, forgetting that they themselves have colonized their own territories.

ETM: What does the image of America inspire you in its entirety?

PL: I have a great admiration for the American people. In 1942, America demonstrated an extraordinary efficiency when faced with the Japanese aggression, and an admirable capacity for industrial and moral mobilization. I have also been very impressed and appreciative of the reaction of the American people when faced with the attack of September 11. All the citizens stuck together and this attitude was expressed through a magnificent show of national unity. In France, the reaction would no doubt have been critical and sectarian.

ETM: Which lesson do you retain from your experience of World War II?

PL: The first lesson is to refuse what is unacceptable. It is not easy; it was said earlier. But as modest as it might be, on a NO, the grandeur and dignity of an individual or even a country, can be decided. In the history of our country, I denounce the stain of the collaboration and the great and criminal fault of Pétain as he led astray many of our respectable compatriots. After the students' protests of November 11, 1940, rising against the German forces of occupation, we were told: "It is not for you, little students, to give lessons to France." And yet, we did it. That is a lesson for the generations to come, to show them that one can refuse injustice, persecutions and racism. In my view, the "NO" of the French people to the bad European constitution in May of 2005 represents a true national surge, an act of faith in the country. One can accept an economic, social and scientific European coordination, but not a Europe that would bring about the abdication of national identities forged through the ages.

ETM: Do you have a message for the American veterans?

PL: We owe them a lot: 1917, 1944. The cemeteries largely illustrate the participation and the courage of the American soldiers. We are indebted to their sacrifice as they are indebted to our participation in the formation of their country. The Americans are bearers of the immutable values of democracy. Having said that, let us discuss as equals the challenges we must face together.

Maurice Cordier

MC: I was born in 1920 in Vincennes, which used to be part of the Seine Department and is now part of the Val de Marne. I stayed there my whole life. My father came back from fighting in WWI. He was gassed in Ypres and I was raised with this memory. He died when I was thirteen, as a consequence of the gassing. That is how I remember him, as a WWI veteran. Something that was not repeated with our generation is patriotism; the aura of victory and all those illusions. I was raised in that atmosphere. My father died while I was studying in a religious school belonging to the diocese of Nogent-sur-Marne, from which many people graduated, some becoming famous. I stayed there to get my high school diploma in philosophy and mathematics. It was quite a performance then, to graduate in both subjects simultaneously. Thereafter, I attended high school at the Lycée Saint Louis, to study advanced mathematics for two years. Then a profound religious vocation fell upon my head like the Holy Ghost. At the same time, war broke out. My generation actually expected it. We all believed that we would be fighting a war, just like our fathers did before us.

ETM: Thus, in the 1930s you thought that war was coming.

MC: Yes, and there was a fierce political fight between the right and the left, such as had never been seen before. For example, in 1934, when I was fourteen years old, there was a street protest by almost all the WWI veterans who were muzzled by the then leftist government. They said the government negated the patriotic values and ideals they had during WWI. This was said to be a fascist protest, but there was nothing fascistic about it. They protested against what they called the negation of all that they fought for in WWI. At the same time, we saw the premises of the social upheavals which led in 1936 to huge strikes and to the rise to power of the Popular Front, which was the expression used then in France and Spain, since both movements were similar. I belonged to the patriotic youth, then led by Pierre Taittinger. We knew little at that time of what was taking place in Germany or its propaganda, but what we did see showed us that our corresponding generation in Germany was being superbly prepared for a great adventure. There also existed considerable Soviet propaganda. The big magazines and revues were always publishing reports on those huge public work projects going on in Russia, the dam constructions, the big steel mills. Power was on the rise there and the Germans were also demonstrating that their industrial and military power were on the rise, whereas we were a leisure society in full bloom. 1936 was the year of paid vacation time and the youth hostels. The young generation in France was discovering tourism, the outdoor life, and camping.

ETM: This would have been ideal in peaceful time.

MC: We actually had in France people who trained at living in a peaceful society, a blind peace, I must say. On the other hand, we had two big powers that were training for war, no doubt. There are pictures of young SS marching on Nuremberg; that was something else entirely. One should not forget those great novels by Jean Giono which were published at that time. They glorified leisure, poetry. One of those novels depicted a person living the idle life in the High Provence region, teaching peasants around him that they should give up growing wheat, which was a form of slavery, and instead grow poppies since they were prettier. At the same time, Giono also published the novel called *May My Happiness Last*. He explained in *True Riches*, a book of reflections, that he had suppressed any reference to Jesus from one of Johann Sebastian Bach's Cantata "Jesus Joy of Man's Desire" since Jesus was the incarnation of suffering, of effort and labour. Thus, we were deep in that atmosphere. There was also a unity movement which denied the existence of any class struggle. I recall marching in Paris as a student, arm in arm with a labour class worker, a sailor, a peasant. We marched together on the left bank of the River Seine; we actually believed in this. No one knew what would happen although we were all convinced that there would be war.

ETM: You lived in a dream state, full of ideals. You knew what the reality would be, but no one prepared for it. What was your personal reaction to France's defeat?

MC: The shock of defeat was what was in the foreground and the background of every soul and every intelligent being. The defeat hit us hard over the head, as if an iron curtain had fallen to cloud our future. For me, it happened at the same time as the revelation of my true vocation but I still tried to become a volunteer in 1939. I wanted to serve, but my conscription class of 1940 was not called. Since I was born in 1920, only those born in January/February and a few until mid-March were called to serve. I wished to volunteer in the armed forces but my spiritual mentor forbade me to do so. I think that he was right because those who did volunteer later felt paralyzed and unable to do anything in view of what happened, and did not have the freedom to react, which later on I did, with others.

ETM: What was the fundamental cause of the defeat?

MC: A lack of overall mobilisation or a defeatist mindset from the start. First of all the conscript of the 1936–1937 classes had little taste for war. They were fully immersed in what was to be a leisure society. Their training was poor. The Communists and the far right propaganda were in full bloom. I personally know of no one inducted in 1939 that was gung-ho. No one was. That "phoney war" was actually a mortal blow because it put the nation to sleep. It is then that we became conscious that the Germans had built a formidable modern war machine. At the same time, there were strikes in the French steel mills. We were not ready at all. The military brass was still in the mind set of the end of WW I. We were late by one war, and it is still true today.

ETM: Was the fact that the parents of the 1936–1937 generation died in WWI and the fact that France had lost 1.5 million soldiers a factor?

MC: It did play a role, but not a primary one. There were no families that did not lose at least one member during that war. My name is that of a dead member of my family, Maurice, the husband of an older sister, killed in 1915. That was generally the case everywhere. We were already a defeated people. I decided to leave on Armistice Day in June 1940. But it proved to be impossible immediately. I have comrades (we will meet some later), René Nordman and another who unfortunately died, Jacques Augendre; he was a friend of mine since junior high. We met one another at the Lycée Saint Louis; both left in 1940. Nordman went to Saint Jean de Luz where he bought a raincoat, managed to pass as a Polish national and left for England on a cargo ship carrying Polish volunteers. Augendre ended up in Saintes with his parents where he took a small boat that made it to England. In 1940–1941 we were repatriated to Paris, after having taken part in the debacle where I pursued my studies in theology.

ETM: As a young Frenchman, how did you personally bear the German occupation?

MC: I took it as an affront, a defeat, something in my upbringing was broken; suddenly the image of the France of de Gaulle disappeared; it was as if a bullet had passed through us. It was the destruction of an ideal. I can recall one instance. In 1941, in Vincennes, the priest in my district told me: we have a German seminarian. He would like a local contact, could you speak to him. I contacted him but I was uneasy about walking alongside him in the street. I tried to tell him but since he was from the other side of the mirror he did not quite get it; I don't think that he was a Nazi. It was an instance where I had a direct contact with a German colleague. I don't quite know what became of him; maybe he also ended up as a priest. I was not proud at all to be dealing with that German. I was deeply embarrassed though I had nothing against him. Our conversations were actually quite peaceful. He systematically tried not to contradict me. As he was assigned to a medical service, he was no war lover.

ETM: When were you finally able to leave?

MC: I was going to leave anyhow. I first tried, with my contacts in the underground, to leave by plane, but being a seminarian of 22 years old, who wanted to leave but had no skills in demand. They had other priorities. These planes were sent from London, landed, usually bringing agents or equipment; on the way back they loaded people on board. It took place in several regions. There was also a rumour that we could pass through Spain. Then November 8, 1942 came. The landing of the allies in North Africa was a trigger for the invasions to come. A detail comes to mind. They landed exactly in the same spot that the Vandals did during the great Barbarian invasions. I am not saying that North Africa tilted that day toward the side of Free France, but it was under the control of the allies and de Gaulle's Free French. The path was traced. First free North Africa; it would then lead to a freed France. We left with my comrades, saying that we were going to join de Gaulle in Free France, but in fact we had no idea where we were going. It so happened that among my colleagues from the seminary, was a captain by the name of Xavier Louis, and one of the *resistants* took us into his network. We were three to make this decision, and we followed the instructions. It was a hundred yards from where we are today [at the Free France Foundation] near the Saint Anne church, in a modest, totally bare apartment. It was a meeting place. I took and passed an exam. They tested us to see if we were sincere and worthwhile recruits. But we had to wait for a long time. It is only during the summer of 1943 that we learned that we were accepted.

ETM: What was the exam about?

MC: The three of us left by train toward Riom des Landes, with fake identification papers usually carried by workers on leave. The train was the Paris-Hendaye (Spanish border), but its course was changed on route. When we arrived, we were welcome by this small resistance group. They were quite brave and they hid us for four or five days, during which an American joined us. He was a cockpit mechanic. His name was Georgi Posinger, from Detroit. His plane was shot down over Amiens and he was rescued by one of these small underground networks who guided and cared for these people whose planes were shot down. He had bought a small scale model of the Eiffel Tower. We were scared having him around because he was a blabber mouth, a typical American. He would stand out from a quarter mile away, but the Gestapo failed to detect him because his papers said that he was a deaf-mute. This Posinger guy was arrested with us in Spain, and later on he returned to the US Air Force. I did look for him after the war. The military officer of the US Embassy in Paris located him after several tries. Unfortunately, he had died three months earlier.

ETM: How did you manage to go from Riom to Free France?

MC: We boarded a train to Biarritz and met in a bistro called La Négresse. The place has disappeared since. All the underground people in it were shot a year later. We needed to cross the Pyrenees. We were lucky enough to meet some resistance people in this bistro who helped us across the mountains to Ascain, then to Sare and finally to Spain. We were first guided by French smugglers then by Spanish ones. The itinerary we took has become quite familiar nowadays. We ended up in a town called Zugarramurdi. We were arrested there by the Spanish police, but we were lucky enough that they did not turn us over the Nazis. And still, we were with our American. After we were freed, we were directed toward Irun. In March 41, I heard that Koufra (in North Africa) had been liberated and for the first time, I heard the name of the General Leclerc. I was thrilled! I wanted to join up with Leclerc whose 2nd Armoured Division had just been regrouped on July 1, 1943 in Casablanca. I ended up in Témara, part of the 3rd Colonial Artillery Regiment. This army corps was *Compagnon de la Libération* (having joined de Gaulle from the start). This fact made me very happy. There I found some officers who knew all about the desert all the way down to Cameroon. We ended up in Yorkshire, a town called Sledmere. There was a castle belonging to the Sax family going back all the way to Hastings. The 2nd Division came under the overall command of General Patton. I was assigned to drive a jeep serving for both liaison and observation. I drove this jeep all the way to Berchtesgaden without ever being maimed. On the other hand the jeep was shot up and pierced. Thus, I took part in the whole campaign of the 2nd Armoured Division. We landed on August 1 on Utah Beach, more exactly in Saint Martin de Varville.

ETM: Were you in Paris at the time of the liberation of the city?

MC: Oh yes, I did it all, the Normandy campaign, from the landing all the way to Paris. This campaign took its toll on many soldiers, on both sides. It killed as many as the battle of Stalingrad. It was a battle of epic proportions. Our Division moved around until reaching Le Mans; then we went back up to Alençon fighting all the way, suffering many casualties. Finally, we got to Paris.

On the August 24, our artillery was on top of Mont Rouge and on the 25th we entered Paris through Porte d'Orléans. I went by there this morning. My unit fought its way between the Military School and the Orsay Station. Thereafter, we were ordered to Le Bourget Airport on the 27th and 28th. It is there that the real liberation of Paris took place because the Germans were trying a counter attack. They were fighting as if they were enraged; they must have been doped. It was a slaughter house. We massacred many of them, I must say. Then, I witnessed the landing of the first American plane on Le Bourget runway that we just liberated. Some ten years ago, I had the opportunity to meet one of the pilots in the local church whose landing I had witnessed. He told me what was taking place up there. In turn, I told him what we were doing down here. It was quite interesting. It was an important landmark date. Thereafter, we went on to liberate Strasbourg.

ETM: Had you already been ordained a priest?

MC: Actually, I was not an ordained priest then. I was ordained after the war. I was then a combatant in the artillery. I actually inflicted many casualties on the enemy. My role was to stay on the front lines with the vanguard tanks. My commanding officer was himself in a tank. I had to see for myself where the bodies were actually falling and also give corrective shooting coordinates for the tanks when necessary. That was my job. The Normandy battle was a brutal encounter and in the process, we crushed three armoured German divisions. With us, there were also the American tank divisions and the allies, the British, Canadians and Poles, among others.

ETM: What were your feelings as you charged toward Paris? Did you feel exhilarated, enthusiastic, and fearful?

MC: Fear was with you constantly. If you want to talk about fear, I always felt fear present. It is a weird sensation. It's like a burden nagging in your head, but I was quite excited to be going. I felt fear but I never panicked, hence I was never paralysed in action. But still, fear followed me everywhere. One time I found myself too far ahead with the jeep, ahead of the tanks and suddenly I saw a German soldier in a moat with a bazooka aimed at me. I told myself, this is it, you are done. He was some 15 feet away and he could have obliterated me. I took the demeanour of someone surrendering since there was absolutely no time to try anything. Then the first tank arrived behind me, making a thunderous noise. The soldier must have faced a dilemma that proved fatal, saying to himself, if I kill him I will be a hero but then I will die; sort of one life for another. He chose to stay alive. He got up, dropped his bazooka. He was actually a Waffen SS, some 6 foot 3 inches. Though big and strong, he was shaking like a leaf.

ETM: And all this took place within a few seconds.

MC: It took five seconds; I think that I was dead scared. As a matter of fact, after that event, I was never scared again.

ETM: You came close to death. You also showed courage.

MC: Paul Tillich, an American author, wrote in a book called *The Courage to Be* about the phenomenon of courage. With most people, it refers to acts of heroism. But, for him, real courage is to fully assume who we are. I came to better appreciate his point of view as I grew older. For me, this is true courage; to assume one's responsibilities under all circumstances.

ETM: And France mattered above all; saving and liberating France.

MC: Exactly. We did not repeat that to ourselves every second but it was present in our sub-conscious. For some of my more simple minded comrades, it was actually something pre-destined, that we all carried in us.

ETM: What happened when you entered into Paris? After all, you grew up in Paris. You witnessed Paris during the occupation. What did you experience?

MC: It was a big mess. There was the shooting at Notre Dame. Some in our unit were assigned guard duty in front of the cathedral on the 26th. I was elsewhere with my captain, on a mission, which enabled me to say a quick hello to my mother in Vincennes, after which we came back. Then, we prepared for the next day's battle, which was the violent Le Bourget battle. I did not personally witness the events at Notre Dame de Paris, but I studied the matter to try and establish the historical facts of the liberation of Paris; Notre Dame being the heart of Paris, its liberation determined when Paris was officially freed. It was done with the help of Cardinal Lustiger who enriched the process. I was the one in charge with my comrades of the 2nd Armoured Division to handle this business. And Lustiger enriched the idea because for him it was a way to associate the Church to all the great events of the nation and not to relegate the religious aspect to the sidelines as many lay people wanted. I had to study this point closely in order to establish its historical veracity.

ETM: How can we pay tribute to the many Americans who fought and died for France?

MC: The tribute for those who died takes place each year. We also celebrated the 50th and 60th anniversary of the D-Day landing. If you go to the Calvados cemetery, it is quite awesome. There you find the spirit of the Arlington cemetery. There, a real tribute is given, it is magnificent. I see the crowds visiting this cemetery. The people who go see the D-Day landing beaches and all those other cemeteries. They could ignore them, but instead they go to pay their respects to the peace that all those sacrifices brought about. This is what keeps the memory of the sacrifice of those Americans and allies alive. In 1994, I was part of a large French delegation that went to America. Bill Clinton was President. We were there to celebrate the 50th anniversary of D-Day, alongside the US Veterans of WW II. We were some 250 French veterans of the 2nd DB. I was the one in touch with the Americans. It was facilitated by a former French commando fighter who lived in New York City. He had also escaped through Spain. He arranged for me to be invited to a US Marines venue. There I was imbedded among Americans. There are some differences between them and us since they don't follow the same rituals that we do. The simple explanation is that, for the Americans the flag is actually a person.

They honour their flag, they honour their dead, and their memory is as if personified. We don't. Furthermore, we found that the veterans were truly appreciated and have quite a following among the population. A WWII veteran in America is an important person; he wears his uniform. We were received by the Cincinnati's, a WWII association named after the head of the Roman Legion

Cincinnatus. For them, being a veteran can almost be a full time occupation. It is quite different from us. How then to show homage? To start with, we need more contact with them. There also is a need for admiration because our younger generations are the inheritors of the "Yankee go home" in the 1960's. Though it is propaganda, the French fall for it. Even now with Chirac, the war in Iraq and other things, we should talk to each other; there exists no grounds to accuse the Americans. Though some Frenchmen tend to point a finger at the United States, most do remember that they are the super-power that liberated us. The popular success of the D-Day landing celebrations tend to show that deep down, even for those who ignore History, there is admiration. The books relating to WWII have kept intact the memory of the American GIs in France. We saw them in the snow while we stood on our tanks. I was there; they had a lot of courage.

ETM: Without America, would France have been freed?

MC: We would not have been liberated. There is no doubt about that. They were gracious enough to let the French troops enter Paris first and in Berchtesgaden also. The Americans were just behind our units. I wanted to go uphill to Hitler's "Eagle's Nest" but it was already guarded and I would not have taken the risk of getting killed for the pleasure of seeing where Hitler had had his tea.

ETM: What lesson should the French youth take from these events nowadays?

MC: In my opinion, there is a collective image: Koufra. That was the fortress which directed the communications through the Sahara. That was an important position since the caravans which supplied food to the army of Montgomery passed by there. That was an important strategy point, very well-armed. Koufra was seized by only 100 men in an extraordinary situation; it was necessary to do 400 kilometers through the desert. It was also necessary to transport fuel in both directions. That was a problem of organization but of resistance as well. It was excessively difficult; the material was of bad quality, the tracks were not well-marked. That is why one can call those who arrived there with Leclerc: "the miserable of the desert." There is a biblical image which comes to mind. They seized Koufra, and the same ones became the core of an armored division which debarked at Utah Beach and which carried out the campaign in Normandy. That was the division which was in the lead of the liberation of Paris, of Strasbourg and which reached Berchtesgaden. Hence, between Koufra and the end of the war, you see the image one can extract from it. I believe that this is the spirit that must be inculcated, in our youth. When one recounts this moment in history (we go into the high schools every year regarding the question of the Resistance), students are immediately fascinated, and small details become so important. That is what happened after the defeat of 1940. France was nothing anymore. De Gaulle had nothing, and the result is positive, however. I think that this is the example. And the quality that you yourself put your finger on is courage. I believe it is a question of courage. The courage about which I spoke is to refuse self-sacrifice in battle, and to end up alive. Courage is at the same time intelligence. I believe that this is the lesson we should learn from this period.

ETM: What message do you want to send to the American veterans and people? And the second question concerns your experience as a man of the cloth, the question of the future of humanity and the friendship among people.

MC: I would like to tell the Americans that they must continue to be involved with a sense of planetary mission. It seems intelligent and absolutely necessary. The only thing I would like to tell them is not to become dominated by money or ideologies more or less political, or even by religious tendencies. I am not only thinking of Bush but of other Americans as well. One should try to transform the type of domination for which they have a vocation; that is to say, to think about changing people before changing the organizations. It is necessary to change the people; one cannot apply the American organization which functions as a huge machine (I see it this way), on people that are behind by one thousand years or have a spirit, completely filled up by traditions that are stuck in frozen conceptions. The Americans should try to help them advance their civilization before building up their industry. In conclusion, in order to assume the immense progress of which they are the holders, they must be psychologically ready and capable of not becoming intoxicated by their power. They must make progress in human terms. The human being should be their first goal before economic, industrial, and even scientific concerns. I believe that if America was penetrated by these things, they would be the ones in possession of the world's future.

ETM: But that is also the challenge of humanity.

MC: That is the challenge of humanity. But America is the only people that has enough power at this moment, despite the youthfulness of its democracy, enough thought, and enough experience to do that. When you talk about the future of the world, they cannot transfer what they live through to the people who are not prepared to receive it.

ETM: And there are the difficulties that are faced in Iraq, for example.

MC: You mention Iraq, why Iraq? It could have been something other than Saddam, why Iraq? Iraq holds a part of the world's energy resources, like Iran. There could eventually be a phase in Iran as there was one in Iraq. These countries are rich, Saudi Arabia, etc. At this moment, the richness is in the reserve of energy which one can make available or with which one can negotiate. When they attacked Iraq, was that because of Saddam Hussein? No, that was because of oil. They could have attacked someone else, particularly Iran. The Americans are obliged to intercede, at least to put pressure on the government of Iran. But when they are somewhere as they are in Iraq, what are the Iraqis saying, even those who were against Saddam Hussein, or those who were otherwise tortured or reduced to slavery by Saddam Hussein? They demand the departure of the Americans. It is striking, like we, the French, demanded the departure of the Americans although they had liberated us.

ETM: Some argue that democracy in Iraq is possible and that it may provide more stability in the region.

MC: I am skeptical. Elections alone do not bring democracy. The Germans had elected Hitler. It is not a question of political system. I believe that it is a question of changing mankind. When you see immense countries which are poor, since they do not have sufficient energy resources, because they cannot sell anything, and the little they could sell, they are obliged to sell it at low prices. These are systems which completely block human progress. How do you want them to believe in the Americans and the "civilized" nations, if when one is present somewhere, it is for economic reasons. Soul is what these people need.

ETM: You said that America holds the world's future; but America realized in 2001 that even though it is a power, it has its limits, it is vulnerable.

MC: Terrorism, as it is presented here, exists only because there are people who are capable of conceiving this terrorism, to put it in action; consequently, people who have evil in themselves. There is evil residing in them. People like Al-Qaida, there are intelligent people in it, there are people who are capable of organizing. There is potential, so they could put their potential to the service of something else. God knows that in the countries where they live, there is poverty, there is non-civilization, and there is injustice. But no, they decided to attack the Americans because of their ideology. They are the rich, the big power, we must knock them down. In my opinion, it is that stupid. That is why I would advise, not only the Americans, but particularly them, because they seem to me the strongest, to try to find how to change the mentality of these people. I have always been impressed by Saint Paul's Epistle to the Romans, a passage in which he says: "I feel inside me two laws: the good that I would like to do, I do not do it, and it is the evil that I hate that I do everyday. Who will deliver me from this step toward death?" It is our problem. People who do terrorism are capable of extraordinary things; like Hitler's Germans and the Russians as well, I believe. However, they were delinquent. In so far as people do not work on changing mentalities, it does not occur in 24 hours, they will not succeed. And if we want this to go to the four corners of the world, it involves the changing of mentalities. One must make the good within us the dominant force.

ETM: It concerns a mission you are talking about, but that mission is as necessary here, in Paris, as it is anywhere else in the world.

MC: Of course. It is a spiritual revolution that is necessary even if it is not religious. You know that nowadays it is impossible to force people be Catholics. But the human soul is nonetheless the human soul.

ETM: What did De Gaulle have in mind when he spoke about the greatness of France? What is it for you, and what should that be nowadays?

MC: When De Gaulle was talking about the greatness of France, he was talking about it like about a person: Our Lady France; he said that. These were his words. One preexistent person; in other words, a young man, born in France had a filial commitment and his mother was already a person called Our Lady. This is a doctrine which does not exist anymore for us. The Americans preserved what has come to us from previous centuries and which comes from a certain conception of Christianity. One cannot doubt it. Even outside religious opinion, it is a way of feeling, consciousness of oneself, and consciousness of one's relations. When one says France, when one says the United States, one makes reference to that there is a nation, there is a homeland. Is there a difference between a country and a homeland? Notre Dame (our Lady) is a term of veneration, of respect. That is a rhetorical figure. I do not believe that it is religious, except for the allusion. When he says Notre Dame of France; he says it differently; he uses this expression in a little book called *For the Children of France*. There, one understands him better. All that is an ensemble at one and the same time: the heritage, present life and future life. I got that from De Gaulle. And I have adopted this as my own philosophy about the nation and the homeland. That is a heritage. Strong with the heroes of the past, strong with memories, with the example of our heroes of the past, we live in a present that we need to go through at least with the same dignity as they and even make it all progress, and this in view of a future that will be renewed by the following generations which will make their own contributions. And all that together, you will find it among the Americans and we do not find it anymore among ourselves.

ETM: What I found among the Americans is a vision of America, and that is what I do not find in France at this time.

MC: Exactly, I agree with you. Since 1968, we question everything and have scratched out the heritage. In the spirit of De Gaulle, we are inheriting from the past, we are living from the past, which is a collective sharing, with all its vicissitudes, its denials, its quarrels, which is like an enormous unraveling carpet and then I arrive, I live from it, I would not exist if there was not that past; and although I don't know some of it, my role is to make progress in my relations or in my family, in the usefulness that I have in the world, and to pass it on to others, so that they can bring their own innovation. Hence, we have a vision where time and place join together. That is, I believe, what De Gaulle called our Lady France (Notre Dame la France). I think that the current generations in France are not well understood. Even the specialists, the investigators have poorly understood the upcoming generations. They are certainly very different. They are not saying very much at the moment. The revolts which have taken place in the suburbs do not represent the revolt of all youth. The young French hide their revolt. And when they are in power, what are they going to do? Something very different; what, I do not know.

ETM: In order to know where we are going, we should know where we come from.

MC: When we made this trip to America ten years ago, we were received a bit everywhere and there was a reception at the French Embassy. It was very comical because it took place the day on which Chirac was elected. Moreover, we had voted by proxy and we learned the news and the same night we were received at the French Embassy and our friends from 2nd Division took down all the portraits of Mitterrand, which were in the embassy, in order to hide them. The Ambassador did not dare to say anything since he was involved in the PS (Mitterrand's Socialist Party). However, his wife was not at all on the same side. The following day, the Ambassador welcomed a part of the delegation for a lunch. Then, it turned out that the table presided over by the wife of the Ambassador where there were chiefs from the Pentagon, the General de Boissieu, and other important people, began to talk about a subject analogous to the one we are discussing: the United States and the differences with France. The Ambassadress did not say anything. We talked about unemployment and working class French people. She let us talk and finally she told us: listen, I will give you an example which will show you that there is a certain difference between the mentality of the Americans and that of the French. She said, I have a friend who is a professor and she had a Chair in a university close to New York. She was teaching this very specialized discipline, and suddenly, the Chair was abolished because there were not enough candidates, and then the professor was dismissed. You realize, a professor in France, dismissed like that. It cannot happen in France. The unions would not permit it. So, what did that lady do? Since nobody was offering her anything else in her area of specialization, she started working at McDonald's. Since she controlled the situation, she became a manager of one of the McDonald's. That continued many years, something which is inconceivable in France. And then, one nice day, a university 2000 kilometers away, offered to create a position in the specialty in which she was well-known, and the whole family moved there and her husband found a job there. In connection with that, I see a big difference between the Americans and us. And if I have said earlier that the Americans were unique, it was also because of that. However, what surprises me a lot is their inability to get adapted in Iraq, for example.

ETM: The example you gave shows that the Americans possess a great ability to adapt to different circumstances. The last comment you made however also reveals that they may not sufficiently know the world in its complexity.

MC: Obviously, they did something different from what they should have after the war. They had to go to war in my opinion. People will point at me if I say that. I think they were right. It was necessary to go into Iraq. But they did not get adjusted to the situation. In order to manage to do something, with respect to Iraq, one can use numerous solutions but one cannot accuse faults as if they were crimes.

Chapter 3
The French-American Dialogue:
On Reconcilable Differences

The focus of this chapter is on the points of contention that exist between France and the United States, and their possible resolution. In these interviews, conducted in Virginia, Wisconsin and New York, I examine the significance of D-Day in the context of the post-September 11 world in light of the disagreements between the French and American governments on Iraq, while taking into consideration the common challenges and visions that both nations share for the future. The aim of these interviews is to shed light on the diversity of opinions that are forged on both sides of the Atlantic but also within each country, and to explore how these divergences could be reconciled. The veterans come from a broad range of states including the District of Columbia, South Carolina, Wisconsin, Ohio, New York, Michigan, California and Pennsylvania. They all have fought in Northern France during WWII after the landing in Normandy.

Cass Leigh evokes French-American relations and the questions at hand based on the visits he made to France and Normandy right after WWII thru today, and on a cultural and historical viewpoint. Jesse Oxendine considers his knowledge of both countries by way of his Native American heritage and gives a vivid illustration of what the relations between people and nations around the world ought to be today. Doc Stolp also explores the character of America and France through the history of his family and the role of his country internationally, while Robert McCann summons up the story of the American sacrifice during the Battle of the Bulge. John Aloisio, Ed King and Howard Comstock chronicle their war experience in Northern France while reflecting on the complexity of the situation in Iraq, with in the background, the repercussions of September 11. For their part, Gene Frice and William Kotary examine the role of France in the aftermath of the war on terrorism, and whether there is a justification for the commitment of American forces abroad today.

Cass Leigh

CL: I turned 20 on May 8, 1945, the day the war ended in Europe. That was my birthday present to say the least. That was quite a, quite an experience right there. We were actually being briefed to go into Denmark from where we were in Northern Germany and an officer came up to the gentleman who was conducting the orientation, said something to him and turned around, and the officer who was conducting the orientation said: "Gentlemen, the war is over." I get emotional when I think about it. We thought we were definitely going to go into Denmark to get the Germans out of there and when he said "Gentlemen the war is over, you are excused." It was a relief to not to have to continue.

You would have expected a massive celebration but we walked away by ourselves and I said nothing to anybody. It was a reflection, thank God I made it. I still get emotional when I think about it and so, nothing really happened; but that night, oh the celebration began, and in this particular town, there evidently must have been a place where they manufactured some sort of booze. I don't know what it was, but it was in clay bottles and what they'd done, they turned these clay bottles over and planted them. So, of course the celebration began.

ETM: It must have been one of the greatest days of your life.

CL: Well absolutely, no question about that, and then of course when the war ended, our division was sent to Bremen for the occupation, and some of us went to smaller towns outside Bremerhaven. It was a farming community and of course we stayed in a house, it was a very nice home as a matter of fact, and they made their own cottage cheese and they would share that with us. It was very pleasant and, and at that time, there was no fraternization, you know, to be with the Germans, none whatsoever. But, eventually, that began to change, as time went by.

ETM: What was it like to grow up in Washington D.C. in the 1920s and 1930s?

CL: It was a very small Southern town. Washington was a very laid-back Southern town until World War II, and then it just began to grow and of course I lived in Chevy Chase at the time when area was developed. It was still a dirt street and it eventually was paved; but it was a small community, and we walked to elementary school which was probably a half a mile away. I remember seeing Roosevelt. My father was in the real estate business and a very good friend of a big builder in the city of Washington. They were very close buddies and he had one of these great huge Packard convertibles, a limousine, and the White House borrowed it one time from him for Mr. Roosevelt on the occasion of a short trip he made in Southern Maryland. I saw him on that day when he came up in this big Packard limousine. It is interesting that my father voted for Mr. Roosevelt for the first term because he felt that he really saved his home. It was the time of the Depression and being in real estate then was difficult so he voted for him, but then for some reason, four years later, he didn't vote for him the second term around.

ETM: What does D-Day represent for this country in your view today?

CL: Well, as a young kid, I don't think I really knew the significance of it to tell you the truth. In reflection, it's an entirely different matter. I feel thankful that I was wounded once and that the injury was not major. You know, in those days, they sent you to the medic station and they cut you up. I was wounded on the 8th of July, something like that, in the Battle of Saint Lô. We were overrun by the Germans, and somehow, we were left unprotected by the rifle company and the Germans came over the hedge row and I was just this close to a German as I'm looking at you right now. With all the action and bombing going on, I think that he was scared as much as I was and then I got hit in the leg with shrapnel. As for the significance of D-Day and what it means today in terms of America's place in the world, I think we've lost a great deal of respect from a number of countries that we had at one point. I went to France probably two weeks after September 11. I planned the trip and the people were just absolutely incredible, good and kind to us. This was to Paris.

ETM: You said you came back for the first time in Normandy in 1947.

CL: Right after the war, I went to Europe a number of times during college. I returned to Saint Lô and I was told before returning that the people would not receive us with open arms because the city had been bombed and flattened during the military campaign. But I got there and the people could not have been more pleasant. I stayed in a hotel and they gave me a bike and I biked back to the beach. I may have been one of the first to return. But there was nothing there, now there's a cemetery. It was just beginning to be developed and rebuilt and the people couldn't have been nicer. They gave me a bike to ride back to the beach. And they seemed to be happy to see me. The fraternity brother that I went with had not been to Europe during the war and he was amazed at the damage and the total destruction. He couldn't believe it. It was in a terrible shape; but then I went back again on my own in 1951 when I got out of college. I encountered animosity and indifference on the part of the people in Paris and I vowed I would never go back again. So, I didn't go back for many years until the Channel train started going from London to Paris, in the late 1980s. I was really upset. And I said well I'm going to go. Well, it was like night and day. The people were delightful and I've been going back ever since.

ETM: The 1950s in France was a gloomy period, in part because the country was in a rough shape. But there was also a kind of psychological depression after the war.

CL: Yes, and that could be part of the reason for it. I tried to blend in with the country because at one point, there were a bunch of Americans going over that I was embarrassed to be anywhere near. But, to go back to the question on the significance of D-Day in light of today's America, we were not the leaders of the world so to speak until after World War II. I think that's when we came to the front. And we were looked to; before this, they felt that we were a soft nation. The army was made up of young men who had never held a gun before and were taught to kill. I remember, I went to a military school, prep school, boarding school, in the Shenandoah Valley, Virginia actually, not too far from Roanoke, and I remember that we had guns, regular guns, and they had to take our guns for the military school to supply the Army. They just didn't have the guns. That was in the early 1940s, right after Pearl Harbor. I'm very proud of the fact that my father immediately wanted to go in the service, you know; but they said, no, you're a little bit older for it now. He was ready to commit in his 40s but they considered him too old. He was ready to give up a very successful business to do it. All in all, it was different from today. I don't like what's going on right now to tell you very candidly; the situation in Iraq is very disturbing. I think we were misled into going in. I support the troops but I feel sorry for those young men who are over there now. We knew who our enemy was, but they don't. I mean, it could be a 14 year old kid, and now I'm hearing that some of the troops, or some of the officers or the police force, are also part of the assailants. So you don't know who you're really working with, who you can trust. I live in Washington and I was just reading the paper here in Roanoke today. By contrast to the Washington Post which I subscribe to, you hardly find in Roanoke's newspaper anything about Iraq, other than the fact that one of the regiments of the 29th Division, the 175th, is being deployed there in the next two months. They need additional training.

ETM: Do you think that the troops should pull out?

CL: You know, I have very mixed emotion about that. By putting a time frame, you are just letting the enemy know. But, why should we be losing our men in the middle of their fight? I don't know; you can't force democracy on some people. You have to have a different temperament I think to have a good democracy and the insurgents are doing a very good job of creating instability. I don't think the capturing of Bin Laden is going to end it; frankly, at this stage, I really don't. We went in Iraq with the idea that there were weapons of mass destruction. I just think that the Iraqis must be wondering whether they are better off now, or worse off than they were before we came in.

ETM: Regarding the threat of terrorism in a post-September 11 world, do you think if Hitler had had the capability of using nuclear weapons he would have used them?

CL: Oh yes. I definitely think he would have, if you consider the V-2 missiles that he launched; if he had been able to succeed, he would have used them and you know, I had no qualms about going to war in Europe at all; none whatsoever. I have two of my friends who are very bright people and they support the administration 100 percent. I say, how in God's name can you do that knowing what's going on, what's happening. And they say, you will see. They support the president in whatever he says.

ETM: The American people I've talked to consider that they were misled, that the country should not have gone to Iraq, but at the same time, they consider that the troops should not pull out. What kind or relation should France and the United States have?

CL: Well, you have a new president and he seems to be favorable to the American people and not so much critical of the President and current administration. I was just thinking back to the atomic bomb and mankind possibly destroying itself. I think that intelligent people know, if we drop the bomb here, they can drop it there. But put that bomb in the hands of a nut, like they have in Iran now, and it is another matter. Now with respect to French-American relations, I hope we can continue to work together. I thoroughly enjoyed your countrymen and they've been very pleasant to me; and you know, reading a map in Paris made me frankly more conscious of the tourists in Washington. One day, I was reading a map on the street, looking where to go, and I had a Frenchman come up and say to me: May I help you? I took French in college and I can understand it better than I can speak it, but I remember that. That's a nice thing to do and I did not say please come over and help me. They just automatically came over and made me conscious of the fact that I was welcome.

ETM: You have landed in Normandy and have participated in entire campaign with the American Army. Do you have a message for the younger generations in France?

CL: Yes. The American youth had a pretty good time like the young kids today. I really feel that the young kids ought to get out there and get involved. I do volunteer work at a local hospital and I'm in my 80s. I'm retired from my business, but I still do volunteer work and I think that it is important for the country that these young people do not only take, take, and take. They really haven't given too much. I don't know what it's like in France, but giving your time to others less fortunate is very important. And even internationally, we're interchanging, we're seeing that our kids are going over to foreign countries and we have young people from other countries coming here and some are staying. People are traveling back and forth together. We are one together. The world's getting smaller and smaller; we have to think along those lines.

ETM: We have to reach out?

CL: Yes, we should. Try to understand and not say: "Well, we're the best," always. We ought to respect each other's lifestyle and experiences. I think that's important and I'm very proud of the fact that I'm in America. I feel very fortunate and I think we're very fortunate in this country. A lot of people don't appreciate that, I'm afraid. I say: "Go abroad, travel, and see for yourself." There are many advantages, things that we take for granted that other people treat as luxuries elsewhere today. We've been very fortunate.

ETM: What road do you want this country to take in the next 20 years, 30 years?

CL: You know, I've never really thought about it. It's terrible, but I haven't thought about it. It's a good question. Well, I tell you, I'm worried for my grandchildren. I mean the pressures they are going to be under. I don't know what they're thinking about it. I've never discussed it with my grandchildren and I'm just wondering what's going on in their minds concerning this. I volunteered, nobody was after me. I did it because I wanted to. I graduated in June 1943 from prep school. I turned 18 on May 8, and I left a month after I graduated to volunteer. I just felt it was my duty. I remember now just talking to you, I was in elementary school and I think I was in the 6th or 7th grade, something like that, a young girl came from Germany and I'm sure that her family was Jewish. They had gotten out of Germany while they could, and she was so bright. I was in awe of her brilliance. I mean she spoke good English and here, you know, in our country.

ETM: She was your age?

CL: Yes she was, as a matter of fact, and I don't know what her parents did. I was that young, but I had an understanding of what was going on in Europe. I was in a football game the day the Japanese bombed Pearl Harbor and they started calling us, and my dad said, as we were walking back to the car after the game: "I'm sure it's war with Japan." Of course it was, and I had no idea that he was trying to get into the service. He didn't mention it to me until he finally said that he had tried, but couldn't get in which I was thankful for to say the least. But, I just felt very strongly, I just wanted to get in and do what I could. Now, I wouldn't want my grandson today to join the army for all the tea in China, under any circumstances. But I support every one of them. I mean, when those poor guys came back from Vietnam, it was terrible the way the country treated them and I think we learned a hard lesson and, even though we're opposed to what's going on in Iraq, we're supporting the young men and women who are there, and we should. Life goes on but I almost feel guilty sometimes.

ETM: You did your duty.

CL: I guess. I was glad to do it and I don't need any glorification or anything like that. And we get together with the fellows like today, we talk about it. We have a common bond. But other folks that never experienced it can't understand it. And I still to this day have nightmares about it, out of the blue. It still comes back sometimes and a number of us talk about it. There are funny things that happen that you can laugh about, but in the back of your mind, that's going to trigger something else that wasn't so pleasant.

ETM: What are the nightmares that you have to this day about?

CL: "What ifs." Do you understand what I say, "what if?" If I had stepped here, I would have been gone; one step further . . . what if I'd stepped . . . what if I hadn't done this, what if? What if I had stayed in that hole where they blew up after I got out of it? What if? The "what ifs" are the ones, the things that bother me more than anything else. You are not even thinking about it. It goes through your mind and, "what ifs" are the worst parts about it, I think, at least to me. Death is potentially around the corner at any second. But fortunately, just being young, I never thought that I would not make it. It never entered my mind at the time that this was all going on that I wouldn't survive. More than once I was scared to death, but I always felt I was going to survive. I never thought I wouldn't make it. That's my positive side.

ETM: You said earlier, we cannot understand what it meant. It's true. I'm like a blind person or a person who is deaf. I don't have the sense or smell of war. And so, it's impossible for me to grasp its brutality.

CL: Well, it's a terrible thing to have to go through and see human bodies, whether they are the enemy or your own, charred to the bone, and these are terrible impressions to have in your mind as a young person and those images never leave. I still see, you know, just horrible things and you just can't imagine what it's like. That's all, but fortunately I can clear out; today, they talked about the young men who returned with psychological problems. They called it shell shock, I think, during World War II, if I'm not mistaken; and there were incidents where young guys couldn't handle it and either shot themselves or did something to end it all and you can't criticize because everybody has a breaking point. Everybody's got a breaking point. But, the only thing, when the war ended, we were kids and there was a lot of emotion there that we hadn't been able to express as young teenagers, so to speak. And after the war ended in Europe, there were not much recreation offered. We sat around and played cards. When we were not on guard duty, we, you know, drank a bit, and German schnapps and so forth. And I remember going home, and 10 o'clock in the morning or 9:30, I would go to my family's liquor cabinet and be drinking it. I had marvelous parents and they handled the situation beautifully. And I just remember one day my mother said: "Son, don't you think it's a little early to be drinking?" She didn't say stop. She said, don't you think? I never touched it again until "happy hours," so to speak. I guess that did it; but they handled it in such a way that I didn't rebel in other words. I could have rebelled if they said "don't do it." I could have said "well, I'll do it." But no, it is a little early, don't you think? That was the only bad time. When I was at George Washington University, I remember coming home one day in my car after classes. I just felt like I wanted to scream, you know. Just all of a sudden; and for no reason whatsoever. I went to the family doctor the next day and talked to him. I had a long talk and I said "whatever you do, don't tell my parents." Of course, he did. I mean, he was the family doctor. But that was the only time that I felt I might have been having a little, you know, reaction from it. But, with understanding from parents and friends it worked out fine. And fortunately, I don't have any problems with it today to speak of. But during the war, I never lost it. I never thought I was not going to make it. I was that way. And I think that sustained me through a lot. You might think this is crazy, but I mean, it probably is the most exciting part of my life that I have ever had.

ETM: That's one way to look at it.

CL: Yes, you have to. And, I don't think I'll ever cap it, so to speak. I could have done without it too. I mean, there's no question about that. I could have done without it, but the association and the fraternity of these guys that I'm with here with today, I wouldn't be here if it wasn't for the closeness that we all feel for each other and it's something that we did share together; nobody else can share it with us.

ETM: Thank you for your time.

CL: Thank you; and I appreciate what you are doing.

Jesse E. Oxendine

JO: I was born and raised in a small farming town called Pembroke in North Carolina, about 100 miles from the East coast. It was a really small town. I was the youngest of four brothers who served in World War II. One brother volunteered in 1939. He went into the Air Force. His name was Simeon Oxendine. He served in the 8th Air Force. Simeon was a gunner on a B-17. He flew out of England and he completed 25 missions over France, Germany, and Holland. He participated in the first raid over Berlin. That was March of 1942. When we would get together, he would talk about it because he saw quite a bit of aerial combat. He also took part in the Schweinfurt Raid. That was the biggest raid they had in the war. They lost 65 planes in one day. He also participated in raids outside of Paris, over the Chevrolet plant I believe.

ETM: What was it like for your parents?

JO: The Schweinfurt Raid made the news because we had lost many planes. When he got back from the raid he wired my mother and all he said basically in the telegram was: "I'm okay." When the telegram arrived the next day, we knew he had survived the raid. There wasn't much discussion about the war when all of us came home. I remember asking him one time what was the worst raid he had ever been on. He said: "All of them were bad. Every raid we went on, our plane was hit." He completed his 25th raid in March of 1944 so he came home before Normandy. He was one of the first men from our area who had been overseas, seen combat and was back home. I wasn't even in the service then. My oldest brother who was drafted served in Europe with the 630th tank destroyer battalion. His name was James Howard Oxendine. The third brother, who was right above me, was a gunner on a B-24. His name was William Earl Oxendine. He served in the China Burma India Theater of Operation. I finished high school in 1944 in my home town. When I was in high school, I ran the projectors at the local theater. That was about all we had for entertainment in this small town.

ETM: How big was the town?

JO: We had maybe 2,000 people living there. This was an Indian community. I am a Native American and this community was mostly inhabited by Indian farmers. The name Oxendine is Lumbee, from the Lumbee tribe. It is believed that the Lumbees are the descendants of John White's Lost Colony.

ETM: There was mixed blood, Native American blood and European blood. The sacrifices that your generation has made and the positive impact that this country has had on the world, particularly during WWII in Europe and France, are extraordinary. At the same time, one must consider when one looks at how the people who came from Europe founded this country, how many Native Americans died as a result of their arrival. How do you reconcile the two?

JO: The Indian people were discriminated against. Let's face it. They took our land and we were mistreated, but this is part of growing up. We had our own school. We had schools that weren't up to standard with the other schools. I have seen that in my lifetime. Things have changed. It's not like that now, you see. I have seen some major changes. One thing that kind of bothered me, and we used to laugh about it, the Indian people used to live in such shame and disgrace; and after the war, it was hard for us to get into the university; but yet Germans who migrated to this country after WWII could come over and get priority in universities. They had better priority than we Indians who had gone over there and fought them, and that was part of the American way, a lot. It's not like that now. It is such a shameful thing; we, the Indian people joked and laughed about it. It's better than crying about it. At least we could laugh about it.

ETM: How can we settle the principles of this country's foundation, the idea of freedom, equality and justice for all, and on the other hand, the reality, the experience, the oppression, racism and prejudices your people experienced? What do you say about that?

JO: I just don't know. As good as this country is we have a lot of blood on our hands so to speak. To me it's the best country in the world, but we can't talk about other countries and what they do and look back at what we've done. But at least we are trying to correct these things. We know we've made mistakes in this country. Herman Goring, founder of the Nazi Gestapo and Nazi leader, brought up the following at the Nuremberg trials: "How can you condemn us for treating the Jews as we did, look at the way you treated the Native Americans?" He had a point there. In the 1800s, the US Calvary went into Indian villages in the western part of the country and shot point blank, men, women and children. A lot of those people in the Calvary were born in Europe. They were immigrants who had come over here. They were Americans, but they were European Americans.

ETM: That goes back to the question of what it is to be American and what is America? What strikes me in your comments is that you speak today as an American and you say: "We have made mistakes." It is quite extraordinary because your reflection transcends differences and you place yourself among those who committed the crimes. In a sense you could even say to this country: It is not "the others" who have committed these crimes, but it is us as human beings, and this is a great leap to make. That perhaps is something the 20th Century has allowed us to do; to make this leap, and transcend our racial and cultural differences.

JO: I am very proud of my Native American ancestry, but I am first an American, second a Native American. I consider myself an American first, unlike the German sympathizers back in World War II. A lot of them were sidetracked, and they considered themselves Germans first and Americans second.

ETM: What was your experience when you were in Germany in March 1945, when it was almost the end?

JO: When I went into the service, I had traveled more than most of the boys. When I was in basic training, I had been to Philadelphia, a big deal. I had been in South Carolina. A lot of the boys who I was with in basic training had never been out of the state in which they were born and raised. People didn't travel back then. Few people had automobiles. In my hometown, people used to come to town on Saturday and you were invited. We didn't travel back then. It hit me first when I was in training in Ft. Bragg. They didn't tell us where we were going. We went through South Carolina. I woke up the next morning and I realized my parents didn't know where I was and I was 18 years old. Normally, my parents knew where I was. I went down through Georgia, Mississippi, came back up to Memphis and across the Mississippi River. That was a big deal for me. I had studied that river in school, and here I was seeing it. I didn't think I would ever see it or be that far from home. When I came out of camp, I found I traveled a lot more that the other guys had. I took my basic training in Camp Robinson, Arkansas. The Lieutenant came up to me one day after two weeks; we were marching back into the Camp. He said: "Oxendine, you have had military training before haven't you?" I said: "No sir." I was in the Boy Scouts for several years. I joined the Scouts when I was 12 years old and made Eagle Scout. It's the highest award in Scouting. He said: "Well, I want you to be my platoon leader." That automatically put me in charge of about 48 men, right on the spot. So, during basic training I was a platoon leader. I found out then that I was smart, as smart as these other guys who were supposed to be so much smarter than me. We didn't have integration back then and all the other guys were white, you see.

ETM: These young guys, did they know you were a Native American?

JO: Yes, yes. We got along great; that was no problem. It meant something to me. It told me something. We took our basic training, twelve weeks, came home and went up to Baltimore, Ft. Meade, Maryland. We stayed there for two or three days and went up to Boston, Camp Miles Standish, right outside of Boston. We went into Boston and the train pulled right up to the boat and we went on the boat and a little farm boy coming from nowhere was seeing this huge ship, going up the gangplank and all of that. We loaded all day and took off from the harbor late afternoon and this blimp came over us. I figured we would get out of the harbor and get in with a big convoy. I knew the blimp was there watching out for German submarines. The next day, I got up and went out there. We were there by ourselves. The blimp was gone and we went zigzagging across the ocean. We landed in Liverpool, March 7 and that was the first time I had seen any results from the war. There were smokestacks sticking out of the water where all the ships had been sunk. So we zigzagged into the harbor, left Liverpool and went down to Southampton. We spent one night there. The next day we went on this old French freighter across the Channel and tried to get into Le Havre. The ship got tangled up on a sunken ship so they had to send out landing crafts to get us. We got off the ship, got something to eat and they sent us by truck to Givet. It is up on the French-Belgium border. It was an old fort they had built there during Napoleon's time. They said that Napoleon had spent the night there.

ETM: What was your experience there, being in a new country?

JO: Well, the fort, I couldn't believe they were able to build something like that. Here again, I was a little old farm boy who had never been any place and to see a fortress built on a mountain like that I just couldn't understand how they could be able to do that. A day or so later, I was told that I had been assigned to the 82nd Airborne; well the gliders. The biggest glider base in the US was only seven miles from my hometown. I was used to seeing gliders fly by my home on a daily basis.

ETM: What was the worst combat situation you encountered?

JO: I got with the 82nd Airborne and we had been there for a few days and we were set up in the Cologne area. That's when the Ruhr pocket was established. When we were in Cologne one night, I was guarding the headquarters, they were crossing the Rhine up at Wesel up around Dusseldorf and I had run the projectors at the theatre and I had seen a lot of the war and the news reels. I was sitting out there one night and they started shelling the Germans. I knew they were close, with all that shelling. But all night long all this artillery firing was going on. I was thinking that I have seen this in the movies, I have seen this in newsreels and now I am here witnessing it. I remember one day up in Cologne this plane came over, a reconnaissance plane came over a B-25 bomber, light weight bomber and this one German started shooting at us and flares were popping all around us. We stayed in Cologne for a couple of weeks and then they pulled us out of Cologne and sent us back to Euskirchen, a few miles Southwest of Cologne. Later on, when we crossed the Elbe River, we were under rifle and machine gun fire.

ETM: Were you in touch with the German population?

JO: There was a German family that came to headquarters one day and wanted to go down along the river to get some bed clothing. The Lieutenant called me out and told me to go with them down there. There was a big boulevard going straight down to the river. So there was a man, his wife and daughter. She must have been around my age, 18. I made them walk around me and we went right down this boulevard right out in the open. I knew the Germans would not fire at me because of the fear of killing them, you see, so I felt safe. So we went right down in the open. The Germans were on the other side of the Rhine river and the city was pretty messed up. They would fire mortar shells at us and we were shooting artillery shells at them all the time. You would look up thinking that you would see the shells; they were barely above our heads so to speak. They were hitting along the edge of the water on the other side.

ETM: Do you think differently being a Native American about war and peace issues, about international relations, about people around the world?

JO: I think basically all people are the same. I really do. This is jumping forward a long way, but I remember, I was going to Paris in the 1980s and people were saying: "I wouldn't go to France now because those people hate us." It was either in the 1970s or 1980s. I was almost talked out of going on the trip. They were saying the French really didn't care about the Americans, but I went on the tour anyway. I was sitting one day in this restaurant, talking to this French guy; he worked at the Hotel. We were discussing the matter. An American couple came in. We were just observing them, how they acted. I said that is a French couple and he said no, they are Americans. They were, but I didn't want to admit it. I think the more education we have, the more we can understand these things better. We went out to eat one night and we wanted to get away from the tourist area. We went to this French restaurant; there were six of us, three couples. We sat down and read the menu. Now, I can't read French, so I began to look around to see what the other people were eating. I got up and started walking around and looking at different plates and the people began to catch on to what I was doing. When I walked by the table, we began to laugh at each other. It just established good relations. They got a kick out of that. That's all it took. I broke the ice.

ETM: You went to war when you were 18, you went to Germany in March 1945, and you witnessed the destruction that the war brought in Europe and Japan, the Holocaust and many other calamities and disasters. What would it take for humanity to build a world of peace? What is it that we need to do?

JO: I think the best thing we can do is learn to talk. We will always have wars. There are so many wars that could have been prevented by talking. You got two sides and they won't communicate, what are you going to do? People are going to have to learn how to talk. You take the Israelis and the Palestinians; not only talk, but learn to negotiate. It is going to be a give and take situation. If you are going to go in there and say I am not going to give anything at all, you don't do that. I believe in prayer, I am religious. How can anyone have a God or profess a God that doesn't believe in love? I have a lot of Jewish friends; I have a lot of Arab friends. I am a pharmacist by profession and I have dealt with the public. I have met these people. They are good people, good Jewish people, good Muslims and all. I'd like to say they are basically alike, what they all want in life is to be able to make a living, having a family, have a home and have a job. That's basically all everyone wants, no matter where you go in the world; basically that's what people want. But, if we talk and try to help each other, if I try to help you do something, I am going to make a friend out of you or anybody else. We need to learn to talk and negotiate. We need to find out why those people over in the Mid-East are doing what they do; there is a reason why they are doing it. We need to talk. We need to find out what is the problem. Do we understand what their problem is? Some people might say that communicating is a sign of weakness. To me it is not. It is the intelligent way of addressing the problem. What is your problem? You tell me and I will tell you what my problem is. Maybe we can put everything on the table and talk about it and negotiate and agree to give and agree to take. That's what it is going to take. Nobody wants to have a war. Nobody wants to fight. They want to be home with their families.

ETM: The stakes are high today.

JO: Who wants their home blown up? Who wants to be away from their family? They want to be with their family. At the same time, they want to be able to support their family. Look at all the poverty in the world. There are countries that have all the oil and nothing to eat. Does that make sense? Here we are paying $3.00 for gas. Where is that money going? Take Hussein. He was living like a king despite all that poverty there. We were trying to correct that and things fell through. I don't know the answer, I don't know you see. You have to know, to judge a picture; you have to see the whole picture. You can't look at one fourth of it and make an assessment of it. You have to look at the whole picture to make an assessment of it. Basically, I would say, right off the top, we have to learn to talk. Until we can talk and discuss things, we are going to have these problems.

ETM: I think that is a great answer, a very good answer. Thank you very much for your time. I really appreciate it.

JO: You are welcome.

Doc Stolp

ETM: You said during our previous conversation that the uniform you are wearing dates from WWII.

DS: Yes, from the early 1940s. There are all kinds of vague indecisions in the army like in medicine; people have to express a lot of criticism before they get anything done.

ETM: We also talked about the first use of paratroopers during the invasion of Poland by Hitler's army and then you mentioned Ben Franklin.

DS: Because he was the first to conceive what this set up could do to an enemy; because in the 18th Century, there were no planes or flights, so every weapon that was invented immediately inspired anti-weapons. You have airplanes; hence, you need to have airplane guns. Ben Franklin envisioned a thousand men falling from the sky behind enemy lines and what mischief that could cause. He had it right.

ETM: And then we talked about Leonardo Da Vinci. And what did you read about him on the subject?

DS: I thought about his sketches and his engineering drawings. He drew many sketches on flying besides painting the Sistine chapel. I don't know what material he would have used but he had a great imagination and it probably would have worked in practice. I of course was able to appreciate his work at the Louvre Museum in Paris.

ETM: Do you think he was thinking in terms of military strategy?

DS: He probably envied the birds' ability to fly; everybody would later be trying to fly. There were all kinds of people that flew above buildings and got killed. What comes to mind is also the ancient myth of Icarus who had fixed wings to his arms with wax. He flew too close the sun because of his ego.

ETM: We can think of flying in terms of military strategy. But we can also think of it as a myth, a science, or a way to reach the moon and explore space. In a sense, flying is an escape, as an experience of the world, even through the imagination. What has being a paratrooper meant for you in your life?

DS: It meant a tremendous amount. In terms of travel and discovery, many of my relatives go back to a period that precedes the French exploration of Canada.

ETM: We know about Marquette and Joliet discovering Illinois and going down Lake Michigan and the Mississippi River. It is a distinctive route to America that is not as traveled as its highways. The path I have chosen here to tell the story of America is through the veterans of WWII. Their experience gave an illustration of its character. I am reminded also that the first Europeans to discover America and settle in the Mid-West were from France.

DS: You know that you are only 100 miles from Portage, WI; it's right up there. When they could not go further with their canoes, the explorers carried them from one river to another, hence "portage." They went over the Wolf River, the Fox River, and over to the Portage city area, right over through the Wisconsin River and down to Prairie du Chien and the Mississippi River. You know where the Mississippi River starts?

ETM: Oh way up in Minnesota; in fact, I was on a flight in this country some time ago. At the time I was living in California. I was in my early twenties. I was sitting next to a person from Minnesota and she told me that she was from the area right where the Mississippi begins. It is a very small stream in center in Northern Minnesota. Exploring the geography of America gives an idea of its vast land and leads us to its source. I also recall the story of Lewis and Clark's expedition and discovery of the West and the route to the Pacific. At the same time, the discovery of America is never completely achieved. It is an endeavor that has not end; like discovering who we are. And for you, where does it all begin?

DS: My lineage begins when my people were enslaved in Sweden. And this has been documented. That's a long story. Do you know Northeastern Germany? Well, way up in the northeastern corner, there is a town called Stolpmunde, and there is a huge monastery in the area. My ancestors went back and forth in the Northern Sea and they were called the Nordics, the Goths and Visigoths. Well, there was a man up there (and this was in old Sweden, whatever race group that was before the reindeer); and he had no children and nobody left but him. He had a little farm and a guy who worked for him who was exactly that, a slave, a nice handyman that tended to the fire and all of that stuff. The time came when this elderly gentleman could see his end was in sight, and he said one thing, to paraphrase: "I don't want to give all of this to the government!" He was smarter than we are. So he called this slave guy in and recited his year of faithful servitude. And he said: "I am going to make you a free man and then I will leave you my property." But the slave said: "I don't have a name" and the man said: "I will give you a name, because you held up my roof," meaning his farm. So, he said: "I will name you Stolp." The name itself refers, in some language, to the roof beam that supports the house, the ridge pole. And so this is how Stolp came to be a free man and where the name originated. And there was a man named Pieter Stolp living around 1610 or 1620, in the era of the Plymouth Rock pilgrims. He shows up in literature. Up until after the Revolutionary War, there was but one family line by the name of Stolp in the United States. They moved out like everyone else to the West to open the new country.

ETM: The word "French" refers etymologically to being free. When we explore the medieval world, the notion of freedom, of actually owning ourselves was a reality for very few people. The story of your name and family heritage is interesting from this standpoint because it shows how the question of liberty is something that is very present in the American consciousness, and how Pieter Stolp is very much a part of that history.

DS: The pioneers were always in a state of unrest; despite where they were, they wanted to see across the next field. They wanted to see what was beyond. And do you know the story of Horatio Alger? That is a significant part of America. It's about a young man, somewhere, before the Industrial Revolution. Charles Dickens wrote about all of these poor debtors in prison who could not pay their debts. But Horatio Alger is almost a myth. He was a waste nothing kid, and he went to work in whatever capacity, sweeping the floor, who knows!, and he became a very nice hardworking man. Though he did not know where he was going, he knew he had to do what was necessary to survive. Anyway, this boy arose though the corporate ladder and became the president of a company. But he had begun just emptying waste baskets. I had a grandfather who ended up doing just that, right after the Civil War. I have to put in an inference here: my ancestors have all been in every conflict including the French-Indian war. There is also a "Stolp story" in every civil unrest or outburst for freedom that the United States has ever had before and through the Civil War.

ETM: Was the Civil War about freedom? How about the end of slavery? How about Lincoln? How about this vision I have of the first explorers who came to this country to discover its geography, and later went beyond the horizon to seek prosperity and liberty. It is the story of a people moving west, a story of discovery, and that is in some ways what we see in Normandy. Flyers and parachutists looking at the horizon, and trying not only to look beyond, but to make what will be beyond, to create another world, a better world. That is also the story of America. What could you tell us in light of this vision?

DS: Well I think there is one thing that springs eternal in a man's heart, one thing that is human. I know a word that filled their presence, their being, their soul: it is hope. Why did the American paratroopers knock themselves out beyond the next hill? What was that other religion in France and Holland, the Huguenots? They did not like where they were. What gave them the courage, and the pilgrims as well including Pieter Stolp and company? It was hope! For us, Nazism was anti-religion, it was evil!

ETM: Ideology has not been as strong here in America as in Europe which is, to give an example, the cradle of Marxism?

DS: It is like an artist painting a picture; you have the charcoal outline, and start putting on the color, and it may not be the whole point of the picture, but without the color, there is not much of a picture, right? My story would be one hell of a story, ok, "formidable!" The story of my life has been intermixed with so much but underneath it all, it has been love of country, this country, all of it. And like I was saying, my "Horatio Alger" type grandfather rose to be a very prosperous man. From a small position of an office boy, he became vice-president of the Asian Railroad Trade and made trips to Japan.

ETM: Changing perspective, you told me yesterday that on June 6, 1944, you were in England. What was your reaction when you heard that D-Day was on?

DS: We were the replacement guys in Liverpool. I prayed. I am not that kind of religious but God and I have an arrangement. It has to be. Otherwise what do I have?

ETM: When did you see action for the first time and what was it like for you to be in combat?

DS: It was on September 17, 1944, in Holland. I did not want to die. We got our nose hit real quick. And you have to know the whole geography and dynamics of that situation over there; and of course General Gavin, "superb!" Have you heard of the causeway five miles south-west of St. Mère Église in Normandy called La Fière? Across, there was this big swamp with a lot of water in it. The Germans had flooded the area and the paratroopers had been landing in it at night. General Gavin and others had landed nearby and he was trying to push that damn tank out of the way so that other people could come through. General Gavin was a front line general. He was always three, even in the middle of the night; he would challenge us. Our first night in Holland, of course, we were all scared; we don't need laxatives anymore! And I had no reason to not be scared because I had not been brought up in this kind of violence. We got the password passed down for the night. The password was "doing" and the counter sign was "fine." General Gavin told us the whole story in two little words: "doing fine," meaning have confidence, go for it! and we went for it. This war experience assailed my knowledge, my soul, and feeling about camaraderie, about brothers, about families, about other human beings, and I am a damn fool! They asked me to search the first POW we had. So I did, and he took out his watch and gave it to me. "Put that back in your pocket," I said, "I don't want your damn watch!" We had guys who were stealing watches and cutting off fingers to get rings, doing any damn things they wanted to do, which was very inhuman; but they had learned in Normandy that that's what you do, not because it is nasty but because it produces a feeling of superiority and power and an ability to control. And they did it. They had also developed a significant hatred of their enemy who had caused us to be there doing terrible things.

ETM: Do you recall shooting at people and killing?

DS: Yes, I do, yes I do!

ETM: And so, it is kind of a silly question.

DS: No, it is not! I know silly questions!

ETM: How do you reconcile what you must do with Christianity?

DS: You don't reconcile it with Christianity. I have to reconcile Christianity with it. I have to say an eye for an eye. It is in the Book; it depends how you want to read it.

ETM: If it is not him, it is me.

DS: That is right. And we knew that; but in spite of that, I made friends with them. I am not a person who is vicious. I will do what I have to do because that's the dynamic.

ETM: And this situation in which you can either kill someone or be his friend shows the absurdity of war.

DS: Yes, and the reason for resorting to it! I had a German POW from Baden under my control with a gang of other POWs and I got to know him. By and large, I am a typical human being. I thought they were all like me. I was trying to be understanding, considerate, and helpful. Because I spent my entire professional life being that, I lost too much money doing it and my family has suffered a lot. I am probably too considerate, too easy. I am human.

ETM: You also embody perhaps the kindness of the American people, the decency, Lincoln says, of the American people. And you are also a learned man; you know French. The first time we met yesterday, you said a few words. And so what did France represent for you at the time?

DS: To my knowledge, liberty, equality and fraternity. Liberty is not licensed. Voilà, it is almost that simple.

ETM: If it is not licensed, then, it is the necessity to recognize the rights of others.

DS: Certainly, absolutely; and being responsible for someone who is not even there, as in driving. I always say that you can tell the culture of a country if you drive on its highways, because carefulness and considerate attention are as important as any other form of responsibility.

ETM: De Gaulle mentioned France's grandeur, and he said that France could not be France without it. But what is grandeur? Is it nobility and being able to give your life for your fellow human beings?

DS: What would be a definition of the word "grandeur"?

ETM: It is perhaps what elevates us as human beings. One who can show the way out of darkness toward the light. But it could be also the authors. We mentioned yesterday Victor Hugo and also Émile Zola.

DS: Yes, "*J'accuse!*" as Zola wrote when he publicly denounced, in a newspaper article, the key role played by members of the French government in the Dreyfus Affair who had knowingly condemned an innocent man.

ETM: Every country has its own grandeur and America certainly has its grandeur. But what did France represent at the time?

DS: To me France, as I remembered, was part of (I should not say the romance), the grandeur if you want to say so, or the development, the "opening" of this country. In contrast, we are all held up with the terrible example of mistreating the Natives. Nobody ever stops to reason or criticize by putting in perspective the time during which it was done, and time means everything. At that time, you could kill people in the west with a fast gun and, who cares? Most people did not really accept it but a lot of it was done by people who did not care.

ETM: You use the word romance when you talk about France. If you look at its history, this may be true. Today however, people talk about not the grandeur of France but about its decline. Some "intellectuals" discuss the decline of the west in general. I am more interested in grandeur myself than decline.

DS: Maybe you are more American than you know. Maybe Americans and French are not that far apart because we do things we love and want to have meaning in our lives and take responsibility. Those things are there. I trusted the French people, implicitly. I have known the French people back here. My cousin who was adopted was a French Swiss. The last name of one of her acquaintances was Aujourd'hui. It is kind of an interesting use of a couple of words; it means, I think, "the day that is today." I love the French language and I love words! Obviously! That heart, that soul, and the fact that we are not one people or nationality but, in fact, we are becoming one nationality. It is a tremendous mixing ball, and politics is screwing it up!

ETM: Is politics in your view screwing up the romance?

DS: The kids I have talked to here today are retuning to Iraq for the third and fourth trip. These are children for Christ's sake and they are going back and they are glad to go. They have the flame in them because they know why they are there and they know what they are doing and they are not fooling around. The biggest complain they have is the political attitude, of what has been called "politically correct" in this country lately. The bottom line truth is they have one solution for the problem: "Kill the bastards!" If I were over there, I would agree because they are going to kill you if you don't.

ETM: The "bastards" being not the Iraqi people, men, women, and children but the terrorists who put the bombs and want to prevent democracy from taking roots. And so, from your point of view, is the mission in Iraq today in line with what your generation accomplished in 1944?

DS: The same. You never see America really go somewhere, brutalize somebody, and take their country. We have never really done that.

ETM: All these young soldiers who are here attending the conference are from the 82nd Airborne and have been sent over there, and they are going to be sent again.

DS: Some are on their way tomorrow.

ETM: How come then, is there so much opposition to the war?

DS: That is the pathetic part, because there are many ways of coming to that subject. I always tried to be a useful person to society at large. I ended up being a dentist and I wanted to be a physician. I was born to be a physician and I do a lot of psychiatric work. I can cure menopause in women from their collapsing nervous system. I can cure agoraphobia, for people who cannot even go to their mailbox. I wish I had time to tell you more, we could talk all night.

ETM: Your theme here is that, what these kids are doing is a reflection of what America has stood for since it was created, and the reason of its engagement in combat is not to seize power and countries. Now, you are a dentist by profession. What do you say to this dentist in Baghdad or in Cairo, or in Tehran, who is not involved in politics and who wants to make a decent living, and do good, and wants his family to be happy and fulfill its needs? What do you say as an American to your fellow dentist?

DS: Well, that's a pretty bad can of worms to open because I am not very happy with my fellow practitioners.

ETM: Yes, but perhaps you have never met a dentist from Baghdad or Tehran. But you see my point.

DS: Yes, I do. He is an innocent man in your eyes, right?

ETM: Well, in my eyes, nobody is completely innocent.

DS: I agree because I have always said there are no innocent people. We all consume, we all waste, we all screw up!

ETM: Yes, but my point is that many people in the Middle East who are not involved in politics suffer the consequences of their leaders' actions. At the same time, from their perspective, they may see foreigners coming to their country like in Iraq and they may be troubled, and not understand. They may also see great danger in local politics. We see that everyday. How do you explain to this dentist in Baghdad that the effort is worth it, that what America is doing is noble, and that it is for the good of his country?

DS: I don't know why they would have a hard time seeing that. Certainly the very "apparently" religious heads in their sand pile have a hard time, and we all get right back to religion.

ETM: But I am talking about this dentist and what would you say to him from here, from Wisconsin?

DS: I will try to tell you something that will help a little bit. Every revolution in the world that I have ever studied has, at its base, a very important member of the group, and he is always a dentist. Dentists are very ambitious, dynamic and irritable people.

ETM: The tooth is immediately in contact with the nervous system. Would you tell him that you are a dentist in Wisconsin and an American World War II veteran, and that "we understand that you are suffering because of this but I am with you and I want your happiness as much as I want mine"?

DS: Right, I would say that. I would say that now.

ETM: "And I want you to have the freedom that I have, not necessarily the wealth but I want you to have the freedom and happiness that I do have."

DS: The basic values . . . basic values and freedom. And I would say to Jane Fonda who has had everything, these liberals who are pursuing everything on the street with "alligator tears," that's a whole other thing to discuss and we should because you could teach me a lot!

ETM: Given your experience, I am not going to teach you anything.

DS: Oh yes you are! You are asking good questions. I have one daughter who is a flamboyant liberal. And I have one daughter who is a flamboyant Republican. And she makes sense, and conservatives make sense. Liberals do not make sense, liberals are emotional. They know what they are told.

ETM: I traveled last year to China, to the other side of the world. It reinforced in me the notion that the world does not stop where we are, that somewhere, in Buenos Aires, New Delhi or Baghdad, there is a dentist who is closing his office, or opening it, or walking down the street, or working on his patients, who wants to do his job and have a good life. What you are wishing him is the same happiness and success. What do you think is the legacy of the WWII veterans?

DS: Let's say, by accident or design, the world is clearly better off because Hitler was evil to the core, worse than evil, there has never been anyone like him in the world. Yes, pure absolute, unquestioned evil. And I would certainly call it that. And what we are trying to do now in Iraq is for the same reasons, more or less. Pretty much; for the same reasons basically.

Robert McCann

RM: I was born 1920 in a little town called Rarden in Scioto County, Ohio. It was just a small community at that time, around 300 people. I was really fortunate because my father was employed full-time by the Railroad Company during the Depression. He did not make big money but he had his family well taken care of. Among my neighbors in my village there were two boys who were about my age. I had two cousins and two other friends in the village and during the summertime, we would all get together and split up in two baseball teams. We would play in the church yard which was not too large. In fact the back of the church had a large stained-glass window but we never hit a baseball through it. We hit the church a lot but we never broke a window. We would play baseball from daybreak to dark.

ETM: Did you see the movie *Field of Dreams*?

RM: Oh yes, we had our own field of dreams. The main thing that I learned from my parents was to always be honest, tell the truth and respect your elders. They instilled that in us. I had some relatives who had fought in the Civil War but I was not too familiar with their background. Like everyone who lived in America at that time, I was very upset and very angry at the Japanese when they attacked Pearl Harbor, and at the Germans too; at that time I was working in Air Service command at Patterson Field in Dayton, Ohio. I was in Air Corp supply and when I was drafted into the army, something got messed up and I ended up in the infantry. I took my basic training with the 42nd Division in Camp Gruber, Oklahoma. After my basic training, I was back to Ohio and they were spreading the Division overseas for replacements.

ETM: Your first experience overseas was in England?

RM: It was in Liverpool, England, where we docked after about a week in the Atlantic. They told us that we would be sent to different companies so they called our names out in the morning and they said you go here, and you go there. We got on a train and I asked somebody: "Where are we going?" They reply was: "We are going to Lester." I said: "Lester, England?" They said: "Yes, you are going to the 82nd Airborne Division." I said: "No way! You have to volunteer for that!" None of us had volunteered but that is where we ended up as replacement of the casualties in Normandy at that time. I can remember to this day the morning of the landing. We were stationed in a little tent, and you could look from one end of the horizon to the other in all four directions; all you could see were airplanes in the sky. It was wing to wing on their way to Normandy.

ETM: What was your first engagement?

RM: My first engagement was in Operation Market Garden in Holland. We landed in a glider. The trip over the Channel was nice through a little rough at times, and when we got over Holland, the Germans were throwing everything at us: machines guns and anti-aircraft fire. Some of the gliders were hit and others went down with everybody in it. We were fortunate and no one in our glider was hit. We made a nice landing in a little field. I had heard about the landings in France and how terrible they were, and the first thing I was looking at when we hit the ground was a hedgerow coming at us, and then an irrigation ditch. The glider turned side ways on the edge of the ditch as it hit the ground. Some of our units had quite a bit of combat. But when we got there, our duty was more of a holding position. The Germans were all around us. It was a front within a front.

ETM: What was your mind set at that time?

RM: The only question that a soldier has in mind is: "Am I going to be here in the morning?" I knew what we were fighting for. We were fighting to put down a tyrant; that is what we were fighting for because everyone could understand what Hitler stood for. We discussed this among ourselves and felt that something had to be done. Then we fought in the Battle of the Bulge. We had many close calls up there. I recall how I lost a friend there by the name of Fran Townsend. He was, if I remember correctly, from Massachusetts. On Christmas Day, we were in a little town but I cannot recall the name. It was on the German-Belgian border. There were four or five houses; it was a town. We were dug in outside this town. My friend and I were in a foxhole, as security for a machine gun which was set up to our right, and we were looking at a plain field. We stayed there getting shelled at times by our own artillery, and we were sleeping there for a couple of hours. I was there in the hole, and my friend woke me up and he said: "Mac, there are Germans all around us," and I woke up and I said: "Be quiet." And they were yelling with their machine killing crews. And Fran said, "What are we going to do?" and I said: "Fran, you go along the line where our boys are dug in, and tell our men that the Germans are coming down through here and I will go down to the Command Post and tell them about it." And when I got down to the Command Post, they sent me and another boy across the backyard of a house, to another building so that we could cross fire them between the two buildings when the Germans crossed through there. While we were there, a little German came around a building pile shouting "Shit on the SS, shit on the SS!" That's what it sounded like. Well I grabbed him by the arm and took him over to the other house where the officers were and turned him over to them. And I said: "Has anybody seen Townsend?" "Yes, he was here a while ago but he went outside." And when daylight came, I saw Townsend lying down in the corner of the house with a bullet in his forehead. Townsend had already been injured in Normandy but he had recovered from his injuries when we got together. He had landed in Normandy in a glider.

ETM: This idea of sacrifice is essential to understand your generation.

RM: That is right. I do not feel animosity toward German people. You know as well as anyone that there are good German people and if they had stood up for what they knew was right, I don't think that the situation would have got to where it was. But they followed a bad leader. I never did get to go back in Northern France. I would have liked to go back. My friends in the 325 have made many trips over there; in fact, a former captain of the company, Wayne Pierce, has made many trips and they are very welcome, more than welcome. Every place they go, they are treated real well. I think the situation in Iraq started off as a good cause. I mean, the world is better off without the leader of Iraq. But our involvement there is a different war all together. Our government I think makes the biggest mistake. They get us involved in something like this, and then they want to run the whole show; and in a war, you cannot do that. You have to let the people who know what war is about to fight the war.

ETM: In a sense, generals do win wars and not presidents.

RM: That's right. Congress does not win the war either. The main decisions were made by the generals and they have not since Vietnam. The French people may be our friends but I don't think the French government is our friend like they should be. I don't know why they don't appreciate the United States who fought two wars over there.

ETM: I give you my take on it. From my perspective, I think that many French, Americans and Europeans disagree right now on the current policy. I don't think they have anything against American people, but rather the American government. Reagan for example, who was a Republican, had a high rate of approval in France as did Bush Senior. But the people disagree with the current leadership. The decision made by the French government may not show that it has an appreciation for this country, but they feel very grateful and refer to

Americans as our friends. When the decision was made in the French Congress to take a different route on Iraq, it was greatly debated and not made in a cavalier way. I think they felt that going to Iraq would cause more problems than resolve them. It is not only one opponent in front of you, but rather a civil war and there are several factions fighting.

RM: It is a hell of a mess.

ETM: Some in the current American administration were saying that American soldiers would be welcome with flowers. But it did not happen that way. Liberating Europe, as challenging as it was, was not the same war. You knew who the enemy was but here.

RM: You don't.

ETM: It is very complex. I think that to a large extent, this is what they thought. It was not just about being against American policy. There was a reason and their reason was that having been involved already in Algeria, they sensed that it would be difficult. This is how I see it even though Algeria and Iraq is not the same thing either. At the same time, as you know, the French government has expressed support for the US involvement and hope for success. And there are French troops in Afghanistan because they think that this is where the war has to be won, where the training of fundamentalists is taking place. I wanted to mention this because of what you said and you may have a point: sometimes it seems as if the government and some people in France don't have an appreciation for what America has done, and I hope that what I say sheds a different light on the matter. Now going back to you, what is the legacy of your generation from your perspective going back to Ohio, the land where you were born and returning to after the war? The experience was of joy, I am sure, when you returned?

RM: That's right. Joy of being with the family and start a family of my own. All my life I worked in the Savings and Loans business. In fact, I worked for several of them for about thirty-five years and after I got out of it, I worked part-time for thirteen years. I have a wonderful family and I had a wonderful wife named Betty whom I was married to for fifty years before I lost her. We have three wonderful children, one daughter aged 53, and two sons aged 51 and 47, twelve grandchildren and eight great-grandchildren.

ETM: This noble endeavor in which you partook over sixty years ago, it is also the endeavor of America; it is the idea that liberty is a cause worth fighting for. And it is also a generous country and the action of your generation certainly illustrates that; this friend who died on Christmas day.

RM: I could tell you about many more.

ETM: And this is why I wanted to have this interview with you. It is in a sense to pay homage and to thank you for what you have done.

RM: Thank you.

John Aloisio and Ed King

JA: I participated in one of the first raids on June 6, 1944. I jumped from the landing craft with my rifle over my head, and then reached the beach. There was danger. There were planes over us and pockets of resistance. I was in charge of communication. Here in the United States, to lay wire, we used to climb the poles but not in Normandy because the Germans could pick you off right away. And then we set up the guns on the beach. A fellow named Camuso was getting really upset about it: "My wife, my girlfriend, my mother . . . " You had to get away from that. I was afraid too to a certain degree. I went on reconnaissance since I was in communication. I spoke Italian fluently and I understood German. When I arrived in the third wave, it was sunshine at about 11am.

ETM: So when you landed, you could see the people who had given their lives on the shore?

JA: Oh sure, oh yes. I had a friend of mine, Giacalone, and I told him: "Joe, we are not going back to Brooklyn anymore!" That's the way we felt. We lost a supply sergeant. His name was Smith. They backed up the vehicle with supplies on a mine that exploded. He was our age, 18 or 19. He came from Pennsylvania. I think that we worked well collectively: the people, the generals, the soldiers and all the men and women back home. We were both afraid and depressed at times. We were afraid also day by day. That war was a justified war. Hitler was evil and I think that 90 percent of the Germans feared him but we couldn't fraternize with them. We were told that if we were caught in their home, we would be court martial. A young fellow named Nick Pasquale was caught and they gave him a six month sentence and charged him for fraternizing with Germans. But I have been into their houses. I have been to their churches where the priest and the Sisters would cook us a meal, but all incognito, you know. I always felt that governments are governments, and people are people.

ETM: So going to Ed, tell us about your experience.

EK: I left New York for Europe on Thanksgiving Day in 1943. I happened to be home with my brother who was with the 63rd Infantry Division and we were seeing each other everyday because we were both at the same port of embarkation. He told me that day: "See you tomorrow!" It was Thanksgiving eve. Well, we didn't see each other the next day. That was the final day we both saw each other. We went and left the same day and we shipped out on with our turkey on the boat to go over to France. I stayed in England for about a month and then went to France. I was attached to General Simpson's 9th Army.

ETM: You personally brought back this sand from Normandy?

EK: No, no, my son did; and when he went to France, I told him: "Bring me back some sand from the Beach!" That's yours now. This is the soil where a lot of our boys were killed, and it represents a great sacrifice because I tell you, there was a lot of fighting there, and I have seen quite a bit of it later on in the little patches, you know. We did repairs for the 82nd Airborne. I was a welder and a blacksmith, and they used to bring this heavy equipment to us when they didn't have the equipment to fix it. They would bring it to us and we would work on it all night getting it ready for them. That was a little bit above the front line and we did that all the way up to the end of the campaign. When we stopped, the Russians were on the other side and we were there. Then, I went to Paris for three days. For furlough, I drove three days and three nights to get to Paris and of course it was a lovely town. I met a lot of fellows there attached to the 82nd Airborne who were wounded in the hospital, and a lot of them were from Brooklyn. They had taken a very bad beating like the soldiers of the 101st Airborne. On the way, we stayed overnight in a house in Luxembourg. We ate there and they made breakfast and lunch for us, and then the next day we arrived in Paris.

ETM: Was this after the war had ended?

EK: Well, the war was going on in the Pacific. I have some pictures here for you. This was one of the concentration camps we liberated. It wasn't a big place but still, it was awful. There were piles of bodies everywhere. The name of the town was Gardelegen in Germany. One of the fellows I was with took these pictures. You could smell the bodies from awhile back but we didn't know what that smell was. Everyone had died. It was terrible. You could see the bodies there. You could see them all; the piles and piles of people who had died. Some had died the day before, and others a month earlier; they hardly did anything with them. How could it be possible? It was very, very, very sad; we were very troubled and no one was talking. No one said anything. Why? Why? What did these people do? We later had the feeling of having been on the right side of the war. Our country was such a great country then, and you know what I mean. What many did. They sacrificed a lot. When my son put that together for me, he did it in French, I think, and then he wrote the labels in French. My brother didn't land where I landed. I landed in England and he went right into battle the third day. He was killed in a quarry in a town called Tübingen, Germany. His name was James Peter King. He was a year older than me. Here I'll show you a picture. This was in Rouen, Normandy. I was there, and there is a tank that was knocked out. Another battle I took part in was the Battle of Brest.

JA: Yes, that was a big battle and I remember the people all over the country shouted on many occasions after we freed them: "Vive l'Amérique!"

ETM: How do you view this country today and its relation with the rest of the world?

JA: It's wrong. I was a committee man for the Republican Party for a long time and I'm against Bush. I voted against him. When two guys fight you never want to get in the middle of it. That's my belief. We don't belong in Iraq. They have a government of their own, right? If we get out of there, they'll have a civil war. We had a civil war here, and either one had to win. Let them fight their own battles. Do you see what happened with Japan? There was so much damage done because of the war, and after the war, we helped them become rich. All the European countries, Italy, France, Holland, and here Canada, are now in disagreement with the position of our government as far as Iraq is concerned. There must be something wrong if these people say you don't belong there, that's all. During World War II, we all thought the same.

ETM: And what is your opinion on that Ed?

EK: Well, I always felt sorry for the people over there who were being persecuted, you know. I guess the United States meant very well going over there and doing what it did, but it isn't turning out how we had anticipated. I don't think they expected it to be so long. There is a political, ethnic and religious dimension to the conflict. Our trouble is I feel that we try to do too much even if we mean to help. But we can't leave it now; we've got to finish it off. I mean I don't think you can walk out of it.

ETM: What would be a government as good as its people?

JA: Well, we like peace in the world, but we can't fight anything that believes in other than what we believe. I mean, how can you go wrong in this country if you have freedom? We don't need three, four televisions. I told my cousins in Italy, America is a great country if you've got a strong back and a working wife. My parents met in a factory and they migrated to places where all Italians came from similar regions, in Williamsburg and Greenport. I used to go to the shoemaker and they used to say to me: "Speak Italian I don't understand you." Democracy, where you vote for your leader, offers the ideal form of governance. That's the proper way. That's better than kingdom, and that's better than dictatorship. If you get any man my age in France, who talks like me, he remembers. If America had not gone in there, Hitler would have taken them over. You're French right? What do French people of your age think of Americans today?

ETM: I think all in all that the people of my generation in France have absolutely nothing whatsoever against Americans. They still remember history, yet, like many in this country, they may disagree with some aspects of American policy. Having said that, I do believe that people recognize the challenges ahead of us, and that, while they have the same aims, to live in a democratic and tolerant society, they differ in terms of how they can be achieved in the world, in particular in this region. The purpose of my presence at this table is in a sense to bridge a gap that one can perceive at times between our two countries, but that does not reflect the reality. It is to help understand each other better and to partake in a conversation in which the two nations have been engaged for over 200 years.

EK: I think a lot of people feel as though France just forgot about all the good we did do in the war; the young generations in particular. I think they more or less deserted the United States. That's the way I feel.

ETM: It is legitimate for veterans to feel that way in light of the historical relation between France and America. But many young French people go to Normandy each year on June 6 to commemorate D-Day. They have not forgotten.

EK: I believe that. My grandfather from Brooklyn who had fought at Gettysburg on the Union side had come from Ireland during the potato famine. As far as I know, my father also fought during World War I. He fought in France. My grandmother was an American Indian. So, on her side of the family we have been in America for hundreds of years. We know that my grandmother was Mohawk from the tribe in upstate New York, all the way up near the Canadian border. Let me show you a picture of my brother who was killed during the war. It was a terror. He was good, he worked hard, honest and everything. He was liked by everybody. He was a wonderful athlete; he played football. He was valedictorian. I mean anyone who ever knew my brother would say that he was a terrific guy. I was a little wilder. He was meek, he was a gentleman, you know. I've got to show you this here. We found my brother's outfit. This is the tomb of the Unknown Soldier in Arlington, Virginia, and that's his outfit there during a ceremony. They put a wreath on his grave. He's buried in Pinelawn, the military cemetery on Eastern Long Island. In memory of my brother and of all who died, I would say, and I am sure John would agree with me, that our legacy, as WWII veterans who saw action in France and the European Theater, is that as soldiers we helped rid the world of dictatorships. It was necessary so that our nation, America, could remain a free government for future generations. Most European people with whom I came in contact seemed to appreciate the presence of the American troops, realizing that America is truly the land of freedom and opportunities.

Howard Comstock

HC: My family came from England a long time ago in the 1600s. I was 18 when the war was going on and I enlisted. My interaction with city people was mixed. I still don't like city life. I still don't live in the city. I have to but I don't like that. And that's alright. I am from Saint Louis, Michigan. The French may have founded the town; the French have been in Michigan before but the town where I was raised in Central Michigan was settled by a German community. It was the first time I had ever been away from home. I spent three years in the army, and most of it in Europe. And it was different; I was treated differently, too. Well, "Gosh, a paratrooper!" "Ah, Wow!" "Hey wow!" you know. We were taught that . . . Eleonore Roosevelt, do you know Eleonore Roosevelt? I didn't like that woman. She was the one who told the government not to let paratroopers back to the United States until they had been "retrained."

ETM: Retrained for what?

HC: For civil life, because us paratroopers had a reputation. It was pretty wild, and we did not think we were that bad. I was in England during D-Day. We had landed in Africa right after the campaign and I made the invasion of Sicily and we went to Salerno, and we got up to Naples and I was in a hospital when the division pulled out into England. So, when I came out of the hospital, I went to battle at the Anzio Beachhead, and that's the reason why I did not go to Normandy. Actually, I had my appendix out at the time. We had landed in Africa three days after the campaign ended. We thought the war was over. The Germans were kicked out of Northern Africa.

ETM: When you arrived in Italy, it was different. What was your worst experience there?

HC: Well, strangely, I don't know whether I should tell you what my feelings are. When we jumped in Sicily, my particular unit was very lucky. We didn't meet the Germans, we met the Italians, and the day before we jumped our colonel made a speech and said: "You're probably going to be killed, so don't worry about it!" We jumped at night, of course, and in the morning we met the Italians and they were shooting at us and we did not take cover. We just attacked. And they surrendered! They said: "Why don't you people fall out?" and we said: "Why don't you hit us?" We did not hide, we just ran to them! Well, you are 18 years old, see, and you are told "You're gonna die tomorrow, so don't worry about it." Ok? It worked very well with the Italians. Not so good with the Germans. Other units had the Germans and they had a real, real tough battle because our job was to keep the German reinforcements from going to the beach. So we jumped before the Sea Borne Invasion.

ETM: We don't always talk about the Italian campaign but it was a very hard campaign.

HC: It kept getting harder as we moved up and the Germans would withdraw and the Italians would surrender. Then when Italy changed side and became an ally that was a bad thing for us because we didn't have those weak spots. We knew we could take the Italians. The Germans around them stayed and fought, so the campaign got much harder. It didn't work well for the Italians either because the Germans hated them; and we didn't particularly care for them. See, they were going to change sides and fight on our side. They tried that once. The American army equipped the Italians and sent them in against the Germans. The Germans found out who they were; they chased them back and the Americans said: "Ah, they are not worth the equipment." We did not have a good opinion of the Italian army. We liked the Italian people.

ETM: And how about D-Day? Were you at that time in England?

HC: I was in Leicester. The 504 did not go to Normandy because of the heavy casualties it suffered in Italy; we were detached from the 82nd Airborne and later went to Holland. We landed at Grave. Well, there, we got over this idea that we were going to die tomorrow. We may die tomorrow, but don't hurry it up. We were over that real soon. Of course, we were getting older too. We had really experienced one thing with the paratroopers: We never lost a fight! We never did. That is a pretty good feeling to have that when you go into a fight, you win. Every engagement we won; we moved forward and did not lose ground. That gave us an extraordinary feeling of confidence.

ETM: Washington, Jefferson and Franklin were all descendent from Britain? What are your thoughts about the WWII experience with respect to America's foundations?

HC: First, you must understand that there were a lot of people that did not want to go to war. Let everyone take care of themselves! And then the Japanese attacked and the Germans declared war. Oh, wait a minute! They got a lot of nerve doing that! But I think eventually we would have gotten into the war. There is a character there. There's an old saying that I absolutely believe. You put an English soldier on a crossroad. Tell him to hold it and he'll hold it against a whole army. You can kill him, but you can't beat him. And I think there is quite a lot of truth to that. The English army, they lose a lot of battles, they lose a lot of men, but they don't really lose because they want it more. They are stubborn. I tell people that it was my idea that a German and an Englishman are an awful lot alike; but they hate you for saying that. However, the German thinks that he's better than anyone else and he'll take any opportunity to try to prove it. The Englishman is a lot like him. He knows he's better but he doesn't care what you think.

ETM: What makes America different from your point of view?

HC: Well, we come from all different backgrounds, and everybody has their own thing that they believe in. And then the immigrants change things. Some people think that's the way it should be. When the immigrants come in, they take the jobs. They take the low-paying jobs. But what happens to the Americans? Well, they are getting forced into a better job. In the streets of Chicago or in the streets of New York, you see the whole world. You are next to someone from the Middle East, from South America or from Asia. It is the whole world, and that's something that is remarkable about this country. There is another place where you can see that, in London. When you are in the streets of London, try to find an English restaurant. I guess it was the law. The people from the colonies had the right to come home. But we have a problem. Our government is so short termed. How are we going to deal with foreign countries? What is our foreign policy? How many years is it that good for? I think a lot of people realize that. I hope we will prevail, I am sure we will.

ETM: Former President Reagan said that what is right would prevail.

HC: Basically, it is right. We later were on the border of Germany. We were back and forth. I would write home and tell my mother that I was in Germany and she would worry. Well, we were fighting in Holland and sleeping in Germany. It was hard to tell. We were on the border. One day, we were looking for food, and we thought it would be nice to have some chicken. We went towards a chicken coop and an old German was chasing his neighbors' chickens for us to shoot. Now, what is wrong with him? They weren't his chickens; they were his neighbor's chickens. It's hard to tell on border countries; who is who. When I returned home, I wasn't home very long and I was ready to go back into the army. I was lonesome. I thought: "There is nothing going on here!" But I came home with a certain satisfaction of having been part of this endeavor. During the war, I never got over the idea that I probably would be killed. So, I didn't worry about what was going to happen when I got home. We were victorious and that felt good. I was really glad that I got into a better than normal unit and didn't go just to a regular unit such as infantry or something like that. It was so much different.

ETM: Could you share with us the name of someone close to you who died in the conflict?

HC: Well, I will tell you. It seems like everybody I was close to got killed. So, I did not want to form any close bonds. These were all friends, but I was thinking to myself: "They might not be here tomorrow, so you just don't worry about getting too close." And I really never got over that. What is the point of feeling close to somebody knowing that he will be gone? But there is another way about it. We had people from our town who were killed in Vietnam. We have another fellow who was driving to Lansing and he was killed in an accident. He is just as dead. So, being killed in battle, victorious or not victorious, you are no more dead than the man who fell off the bar stool.

ETM: Yes, but dying in war is not exactly an accident. There is a purpose, there is a reason and there is a sense of sacrifice.

HC: About this thing in Iraq, I can say that we can't win there. There's no way we can win there. The longer we are there, the more people come in to kill our soldiers. It's not a war. That's the whole problem. We can win a war, but we can't win something like this. My take is I wish we weren't there from the start. We were not ready. They drew the army down. We don't have the personnel to carry out this war. A big percentage of them are people who have been in the military, the reserves, or in the guard which was created for home defense. I cannot understand what we are going to do. How can you stop a man who is willing to die, anxious to die? How can you stop him from carrying out an act? You say, "Stop or I'll shoot you?!" No. That's beyond me. I feel that we have many more enemies than we had when we were into this.

ETM: What is your take on France and the position of the French government?

HC: There is the problem. We may not like what the president of the French government says, but it's just like our government, it'll change. My wife and I made several trips to France and everybody told us that French people hate the Americans but we were treated so wonderfully. Things come and go with governments. I also look at the "loud" posture some Americans adopt toward the Europeans. Where does it come from? I don't know; people get the idea: I am American, I am the greatest! We have a lot of French people in the United States. We have a lot of English, German and Spanish people and we all share the same values, pretty much. Like from the Germans, we get the good farmers. And they are very stable and they work hard. That's one of the values that they brought. I think we should get all religion out of government. It seems that most of our wars are in part over religion. And why? If I look at some of these people, they are so silly! They look at me, ok, I'm a Christian and I do silly things. Our president George Bush does some things that I don't like. He flags his religion and I don't like the extremism of anybody. I don't think it's necessary. There are a certain amount of people who think George Bush is ideal because of his conservatism, his Christian religion. I just wish he didn't bring it up.

ETM: Every religion has its own value and virtue.

HC: Well, that is what I think and I've had Christian people tell me that all of the great religions in the world are based on the same values. But you would not know it because they started with the same values and grow up in their separate way. I am a conservative, but I am a conservative here [in my mind] not there [in my heart]. There are good things on both sides and to say that I have to be on that side. . . . I usually vote Republican because I like to spend my own money; but I have been so mad with the Republicans for the last two elections. I was ready to switch to the Democrats and they did not put anybody I would vote for. I sense that as soon as you are labeled as a Conservative, you become extreme and I think that's a mistake.

ETM: Could you tell us more about your experience in the Battle of the Bulge?

HC: There were rather strange things that happened there. The Germans were on their last wait but they were ready to put up a fight. One night, we were in a forest and could not sleep; and here come these German soldiers with brand new uniforms and equipment; and they wanted to surrender. We thought it was because of the camp fire. We woke up the colonel and he said: "Let them sleep there," and they lay down to sleep. Came the morning and then we found out that they were not Germans, they were Czechs. They had been conscripted, given a uniform and set up to fight, and the first thing they did was to look for somebody to surrender to.

ETM: The veterans do not talk much about the fighting. They prefer not to. Is that correct?

HC: The GIs had a good time in Europe, but it was not all fun! I feel that I have a very healthy memory. I don't remember bad things. I think the people who don't have that type of memory, they lose their mind. Because if you can only remember the bad things, you have lost it. . . . If they had dwelled on that, they would not be here today. They would not come to a gathering of veterans. They are very few people out here that I know. I was one of the young ones, you know, I was only 18 and most of these guys were two or three years older, not old; paratroopers could not be over 30 years old.

ETM: You said earlier that you came back to Normandy.

HC: There was a school there and they were teaching these elementary students; they were teaching what causes war and how to prevent it. They should do that all over the world. Because wars do have a cause, they don't just happen. You see this is where I think that your French president was right; we should not have gone to Iraq. It was wrong and there are a lot of things that could have been done there rather than going to war. We can win it but the war has been going for many years; we are fighting and more people are dying than ever. The timing was not right. Whether there is a right time or not, I don't know.

ETM: But then how do we respond to September 11?

HC: Did Iraq have anything to do with September 11? The only thing is, were they training terrorists or not? Saddam Hussein was a mad man. There is no doubt about that. He does not seem to have any concept of reality. He still thinks he is the president. Now, during the First Gulf war, they said to George Bush, "you should not have stopped; you should have gone all the way to Baghdad." Absolutely not! If he had gone to Baghdad, you know what would have happened, we would still be there fighting. How do we respond to terrorism and extremism? It is what is in people's head. It is not just there but also in Israel and Palestine, people go out and blow themselves up. What are they proving? It is like when the colonel told us when we landed in Sicily that we were going to be killed tomorrow; he was not advocating that we die, but he said that it could happen.

ETM: He was taking out the fear of dying.

HC: Sometimes, you get into battle and it gets pretty noisy and pretty bad, and anything that would end it . . .

ETM: would be fine.

HC: Yes.

ETM: Please let me die. . . . Is that what you have in mind?

HC: Yea, yea. . . . I actually saw a man I knew, a brave man, I saw him stand up; he threw down his rifle and said: "the hell with it!" and walked away. There, right up in front of everyone. He walked away. The Germans should have killed him; according to all the rules of warfare, our sergeant should have killed him, he was deserting. He just walked away and he ended up in a hospital.

ETM: Thank you for your time and for sharing with us your experience.

Gene Frice

GF: Well, I can say that I was born at a very young age. Actually, my place of birth was Long Beach, California, which is part of Los Angeles in a way. From a family standpoint, I did not have much of one. I had a working mother and I never met my father until much later. Because my mother worked, she did not have much time for me. I saw very little of her; the result of this was I ended up in boys' homes. I spent most of my youth in one home or another. I progressed through every school in the city of Los Angeles, where a Boys' home happened to be located. I attended Hollywood High School and traveled some distance from home to Hollywood. I think my mother brought me home every six months or once a year. When a place looked like it was going be stable, I would be brought to her, and then it would not work out and I would be brought back to a boys' home. So I ended up in Hollywood living in a fairly nice place. I used to take the bus every morning to Hollywood all the way across the city of Los Angeles, or hitchhike. And I got through the second year of high school in the 11th grade. When Pearl Harbor came along, I was introduced to the military, to wearing the uniform, because a certain portion of the Academic program in school was military. I wanted to be part of the military and I was 16 years old. So, I volunteered. I lied about my age and was assigned to security duties in the Los Angeles National Guards.

ETM: Maybe the army felt that the show of military presence on the West coast was important.

GF: We had all kinds of weapons training. And finally they sent us to San Louis Obispo, in Central California, which is one of my current homes today. I thought this really strange, but they figured that San Louis Obispo would be the point of invasion by the Japanese. In those days, we really believed that the Japanese were going to invade California. There was not any foolishness about that. We figured that first Hawaii would go, followed by the mainland, but we did not know at the time that they did not have the amphibious means to get to the United States. They wanted to destroy our fleet by air because that would have had international repercussions and affect our ability to go around the world and carry the war abroad. They did a good job at it. If it were not for the fact that two or three of our aircraft carriers were at sea, much of the fleet would have been destroyed.

ETM: Why was San Louis Obispo strategically important? How long were you there?

GF: Well, the local area had probably half a dozen repositories of oil, and in the Central valley of California, 50 to 100 miles from San Louis Obispo, there is a very large storage of oil called a strategic petroleum reserve. That was our next stop after six or eight months, and by then I was a sergeant. It took eight hours to post the guards; the perimeter of this oil reserve was vast. The Japanese made an attack on San Louis Obispo with three submarines and one of them came close to shore and shelled an oil refinery. That night, I remembered that everyone thought that this was the beginning of the invasion because rumors immediately spread. We packed our trucks and headed south to engage the Japanese on the beach, probably in Santa Barbara. We figured that we might die, but later we found out that it was just a shelling of the petroleum. So, we continued our duties, and we were even sent to Northern California to pick up fruit; there was not a soul on the farms because of Army enrollment. Then I got into a fight with one of my men. I was sort of combative at the time and they were going to court martial me but then after they interrogated me, they found that I was only sixteen years old, so I was discharged. They kicked me out almost to the day of one year in service with the guard. And so, I went to work for Lockheed Aircraft. Then in June, I reenlisted. I was seventeen by that time and lied about my age again because you cannot go in the service until you are eighteen years old. So, in February of 1943, I volunteered for parachute duty and ended up in Georgia for training.

ETM: You eventually partook in the French-American landing in Provence on August 15, 1944.

GF: When we arrived in Italy in early 1944, things were not going well. This was right after Cassino and before Rome fell. We landed in Naples and we went toward Anzio and got our first taste of combat in that area. The fighting was mostly in the mountains. We were in the mountains of Italy in June at the time of Normandy, and then we prepared for the landing in France in the beginning of August and jumped on the 15th in the area of Nice at 4:30am.

ETM: What were the conditions when you jumped?

GF: One aircraft was shot down with the air crew on board. I don't think anybody came out. As soon as I exited the aircraft, I looked down and saw what I thought was the moon's reflection on the water. As I was approaching the landing, I could hear the waves and I thought: "Oh, my God!" I thought I was landing on the sea. It turned out that what I was seeing was the fog. We landed in the mountains about 2,000 feet high, in a very heavily forested area; and when I hit the ground, I could hear shooting not too far away. The war was on. And it took us until the next day to go to the command post in Sainte Roseline, a woman who was canonized there, and we used the chapel as the command post. And then we moved west and had frequent encounters with the Germans. There was a Panzer Division not far away and the 5th or 6th Parachute German Divisions located there. Our first substantial engagement was on day two; we got machine gun fire going through vineyards, coming from the top of a hill.

ETM: What was the nature of your mission?

GF: It was to liberate the territory, create a second front in France, and prevent the Germans from receding from Italy to get back up into Germany and to Normandy. So we were there to block them and we were at the foot hills of the Maritime Alps. There were forts built in WWI on the border that needed to be secure. The Germans gave us a fit there for months on the mountain tops. This was German held; they covered every road, every pass and mountain top, and so my company spent a month taking the high ground around those forts. We went from Draguignan and Le Muy, going west for about 50 to 70 miles, and that took us from August to November. The Navy tried to hit the Germans in these mountains but it was difficult to do.

ETM: What was your encounter like with the French population?

GF: Wonderful. We walked quite a bit because of the terrain and the mountain, the area being so remote. We worked quite a bit with the FFI (French Forces of the Interior), and we knew that some of them were communists but they had an intense hatred of the German soldiers, the *Boches*. And so, they made very good companions. A young man from one family my lieutenant was friend with guided us through the mountains. He ended up getting killed and I felt very badly about that. He was probably sixteen years old, something like that, nice young guy. The people were wonderful. They had little food, bread was sort of an honor, but they had fruit, and eggs and things like that. We would give our canned rations to the families and they would prepare them with vegetables and fruit and everything and we ate very well on those occasions. I never had any bad experience with the French people there; they were wonderful. The only problem we had was the language barrier. Generally you would find some people who had some command of English, much more so today of course, so it became at times a kind of pantomime to communicate. All of us loved the people there, and I still do today.

ETM: What did you do after the war?

GF: I worked 30 something years in the State of California with the Department of Justice, 30 something years in the military, 10 years in the county of Los Angeles as an investigator, five years in the Guard and I am only 23 years old.

ETM: Do you think that France and the United States still share common principles?

GF: I don't know if we do or not. I think that we have so many things to distract us with cars and movies. Considering the lives of luxuries Americans have, I think the American family is a wonderful foundation for our country and what has held this nation together as well as it has over all these years. But the children's minds are elsewhere, the minds of the parents are elsewhere. Most homes are run by a single parent, just like when I was raised as a kid, and in a lot of homes there is no parent. We have a problem with minorities, trying to give them the opportunity that they need to live, to find employment and education. I used to tell my troops that a Black person would need to be twice the man that I am in order to be at the same place because he is Black. It is more difficult for him to get an education, and it is more difficult for him to get employment in the system of business and industry, the corporations, the military and the Church, than it would be for me, even if we had the same education. I think that we need to clean our own house in this country. I hate the gangs that we have; however, there is no escape for them. Generally, they have left school, they are on their own on the street; they have no parents, they have nothing to do, except tattoos, drive-by-shooting, robberies and dope. And dope itself is a problem in America, more so than in any other country in the world.

ETM: As a conservative, you also care for the underprivileged.

GF: Well, I am a humanitarian conservative; because that is where I come from. I was not brutalized at school; I was never beaten. I got slapped a few times, maybe I deserved it. But I recognize that there are opportunities that I have had and that other kids don't have. And so I feel more sympathy, more concern for other people. And even in Europe, I hate to see people die in warfare. I was in Berlin for eight months right after the war. The 82nd Airborne went in right behind the Russians, two weeks after, and I think I saw more dead bodies there at one time than I have ever seen in my life. The canals were jammed with dead bodies, the subways were full of dead bodies; the Russians flooded the subways. Though the adult dead bodies bothered me, nothing was like seeing the dead children. Every time I see something on TV about guys who kill children, I get furious, furious! Although having been in law enforcement, I know the legal restriction that exists to prevent me from skinning one guy alive.

ETM: And this is what makes you say that going into Iraq and removing someone like Saddam Hussein was the right thing to do. What are the greatest challenges that the world faces in the post-September 11 world?

GF: I think that the most serious problem that the world faces now is Iran and North Korea. The leader of North Korea is uncontrollable, and if he develops the nuclear component of warfare and if Iran continues with its program, I think this is certainly a serious matter. A rogue nation or leadership with a nuclear bomb could cause untold disaster around the world. The second problem we could talk about is worldwide starvation and disaster. I also wonder whether with radical Islam, we are looking at the third crusades now, the reverse of Islam battling against Christianity. While I worked for Interpol, the International Criminal Police Investigation, I went to Paris in 1972–1973. I was in the French or British office, and Interpol was right across the alley, and right next door to that was the KGB, everything was clumped together to make it convenient for everybody. We need an international family to address these problems.

ETM: Could you tell us about a person close to you that you lost in war?

GF: Two persons come to mind. The first is Mark Enari; he was my executive officer in my special force A-team. I was the team commander as a captain, and he was a first lieutenant. He was from Estonia. His family of aristocratic background had been captured by the Germans. He was a doctor in Botany and his mother was a medical doctor. They escaped, came to the United States and ended up in Los Angeles after the war, and that is where I first met his family. And then Vietnam came about and he was assigned to the 4th infantry Division. Our family adopted him and he was the first man in the 4th Infantry Division to be killed in Vietnam. So he received the Silver Star and a base was named Camp Enari in Vietnam to honor him. He was not an American citizen and he volunteered to go in the military to obtain citizenship. And so I asked the commander: "Do you know if he got his citizenship before he died?" And I added: "We give medals to people posthumously, how about citizenship?" And he answered: "That's a hell of an idea." The other soldier's name is Joe Brian. He had a sense of humor and drove everybody crazy, but he was a wonderful young man. He was the first soldier in my company to die in Southern France in Le Muy; he was killed from a German Schmiser and he was buried in the Draguigan military cemetery outside Nice, until his mother, a few years later, asked that his remains be returned to the United States. He is buried in San Bruno, near San Francisco. One day in the cemetery, I wondered where he was buried. And I found out that he was not 50 feet away from where Joe Brian rested. Two of my best friends were buried within 50 feet of each other there in San Bruno. That's what I hate about warfare though.

William Kotary

ETM: What does it mean to be part of the greatest generation?

WK: I am 85 years old. I arrived in Europe on June 2, 1944. I was part of the air assault in Holland with the 325th Glider Infantry Regiment. I grew up on a farm during the Depression in upstate New York; in a background that was superior to life in the city. We were more conservative in small towns and we all worked to help everybody in farm work and we did not get rich doing it. Conditions improved after WWII with the GI bill. We are a generation of doers. We worked and got organized for the betterment of society. In contrast, I would say that the Vietnam generation for example is not made of joiners; they don't always show solidarity and they have a propensity to downside the framing of character.

ETM: What does it mean to be conservative?

WK: I have been a conservative for years. To be conservative has meant for me from my young age, to conserve and not throw away, to conserve all the natural resources at our disposal, wood for fire, as an example, contrary to what is done today with credit card spending and marketing. I think we need more conciliation in this country. You see how the country is divided for a Supreme Court appointment. Something to consider I think with respect to the rest of the world is that we are not a vindictive nation. The Marshall plan is an example of this when we made ourselves and our equipment available to others. We also believe in the freedom of people to speak their mind and practice their religion. The pledge of allegiance to the flag is central, in this respect, to American values. And it hurts me to see poverty in other countries in the world and to see people deprived of the rights that we have in this country. Our GIs in Iraq provided a lot to the local population in terms of construction and renovation but our media does not pay attention to this. On the other hand, I regret to see Bush's lack of humility and see his aggressiveness which does not provide a good image.

ETM: You have said that taking away the pledge of allegiance is something that you question. And as a conservative, you talked about the feeling that you have for people in the world, the word that you have used earlier is that America is not "vindictive." Do you think that what is being done in Iraq right now is an example of what this country has done in WWII?

WK: It is kind of hard for my generation because there are so many years that elapsed. I think that in general, our generation supports the idea that a country should be free, free to move wherever, to speak, attend any church, and follow any religion they wish to have. Even with Russia and some of the countries that had been considered "our enemy" in the past, when there is a natural disaster there or an accident, we have stepped up and provided funds and relief; and just recently when they had that submarine stuck at the bottom of the ocean, we sent support over there. Our people are generous, our country is generous, and will continue to be. But to go back to one aspect of our country during WWII, it was united and everyone was in when we got into the war and felt that we had to do it. It took awhile to get in there because we were a pacifist country; we did not want any entanglements with foreign countries; but you could not let England and the occupied countries in Europe suffer the way they were suffering without doing anything and with the bombing and whatnot that these people went through. But I don't believe now that you will ever see this country have a single mind on a subject. We are too darn personal. In the last fifty years, with immigration, we have very different nationalities, and I don't necessarily understand what our country was like going back prior to WWII. But everybody worked for that one thing, a successful conclusion to the war. And then everybody came back and returned to one's own life. Now, we are such a diverse country, we will never get a good single opinion on any subject. Iraq is a good example.

ETM: This cohesiveness originated also from your experience growing up.

WK: Our contribution to the war was materialistic but we also needed people to build up an army. We not only had to supply our own army but we supplied England and we also supplied Russia. Now you stop and think how we were able to keep our manufacturing facilities and the figure heads, to be able to build one ship a day; that was never heard of before. We had to stop manufacturing certain things to manufacture war material. And we had, as I said, to build up our own army and we had to supply other nations.

ETM: Going back to Iraq briefly, would you compare the liberation of Iraq with the liberation of Europe from the Nazis, or are there fundamental differences?

WK: Well, first of all, we had the Japanese in the Far East and the Germans in Europe. I think there is a difference in the background; of course Iraq, their education goes back and their standard of living was tremendous going back to before the United States came into existence. I think the premise we went into Iraq, if we were told this with a straight tongue, was to me a crime; if there is a threat there of a chemical or nuclear weapon, we don't want to be in the hands of some of the crazies like North Korea. So, I supported going into Iraq but I was worried that the bases that we were given might come back to be wrong. And that is what has happened. That is what bothers me about governments. We can only make a judgment based on what information you have, the people in a government have much more information than we do, so you have to go on the basis of what they are saying. I think the circumstances under which those people were living justified going in and removing Saddam. But the basis given for our intervention is on shaky ground. The result is however what you would like to see. Get rid of him! How many palaces does one person need denying his own people's good living for one person and his close entourage? That to me is completely wrong.

ETM: Considering the disagreement over Iraq, do you recognize between France and the United States more similarities or more differences?

WK: Our country is made up of the same people. We have a lot of Germans over here; we have a lot of French. These are the people who came in from European countries; they were hard working people. I was upset particularly with France because they were the most outspoken; Germany was the same way. Politics had things to do with that, it might have been, and we will never know unless we have a close insight. That is why I have never gone into politics; you have people talking on both sides of their mouth. I don't go there. Politics is not my cup of tea. Now, my understanding is that while these countries did not support us going in there, they were providing some help under cover.

ETM: What do you remember about WWII?

WK: I lost some friends in my hometown; we were not in the service together but I lost some friends and this is true all over and when you start to figure that they were teenagers in their early 20's who lost their life, they had not seen life, and particularly as the war went on and we needed the teenagers in the military. In fact a friend of mine who is here downstairs with his wife came in out of high school. He was a teenager and joined us during the Battle of the Bulge; we were getting low in terms of replacements. The fellow who has been the hardest to lose was a sergeant who was killed a day before Christmas 1944. That was in the Battle of the Bulge. We were at a crossroads, and the SS 2nd Armored Division hit us. The 3rd American Armored Division was there and we provided a company for infantry protection. The SS troops hit us for a couple of days, and we repelled them; it was very cold because we had some of our automatic weapons that froze; so on the night of the 23rd, I was going to go get the wounded, and this is when the SS 2nd went on again with their assault. The artillery barrage was tremendous. This kid driving the truck I was in turned around and we followed the trails of tank destroyers and went back. On that night, our company was overrun, I knew two had been captured, one from New Jersey and the other from California. This was in December and the ground was frozen, we could not really dig a fox hole and they said tanks would come up so none of us gave up. It is bad enough to have a people killed but in my thinking the day before Christmas, when a family should be celebrating, what a time to get the news that your son has been killed.

ETM: This was during the German counter offensive.

WK: Well, the 82nd was the first Division called back. It was the 16th of December I think. And I can remember being in camp, I was writing letters, and I think I was the only member of the battalion staff in the camp, the others were in hospitals nearby, and it was about 9 o'clock at night. It was in the evening and a fellow came with the order, and we had to be ready to move in 24 hours, and soon thereafter it was changed to 12 hours. We had come from Holland to Soissons in France, just outside of Reims and our headquarters. I looked at it as a job. Believe it or not, it was a job that we had to do. From my standpoint, I cannot speak for others, when you were told to do something, you did not question it; it had to be done. It was just like going to work somewhere. There was a hazard of course but it did not enter my mind to the point where fear took over. You recognized that you may be injured or killed. We thought that if we were going to be injured, it would be a burden on the family, so to be killed would be all right.

ETM: That crossed your mind.

WK: Oh yes, that was my belief. It did not cross my mind, it was my belief. And all the fellows I talked about felt the same way. I knew fellows who were in fear of being wounded; they did not want to be a quadriplegic; I also said to myself that if it is going to be that serious, I'd rather die. I did not think much about it but Germany had begun the war and there was no justification for them to do that. And of course, we learned that the Japanese had attacked Pearl Harbor and had made an unprovoked attack; but most wars are unprovoked. It is just like Germany which captured the Fort in Liège, to liquidate Belgium, and the same with France and the Maginot Line; there is no strategic position that is safe, particularly today.

ETM: Did you come to close encounters with German soldiers?

WK: Yes, many times, on the morning of the 24th, to go back to the event I was telling about, when my sergeant was killed, our division was so stretched out, we covered miles and we could not occupy all the land. I think there was 1,000 yards between our company and another. We were told to take a high ground; our commander had been hit and we had a temporary battalion commander. I asked permission to withdraw but they refused to let us withdraw. We took the last ammunition and we dumped it on the ground. We had a jeep and a German patrol fired on us. And the only thing left for us was a ditch. The fire went on for a long time. Then our guys began to run low in ammunition. I crawled and tried to open one of the M1 rifles and I could not lift off the top because of the corrosion caused by the water. At least we had the ditch and the Germans were in the open behind trees. I don't remember how long this went on, but finally they gave up, they had some casualties and we took prisoners. Then we got permission to withdraw, so I started evacuating our position.

ETM: What has the experience of war taught you?

WK: Well, you don't want to have another war. It also taught to work as teams. Seeing the injured people made us also appreciate life. I can remember at the Battle of the Bulge, the snow was very deep and everybody was covered up. We were under Montgomery. We were on the north side of the Bulge, in the 18th Airborne Corps. He had us withdraw on Christmas Eve. It was cold, oh it was cold. And we withdrew and got supplies before we could attack again. Today things have changed but we still have these people with their selfish interests like Saddam and other dictators; their people are suffering while they live well, I was hoping we would not see it.

ETM: Are you hopeful for this country?

WK: Not really. We still have to deal with regimes in the Middle-East, Syria and Iran. People don't want us there but they want our support and us to help them out. The American people are great particularly when there is a disaster. We will contribute money, supplies and whatnot; that's our whole philosophy. We don't want to be at war. We try to democratize countries, to give them what we have and enable them to try to live a life, and certainly the

Iraqis did not have that under Saddam Hussein. I listened to some of the TV interviews. They are educated people; it is where early civilization began. One thing that bothers me is that our army did not always intervene when people rose to face regimes like this. But we don't have enough people over there to be able to do that.

ETM: You do not seem as optimistic as you would like to be.

WK: No, I am not. There is such a lack of courtesy and discipline in this country. These rules still exist but are they practiced? No. There is today very aggressive behavior, particularly females who never used to be. They are now. There are signs: "no U-turns." I almost got hit a couple of times with people who are not respecting it. And I have seen mothers with children doing it. You cannot avoid accidents when people do not follow the rules. That is courtesy and discipline. You don't have to be courteous but you have to be disciplined when you are driving in the highway. Back in the 1950s, I had a company, a training company, in an Infantry Division, and I addressed the company as the commander, I said there are two things that I require: discipline and physical condition. I said one without the other will never cut it. And I also told them, you know, there is a good possibility that most of you will end up in Korea because that is where most of the needs are, and you have to have to be in shape to go up and down these mountains. And I said in the whole likelihood I will end up in Korea; if we end up in the same company, you are going to want to know something about me, as I would like to know something about you. And I recall one night, we were in training and one fellow was walking around and the other was looking up. I said, I am going to see how close I can get to them without them spotting me. And I got to them from about here to the wall; and of course it was slow walk and I was very careful, so I just raised up my arm when I was standing next to them and you talk about two surprised soldiers and I said to them: "You know, a chain is no stronger with a weak link, and if you do not stay alert, then not only your life will be taken, but also the one of your friends." Well one of those boys, when he finished basic training, was assigned to the signal section of the post so when we went on the firing range, he was supposed to stop up there and pick up the telephone; and here is this kid, he said "Captain Kotary, you remember that night up there?" He never forgot. So he learned from that experience.

ETM: You talked earlier about discipline and courtesy. Can conservatism be a philosophy of life?

WK: There is today a breakdown in our morals; look at executives of big corporations, look at one of them, he gave a one million dollar birthday party? Where is the morality in this? And where is the integrity? A lot of people in some of these corporations lost their retirement. It did not seem to bother these executives. This is a thing that really bothers me. I don't worry about money because I came from a very modest background. I was raised on a farm. That is why I stayed in scouting for so many years. I have been in scouting for about 40 years. I enjoy it because I am working with youth, and I am hoping that they will take some of the things that I try to stand for and try to teach them.

ETM: Talking now about the divisiveness you mentioned in this country, do you think there are ways to be reconciled as Americans through figures and examples like Lincoln or Franklin Roosevelt? What would you say about a figure like Roosevelt?

WK: He was a Democrat but he came into prominence at a good time, things were really tough. He created one of the greatest things, social security, to provide at least a base of some retirement income; and that is socialistic, but needed. There are people who will spend whatever money they have today, and that to me is a problem; they want immediate gratification. Why do you need a million dollar home? I would not want that mortgage. And today, you never know if you are going to have a job tomorrow. It used to be when I grew up, if you worked for a bank or for an insurance company, you did not make a lot of money but you had a job, and as long as you did your job you kept your nose clean; but you cannot say that today. And that is why I never had a credit card for a long time. My first credit card was for gas, but I pay it off at the end of the month, if I cannot afford it, I am not going to buy it. That goes back to the Depression days. I cannot go along people's philosophy today. I have a son and daughter. I can remember when my son came to me one time and he wanted money to buy a car. And I said I don't have that kind of money. I am better off now than I was in those days. But that is instant gratification. I did help him out later. The problem is also the politicians who to me are more interested in the benefits; and it is the system. The reason they are serving is because of the two things: They have a good income and they have good benefits, better than the average American.

ETM: Ross Perot repeated many times that he wanted to serve, to be a servant to his country.

WK: And he had the personality. That is the thing with Bush. I don't think he came across when he was making his case, about going to Iraq. I did not read any humility in him. Now Reagan was a master, he could win you over. He made a great impression, but not Bush. He is not that good a speaker in my opinion, and certainly his facial expression did not help him. That is my opinion of him. Clinton was an excellent speaker but I was disappointed in his character. Politics is tough; it is give and take but we are too contentious now. There are ideologies on one side and on the other side. And the Supreme Court is a good example. The selection is based on politics and personality rather than capability. And I think too often, it is me against you and you against me; somehow you have to be able to come together. That is what government should be about because there is not one party or group that has all the answers. You've got to try to somehow find a middle ground that both sides can live with. Colin Powell had a good record behind him and I thought that he was a leveler in the Bush administration. But I will say this, these people who wanted to give it more time in Iraq, my answer was, look at Lord Chamberlain, you don't change those people, they have their agenda and they are not going to change, and time is not going to make it any better, so I thought that more time was not the answer. I would have liked to have seen a coalition just like with his father; that would have made it easier. But I did not like the way Bush was trying to sell the idea.

We are now more by ourselves, it is fine; however, it is expensive. And we are going to have to pay for it. And it is going to be for a long time if ever.

ETM: Who could be a good leader for this country two or three years from now?

WK: There was an African American. He played football and he was from Oklahoma. He spoke at the Republican convention. He was a representative for a few years and then chose not to run for reelection. His name is J.C. Watts. He was one I was hoping to see move up. I was disappointed when he stopped but I can understand because if you are in government, that is seven days a week. It is just like being on a farm. Right now, I don't know anyone. I cannot come up with anyone on any side. I was not impressed with Kerry. He may be very capable but he did not make the visual impression of a Reagan, and that is part of being a president. A lot in politics is about image. That is what I tell the scouts; when I ask them to nominate someone who they think is a good leader, they will come up with a name. Often time, it is a teacher. Then I ask why do you feel this person is a good leader? They don't think about that because they don't know what it is that makes a good leader. What is the definition of leadership? What are the characteristics of a leader? I told them one of the characteristics of a good leader is bearing. And I said if you don't make a good impression coming in, you are fighting from behind. But if you make a good impression, you are in the plus side right from the start. So bearing is an important factor.

ETM: What question would you have for me who grew up in France, you having gone to Northern France sixty years ago to fight to liberate the country and the continent?

WK: One thing I always remember, De Gaulle. I think I know the reason why the ambassador who was sent in France by Kennedy was James Gavin. He was in Washington at the Pentagon; he was a Lieutenant General and in charge of research. He resigned because of a difference of opinion. But I think in my mind Kennedy selected him because Gavin was a very successful leader and De Gaulle would respect that. But regarding your question, I heard at times about Americans not enthused by the French and their experience in Paris. And of course if and when they went to smaller cities and villages, they probably have a very different experience. It is like the people going to New York City instead of the place where I grew up. I did not think about this when I was over in France during the war. Our division went to Berlin at the end of the war in occupation. And I can remember going to Berlin and that was beat up. And I remember there were streets, we had to take detours to get around. And I can remember women out there, taking these bricks and chip them off so that they could be used again. And I remember the countryside of France, and of course France has a lot of old communities; and I think that we benefited from the Europeans coming over here and settling. We also had a lot of Poles in Pennsylvania who came to work as coal workers and ended up farming the land. My knowledge of Europe is limited to my war experience. But the making of Europe through cooperation is something that was needed. If you don't, history may repeat itself. You need to have counterbalance. And if you look back at the different friendships over the years, look at now the United States and China and Russia; some people say, well, we stopped the spread of communism going into Korea, which is probably true, but war is not the answer over all. Sometimes it is justified but it could be a better world if we could live together.

Chapter 4
The Legacy of D-Day:
A Global Perspective

The veterans interviewed in this chapter ponder the legacy of D-Day and the fate of French-American relations in the post-September 11 world through their international background and experience. The conversations took place in their homes or workplaces in Chicago, Marble Falls, Texas, New York and Fréville, Normandy. Walter Reed recounts his experience growing up in Germany as a Jew. Sent away by his parents, he flees from the Nazis into Belgium in 1939, finds refuge in Southern France, and escapes to the United States where he enrolls in the US Army in 1942. After landing in Normandy, he returns to his native country in 1945 to find that his family has been murdered. His reflection on French-American relations is based on this long journey, a life spent in America since the end of WWII, and the numerous trips he has made to Europe over the years. In addition, Peter F. Dembowski narrates his partaking in the Warsaw uprising against the Nazis, his capture and deportation to a concentration camp. His reflection on France and the United States is based on his experience as a scholar teaching French literature at the University of Chicago.

As he considers the legacy of D-Day and the American sacrifice of all wars, Harry Deal gives an account of his involvement in the Pacific with the American Navy and considers the necessity of dialogue among cultures today. Henry Stein describes the life of a Jewish-American family during the war that had migrated from Eastern Europe to Chicago. He also details his work at Percy Jones General Hospital as a counselor and history collector taking care of soldiers that had been gravely wounded. George Zenie recalls his landing at Omaha Beach on D-Day and the fierce battle that followed. As an American born of Lebanese ancestry, he discusses with his wife, partly of Iraqi ancestry, the repercussions of the current American involvement in Iraq and their views of France. Jean-Baptiste Feuillye speaks about his encounter with American soldiers in Normandy and his joining with them, at age 13, up to the German border. Working in the service of military graves right after the war, he tells the story of the thousands of American people who have returned to Normandy to mourn the loss of loved ones and revisit up to this day the sites of the landing intertwined with their family and own history. Oldest among the veterans, George Daniels, born in 1917, remembers his flying missions over Normandy, Northern France and Germany, and his witnessing of Lindbergh's take off for Paris in 1927. He uses this event to illustrate the challenges that France and the United States face today, and of the possibility to reach beyond, together, and create a better world.

Walter Reed (Werner Rindsberg)

WR: It is in Wannsee, a town south-west of Berlin, where all of the really bad guys from the top of the Nazi echelon had a special meeting in the so-called "Wannsee Conference." Not Hitler, but his Henchmen, Himmler and Eichmann among others, made the final decision to murder all the Jews of Europe and then began to set up the murder camps. This was in January 1942 and within weeks they began the deportations. They undoubtedly were extremely eager to get on with the killing. But before then, while there were many Jewish people who were killed for one reason or another, individually or in concentration camps, the policy of the Nazis was to get rid of the Jews by emigration. They did everything they could to encourage the Jews to leave Germany. Of course, things changed when they went to war with Poland and began to murder Jews through the so called *Eihsatztruppen*, which were specialized killing squads that did not work in camps. They literally lined up people in front of ditches, and murdered them with machine guns, sometimes thousands. This was not the same thing as the gas chambers.

ETM: These were Polish Jews?

WR: Yes.

ETM: Could you talk to us about your experience growing up?

WR: Well, I grew up in a very small farm village that at the time had about a population of 1000. And, as I remembered from then, and based on the research I have done since, there were about 26 Jewish families in that village. So we were about 7 to 8 percent of the population, something like that. We had our own grade school and elementary school. All the classes were in the same room, and when we graduated from there we went to the so-called *Realschule* which is the middle school in a nearby town. As a boy of seven to nine years old, I was aware that the Nazis were campaigning and vilifying the communists, the Jews, and other people they did not like, and that they were casting blame about World War I, holding Jewish people and certain financiers responsible for causing the Germans to lose the war. The fact is that many Jewish people were soldiers in WWI; I have two uncles who served in the German army. The allegations that the Jewish people caused the defeat of WWI were totally ridiculous, but at that time, many people believed them. The reason is that the economy was very bad; there was the Depression like in the United States which brought on the desire by Germans to follow anybody who would promise them a better life. Of course, Hitler in those days (I remember this like yesterday), was preaching that the Germans needed living space in other countries. For us, as residents, as families, life got very very unpleasant, because pretty soon, many of the German people followed the Nazis; not just a few, not just Hitler's two hundred close associates, but the whole population of Germany, men and women, and children. For instance, young boys that I knew in our small village joined the Hitler youth and wore uniforms, and the girls joined the *Bund Deutsher Wädchen*, the Girls Society of the Nazis. Life got to be pretty scary because we Jews were constantly called names in the streets by the other kids, and they would throw stones at us. If they found you alone, they would beat you, particularly if there were several of them and only one of you. There were people who opposed what was happening but they were in danger if they did it publicly. If they were known to have opposed the Nazis, they would be persecuted. It was quite well known that you did not speak out. It was truly a dictatorship in the worst sense of the word. And so that's how in 1934–35, we already knew that things were bad.

ETM: Was your family a practicing Jewish family?

WR: My family and most of the people in the village were orthodox Jews. That is to say, the majority of the Jewish people population in that village regularly went to Synagogue services, and practiced all religious laws and so forth. It is a little bit like being constantly persecuted. You knew that you were disliked and that things were not good for you. And it culminated in the so called *Kristallnacht*, which by the way is a word that was coined many years later. On the morning of November 9, there was a knock on the door of our house that shook the building, and men in brown shirts, who were the SA (*Sturmabteilung*) from the local area, were outside with a truck, and they shouted "*rauss, raus!*"

ETM: What time was that?

WR: Oh, about 7 o'clock in the morning. They arrested my father and me, I was 14 years old, and took us to the jail in the next town where I was going to school. That was the county seat of that area. The same morning, they picked up all the Jewish men and boys in all the villages in that area and burned down the synagogue while people came out to watch. I was in jail as a juvenile a few blocks away, and did not know that the synagogue was burning. I was in jail for three days and three nights, and then I was released because the local Nazis realized that they had made a mistake by arresting young boys. But the men were all sent to the nearby city of Würzburg, and from there to Dachau, the concentration camp. And other men from that area, many others, stayed in the concentration camp for about a month to six weeks. I am fond of saying I would not be with you today if the Germans had not brought my father to Dachau. Because when he came home, he had been ill, and he realized that we were in danger. I think it is because of *Kristallnacht* that my parents decided to send me away to safety. And as I say, if it had not been for that, they might have just held on and hoped for things to change, which they were doing, and I would have perished along with my family.

ETM: Did you think or did your parents talk about whether other nations would react to do something about it?

WR: The environment where I grew up was very rural, a very small town, a little bit like the small town where you grew up. I don't know about your town but most of the Jewish people who lived in my village never graduated from high school. So their knowledge of foreign countries was not bad, but it was not sophisticated and as a result they were very reluctant to consider migrating to a place where they did not speak the language, and where they had no skills or knowledge of anyone. The idea of emigrating was one that many people hesitated to accomplish. Fortunately, many hundreds of thousands did emigrate in time, but there were many others who hoped that things would improve and they could never foresee that they would all be killed. In fact, even the day the Jews were deported, they and the local people in their village, in many other places in Germany, believed the false story that they would be sent to labor camps in the East. That is what all the Germans were told. And until after the concentration camps, the killing camps, were discovered, after the defeat of the Germans, many Germans had no idea that it had been going on. Some knew, but most did not. I had the experience, fast forward, going back to my village as an American soldier in 1945 after the Armistice, of asking the people: "Where is my family, what happened to them?" and they said "Oh, a couple of years ago, they were sent to the East into a labor camp." I remember them telling me that, and I don't think they were lying. Many of the people that I knew had very little knowledge about the other countries in the world.

ETM: Do you have harsh feeling toward German people today?

WR: I have always had the following attitude about it: The people who perpetrated all these things were not just two or three hundreds close friends of Hitler. There were many people in Germany, many ordinary people, who literally became criminals, killers and robbers of Jewish belongings; those people, I think, all deserved at the time to be punished by jail sentences and by fines. The people who were sons and daughters and who were not involved in invading Poland, France, Belgium and Russia among others, I think just like our sons and anybody else who is living today; they had nothing to do with it and my feeling toward them has always been like anybody else. They are not bad people because their parents were Nazis. On the other hand, I have very strong feelings about what the German people did to other countries. I am not one who thinks, as many do, that the Jews were the special target and that Jews should never set foot in Germany because of this. I have a broader view. I think the Nazis did far worse than murdering six millions Jews. They also are responsible for destroying the lives and the livelihood of Poland and Russia, to name just a couple of countries that are in the East, and invading Belgium and Holland which were neutral, and France which was not. They had no right and business invading France and I was personally a witness, having lived in southern France for a year and some months in 1940–41, to the total theft of anything that was transportable from southern France to Germany. So I really feel that the then living German people were criminals as the world had not very often seen. And therefore, I feel that they were really guilty. On the other hand, I feel very strongly about having friendly relations today with people all over Germany. I have had the privilege to speak to German students in classes in the last few years and it is very interesting because when I speak to them, I have to really think about how I am going to present my feelings. My experiences as a young person in Germany were what they were. I only speak to them from the perspective that it is not something they or their parents have done, but what their grandparents did, or some of their grandparents.

ETM: How was it like to then move to Holland and Belgium away from your family in the context of what was happening in Germany?

WR: You have to remember that I was fifteen years old. I was a young person who grew up in a small village, a very nice place. I go back sometimes but I would no want to live there. I moved to the large metropolis of Brussels and I enjoyed it immensely. My enjoyment was in part, I think, escaping the persecution. But it also was, as we say in this country, like Disneyland, with the street cars and automobiles all over, the museums and parks. My main emotion was really, in addition to feeling liberated and enjoying the city life, an appreciation for the Belgian Jewish committee that took care of us and that rescued us, and sent us to school. But I got there in June 1939 and school did not start until September. And so until September 1939 when the Germans invaded Poland, I was free to roam the city of Brussels even though, because of our age, we were regimented. But still, we were taken on excursions and I was still able to write to my parents; in those days you did not use the telephone unless it was an emergency.

ETM: What was your experience when the German army invaded Belgium?

WR: It is always interesting to talk about things that happened earlier in your life because sixty-five years later, you forget; it is hard to tell exactly what it was like. But I do remember this: we were young teenagers so we were not that knowledgeable in world affairs. We knew Poland had been invaded, from the news, Hitler's speeches and what the Germans were saying, so we were not surprised that they would attack somebody else after invading Austria, Czechoslovakia, then Poland. We were very much aware of that. The Belgians were neutral so they all thought that they were safe, like Switzerland. The other thing was that the Belgians had built fortifications. There was Fort Emmanuel in Liège, and there was continual coverage in the press about how unassailable it was. The Germans conquered it in three hours by coming on top of it, using paratroopers and killing people inside. Nonetheless, there was an attitude in Belgium that I remember in 1939, early 1940, of "we are well prepared." The Belgians felt that the Germans would not violate their neutrality but they were ready to fight and felt secure in the French as their allies. There was a song at that time the people were singing in both France and Belgium, and it went: "Nous allons pendre notre linge sur la ligne Siegfried." It meant: "We are going to hang our laundry on the Siegfried line (which was the German *Maginot* Line)," and it was sung with great enthusiasm. Of course, it was false enthusiasm.

ETM: As we know, the French-Belgian border collapsed in a matter of days.

WR: Right. So it was in this atmosphere that I experienced May 10, 1940 and the thing I like to tell school students when I speak to them is that nowadays when an airplane flies over we barely notice it; but in those days, there was no air commercial travel, and then on May 10 there were suddenly many airplanes in the sky and the radio announced the Germans were invading. At that point, panic set in; all of the fifty or so boys knew what it was like to be in Germany. We all had had the common experience of not wanting to be there. So the Director of our home, whose widow's picture I showed you, assembled all the boys and the girls in a different part of Brussels and ninety-two of us on May 12 or 13 went to the train station. We boarded a freight train and were sent from Brussels to Arras in Northern France and then south. We covered a lot of France in five days with many stops on the way and eventually ended up south of Toulouse.

ETM: What was the name of the organization that took care of you from the time you arrived to Brussels to the time you arrived in south of France?

WR: The organization in Belgium that managed to bring Jewish children from Germany and Austria to Belgium was a Committee of Jewish Women, *Comité d'assistance aux enfants réfugiés juifs*, and they were in turn created by a man by the name of Max Gottschalk, a well known Belgian attorney who started to rescue Jewish refugees from Germany right after 1933. After *Kristall-nacht*, he encouraged these women to form a committee, and he and the committee in conjunction with the Belgian government, were able to obtain immigration permits for about five to six hundred children from Germany and Austria. Just by chance, by luck, I was one of them.

ETM: How much time did you spend in the south of France?

WR: More than a year but I am still not sure precisely. I am going to the *préfecture* in Toulouse in September. We took the train to Villefranche de Lauragais where we were all unloaded (just the ninety-two children and their care-takers, not the other passengers), and went up the hill about six kilometers, to the village of Seyre. I still don't know why or how it was selected. We ended up there in a barn; there was no living facility in the barn, it was strictly a storage facility, and there was no place to cook or wash; there were no toilets, nothing, just space. We were literally like hundreds of thousands of refugees from the north.

ETM: When you were there, what were your fears, your hopes?

WR: Our first emotion when we got there really was relief at having es-caped one more time; we were not too worried at first about the primitive conditions that we lived in. We had also no idea that the food would be rationed very soon, which it was. Afterwards, it was almost impossible to get enough to eat unless you were in the countryside, which was lucky for us because the farmers still had some food. I remember in the summer of 1940, we went on Saturday to the *marché* to buy provisions; imagine, we had one hundred people, and while many were children, they still needed to eat! The first emotion was really one of being saved. The second thing is that there were virtually no French people in that village, just a few. They were even more primitive farmers than the people in my home village. The French people who were there were people who spoke this *patois* of the *midi* (the dialect of the South). That to this day is what they speak and it is totally different from real French. We did not have any interaction except with the owner of the château nearby, Mr. de Capèle. He died about seven years ago but I saw him before he died. He was 90 years old and I am in very close rapport with his descendents. Mr. de Capèle was not exactly very happy either, because France had lost the war and things were going very, very badly.

ETM: What was the nature of the conversation when you met him again?

WR: Before I answer, you should know that I came to America in 1941 and lived in New York and Brooklyn, New York. I went to school there, night school, and worked during the day. After two years, I was drafted into the US Army; this was 1943. The experience of being in a training camp for the first time opened my eyes. I found that there were good and bad Americans, and that prejudice and racism were widespread in America. I became very much aware as a Jew of who I was and what I was. I would be subjected to discrimination in this country, just like the one I had escaped; it was not quite the same, they did not kill me and allowed me to make a living and all that. Soon after I was drafted in the Army, I was offered citizenship and when I became a citizen, I changed my name. After I left the army in 1946, I decided that I would no longer be an immigrant or Jewish, I would be an American. I wanted the same opportunity as everybody else. So, I changed my name, and on the form of employment applications I wrote that I was born in Brooklyn, New York, and that I had lived all my life there. I started a new life and it was not because I had any trauma or any psychological problems like many survival Jews, I just wanted equal opportunity and not be disadvantaged anymore.

ETM: So, your name before was . . .

WR: Werner Rindsberg.

ETM: And then it became . . .

WR: Walter Reed. I chose that name. I wanted to keep the initials of my original name W. R., and as my new middle name, I chose my original first name. My name today is Walter Werner Reed. But I don't use my middle name, I just write "W".

ETM: If you had not encountered these prejudices, would you have changed your name?

WR: Probably not. And many did not. Henry Kissinger did not change his name and he kept his accent; he was different. Many people who immigrated to the United States did change their names for one reason or another. They wanted them Americanized. It is not unusual but in my case it was very deliberate, and as I said I kept the initials with my first name as middle name because that is the name my parents gave me and I did not want to throw that away. From that time on, I no longer had any contact with anyone from the past. I created a new identity, so to speak, with new official documents and so forth; it was probably punishable.

ETM: You did this after the war in 1946.

WR: Then I went to the University of Missouri in 1946 and all my classmates thought that I was born in Brooklyn. Some of them never found this out until about eight years ago because I was literally, as one would say, in the closet. I was in the closet until eight years ago, and this leads me back to the question you asked about my experience in France when I met Mr. de Capèle again in 1997. Well, until that moment or just briefly before that, no one except

Jeanne and our children and her family knew anything about my background. Everybody else thought that I was born in Brooklyn. German people would ask me: "Where did you learn how to speak German so well?" I would say: "In school in America." And the French people would say: "Ah, our Frenchman!" and they called me Gauthier, the French translation of Walter; "Gauthier, où est-ce que vous avez appris le français? [Where did you learn French?]," and I would say: "à l'école [in school]."

ETM: So, when you met Mr. de Capèle, you told him the story, you had to tell him the story.

WR: By that time, I was beginning to be out of the closet and I should tell you the circumstances that led me to meet him. When our children were old enough to be aware of things, we decided immediately to tell them. I should tell you that when I first met Jeanne in 1968 she did not know anything about my past and we were dating for a year before I proposed to her. And when I proposed to her, I said before you answer, I have to tell you something. I am not who you think I am. And she said, well it does not matter; that is how complete my camouflage was. It happened that a friend of ours in 1997 had a daughter who was marrying a young Frenchman in Lyon. They invited us to the wedding, so in July of 1997, we went to Lyon and Grenoble. We went to the wedding, and I proposed to my family: why don't we go to look at the place where I was during the war? Jeanne and our sons knew about my earlier life but had never "seen" it. So we drove from Lyon down to Toulouse, and went to look at the barn from the outside; we took some pictures and as we were doing that, a man crossed the street, sweeping in front of his house. He said: "Bonjour Monsieur!" and I said: "Bonjour Monsieur!" and he asked me what I was doing and I explained to him what we were doing, who we were, and that I was once in the barn. He was a little boy living in the same house across from the barn where we were, and as a result, over the years, a number of the survivors of those days had come back to visit, like I did in 1997. He showed us some snapshots of others who had come back. That is the first connection I had. As we spoke, he said: "You know Monsieur de Capèle is still living in the château," that he was now 90 years old; and Jeanne said: "Oh, you've got to go see him!" and I said: "No, I don't want to bother him, no, no." And the local farmer said: "Oh, you should go, he would be glad to see you."

I really was not going to do it but after some urging we went to the entrance of the château, rang the bell, and a woman came who turned out to be his daughter. She was not living there but was visiting and I explained who I was and what I was doing there. She said that her father was ill and that this was his nap time, but that she would go in and see if he would like to see me. But she said: "Promise me you won't stay more than five minutes." Monsieur de Capèle came down from upstairs and we were there for an hour. He had been visited by other people and it turned out that, a few years before, a German television crew had come to do a TV production about the children of Seyre. Then another daughter came with a list of all the children. This is the first time I saw that list, or heard anything, and he said others had come back. So that's the first time I was really re-connected. So my visit with him was quite an emotional thing for me and for my family, but also in a way for him because he had many memories. He of course was the guy who let one hundred children live on his farm. What person would take one hundred wild children into his farm in such a bad time? So there was this connection, and from there we went to the château de la Hille where there was even a bigger surprise. It is now a holiday accommodation. The woman who owns it, Madame Dedieu, came out, and she put a book in front of me entitled *La filière* [The Network]. The book had been written by one of the Swiss camp counselors who were there during the war and who in the 1990s wrote this book about the experience of the children of la Hille. Here for the first time, I was reading the book in French and getting an idea of what had happened to all the survivors during my teenage years. I had very vivid memories of them but I had not been in touch with anyone or tried to be. I left my business card with the owner of the château. Before we came back to the United States, there were phone calls. The other survivors had been looking for me but could not find me because I had changed my name, and since that time, I am reconnected with them. They were people I knew since 1939. Jeanne and I organized a reunion in Chicago at our house in 1998, then in Toulouse, and at the château de la Hille, and 30 of the survivors came from all over the world with their relatives. By that time, I became the coordinator of the whole group worldwide and this is why I am now writing a book about it. So, my reconnection with Monsieur de Capèle which was your question came as a result of visiting there; and now everybody knows my background, and stories have been written about me. I speak to schools here regularly and a week from tomorrow night, I will be interviewed by a Chicago radio station about this whole story.

ETM: What has it meant for you to find your identity again?

WR: It is like this: I have had a very rich and very fortunate life, and I am very active. I have had many interesting experiences in my business life and private life and my community activities, so it is very fulfilling. I am now financially secure so I can afford to travel and go places. If not, I could not travel and speak to these German classes, or go back to France to the reunions. In my professional life as a public relations person, I have had the opportunity to travel abroad and I have a sense of other countries that nowadays many people have. As a result, I find it very easy to carry out the kind of activities related to my past. So it gives me great pleasure. I am 81 years old; if, at this age, I can do something meaningful, it is very important. I don't have to go out to play golf to have fun.

ETM: At a personal level, was this a necessary step to take in order to complete your life?

WR: One might think that now I am relieved but I always have been matter of fact about putting the past away, not that I was psychologically hurting at all. I early on got over the death of my family. I made up my mind that Hitler had done enough damage to my life. I was not going to give him the pleasure of being harmed for the rest of my life. My real enjoyment is sharing this since I have been fortunate enough to live this long. I am an eyewitness for young people and school groups, and I share something they cannot get in movies. I have become aware that this is really the most important. I see myself as a vehicle if you like. I happen to be still living and I can talk about what it was like when the Nazis began the war. I have no thought of getting even with the Nazis or anything like that. I have a tremendous amount of gratitude for the Belgian people and the Belgian women who did things not just for me but for hundreds of children. I have a great affinity with the people of France who, when I was there in 1940–41, suffered immensely because of the oppression by the Germans both in the occupied and non-occupied zones. The life of the French people in those days was horrible. When we landed in Normandy in June 1944 (I was not in the first wave, I came about a week later), my feeling about the French people was that they had really suffered and been subjugated by the same people as I had been. The other thing is, because I speak French, I have had the opportunity to meet French people in all kinds of ways, not like many Americans who don't speak the language and who judge French people by the waiter they meet at the restaurant. I had the privilege to travel all over France and I love it. My ambition until about 25 years ago was to retire on a French farm. It really was. This was where I found refuge and saw France under German occupation. When we landed in Normandy, in the hedge rows and surrounding fields of Normandy, I remember the morning when the allies bombed St. Lô. I was about fifteen kilometers north of St. Lô in July 1944. There were probably 1,000 airplanes in the sky, and right after they passed us, the earth began to tremble. They were bombing St. Lô. And my feelings about France were deep. The Germans were occupying the country and they were fighting not to lose; we were fighting to take it away from them. So, I have been a Francophile all my life. It actually goes back to French classes in middle school in my rural area in Germany. I was the best student in the class and I remember as if it were yesterday the teacher singling me out because I was very good in French grammar. I was into French language early on.

ETM: What do you have to say about America?

WR: People asked me recently, so what is your feeling? Where is your home? Where are you from? I am from America. I was born in a village or town in Germany, but I am always American and I have a great affection for the ideal America, not the one we are living in today. Jeanne and I don't hesitate to tell people abroad, just to make sure that they understand that not all Americans are in favor of what is going on. That is not the America I am talking about, but basically America and the American people are what I identify with and that's who I am. And if somebody asks me, what is your nationality? What is your country? This is my country; after all, I was an American soldier. I have lived here the majority of my life, sixty-four years of my life, so this is my country. And my feelings about America are based on other things that are too long to talk about. That is, I have had the opportunity in my business life to travel all over this country, working with and meeting people in many places. I really feel at home in rural Nebraska (most people in this country have not been there), and in Iowa and so many places with which I am really familiar. So I am very much like many immigrants. I have affinities with people around the world. Jeanne and I try to understand what is going on with people in other parts of the world; that is why we travel. In the last few years, we learned about people from Peru,

Costa Rica, Australia, Africa, etc. not just in Europe. So that is another aspect about how I feel about myself. I am very active in Rotary and one thing that attracts me in Rotary is worldwide organizations. A week ago in this room, our dinner guests were from Marseille, Congo, Germany and the Philippines who were Rotary officials who were here for meeting. So we do that sort of thing and our lives are greatly enriched by the kind of things that this produces, including sitting next to a French person in an airplane.

ETM: I am very grateful to have met you and for this conversation. I have one last question. What do we need to learn, our generation, what do we need to learn from the past?

WR: I think we need to learn to be humble and to understand that people all over the world, no matter what their nationality might be, are pretty similar. We ought to respect and like each other and accomplish things together that are positive, and I think we need to be open minded about the needs and the aspirations of other people and try to assist them as much as we can. This is very difficult because human nature through the ages, if you study history, has engaged not only in individual battles, but also in collective exterminations and dominations. We could spend hours reciting what has happened. So, I would say we need to be tolerant of and to sustain each other because one of the great things about human beings is we are indeed more capable than the animals, but we too often continue to malign each other, to distrust each other and to harm each other. So what you are doing by examining attitudes and feelings is in the right direction.

ETM: Thank you very much for your time and for sharing your experience with us.

Peter F. Dembowski

PFD: I was born in Warsaw, Poland, in December 1925. I have been an American citizen for many years. I became a member of a clandestine organization during WWII. I remember the date exactly because I pledged allegiance to the group the day the Americans landed in North Africa in October 1942. I was waiting for this moment, to be 17 which was the minimum age, with much impatience. Many young men cheated about their age. I continued my studies but all was done illegally because the Germans were opposed to our education beyond the sixth grade. We met at least three times a week. We were ferociously patriotic and generally we knew that our comrades were in different types of underground organizations, but we did not discuss the matter. I completed my training in the Polish underground army in 1943. I knew by heart the infantry code. The situation in Warsaw had become more and more difficult. The German terror became more and more "efficacious" so to speak, and therefore we became more and more patriotic. During this time, patriotism blended with Catholicism in Poland. What I remember the most is that on Good Friday 1944, I was arrested with about sixty people. We were caught transporting weapons from one depot to another. On April 6, 1944, people were forced to leave their weapons for the night where I lived. That very morning, there was an enormous

German police/army action in the area. When I realized that the Germans were coming in, I took the weapons with me and hid them in the basement of the building at the last moment. But a German solider saw me coming out of the basement around 6am and he told me in German that I had to open all the locks. I told him that they were open. For two hours, we waited and then I heard a loud shout in German: "English weapons! English weapons!" They had been found. What saved me is that I was older than 17 but I looked as if I were 13. I looked like a child. Another detail which I remember is that the German soldier who was of a certain age from the *Wehrmacht* who had seen me that morning kept looking at me closely without saying a word. If he had just mentioned at that moment to the Gestapo that he had seen me, I would not have the pleasure of having this interview today. In any case, I was put in jail with sixty prisoners; there were four people from our floor and they were with us. Unfortunately, some people did not have any documents, and Jewish people were living with us as well. They were talking among themselves and they knew that they were going to die the same day. The prison was located in the ancient ghetto since the ghetto had already been destroyed for almost a year.

ETM: What was your state of mind during these years?

PFD: I began school before the war and it became a clandestine organization. Everybody knew that we were all involved in the underground; we were all inhabited with the notion that the less you know the better it is. We were young, enthusiastic, patriotic and a little old for our age. I recall a striking detail about my education. Our German professor was a German woman who was hiding with the Polish population. It is an incredible story but it is true. She spoke Polish poorly and had fake documents because she had married a Polish officer before the war, and from a Nazi standpoint, she should have divorced him because, according to Nazi laws, it was abnormal that a German marry a "subhuman." She spoke about it but only in German and we liked her because she was a beautiful woman of age 30 and we were 17 and 18, and not good looking, so we liked her a great deal. Once we heard someone being arrested in the street and she made a long speech in the class saying that it was not the real Germany that we had in our country. She was a good woman.

ETM: What was her name?

PFD: I forgot. I only remember her false name that she could not pronounce well. Each Polish citizen was supposed to carry an ID card and if the card had no nationality, it meant it was Polish and if it was Jewish, it was indicated. My studies were interrupted for four weeks when I went to jail and it was the greatest joy of my life when I was released on May 3, 1944, on the day of the feast of the Polish Constitution dating from the 18th Century. People were expecting executions and I thought I would be executed but I was led to the Gestapo and released from the SS. I later learned that someone had paid for my release. I had told them that I had not seen anything and I had sworn on the Virgin of Czestochowa that I was telling the truth; they never asked specific questions even though the inside of my shirt was full of grease from carrying the weapons I had hidden. When I returned they all welcomed me back because they thought I was gone. During that time if you were arrested by the Gestapo, the minimum was Aucshwitz, not to be killed but put into forced labor. In 2003, I learned that someone in the underground organization paid the German Criminal Police, which was corrupted, for my release. There were mediocre public workers and through this process got money under the table. It was possible to pay for someone like me who had just been interrogated and was suspect. If they had really been suspicious about me, it would not have happened.

ETM: How were the conditions for prisoners in Warsaw?

PFD: It was terrible. The first two weeks, we were 40 in a small cell with all kinds of animals and the minimum of food. But the Polish underground had put pressure on the Germans to take care of the prisoners, or else. It was also terrible because of the fear of being interrogated. I was set free on May 3. Later, I received my high school diploma. And the first question of the German lady professor during the exam was: "Sprechen sie Dutch?" and I replied that yes "I speak the cursed jargon." She was a good German and a good Polish woman. She was faithful to her new nationality, in these terrible circumstances. I passed the Latin and French exam as well. I was a good student. Our organization was part of the *Armia Krajowa*, the AK (Army of the Homeland), as opposed to the Army abroad. Insurrection was the only aim to free the shame of occupation which was so depressing. The Nazis behaved like beasts; they would kick you in the street at the beginning. But they gradually began to behave after the German army was losing ground in Russia and the Russian army was calling in Soviet radio waves for people to kill the Nazis. We also heard and translated the Free French radio broadcasting from Moscow: "Death to the German occupiers! To arms!" and we began the uprising and achieved success. We had taken three-fourths of Warsaw by August 1, 1944 at 5pm. We chose the afternoon to take them by surprise because an insurrection usually begins early in the morning. I was in the south area of Warsaw named Mokotów. The insurrection lasted two months. I was with two regiments of 3,000 men of which we lost a third; a lot happened and there are many books on the subject. We were certain until the middle of September that the Russians would come to our rescue. In the end, we did not have enough ammunition and received orders to go underground through tunnels toward the center of the city. The Germans used explosives to destroy the tunnels in which the water began to rise. We were given a choice the day after around noon: to get out or to drown; several of our friends died. I came out and I saw German soldiers around and they killed some among us at random. Suddenly, we remained on the ground and absolutely extenuated, due to the lack of oxygen in the sewer. I thought I was going to die from it; that we would die by losing consciousness; and that they would kill us anyway. My elder brother who was with me said we must say something before we die; shout: "Long live the Republic! Long live Poland!" something like that. Two hours later, on September 29, a German officer said that we were prisoners of war and they led us ten miles outside of Warsaw in a camp with Russians prisoners. Three days later we took a train ride for two days and two nights to *Stalag* XB, near the Holland border. I was given the number 221857.

ETM: What was your experience during and after the insurrection?

PFD: At the end of our struggle, we decided to go downtown where the underground was better equipped. Also, we did not want to die alone. We usually fought the Germans at the beginning of night, unless they were attacking us. We were hiding because the Germans were using their Air Force to bomb us, but they were afraid to bomb their positions also. There were about 40,000 taking part of the insurrection in Warsaw. The average age was less than 20. When I look back at our clandestine activities, we were more protected than the population because we were well informed. There were a lot of reprisals and the civil population did suffer a lot. It was terrible. The insurrection was an enormous tragedy and it gave great rebirth to the Polish resistance. For example, later in 1986–1987 when Solidarity, the Polish Union Movement, began its rebellion against the Communist Regime, it used the rhetoric of AK because it was part of the heritage of the Polish land. There were Communist troops with us who participated in the insurrection and they did not know that the Soviet army would later betray us. At the camp there were Polish. I also made friends among French soldiers and met American soldiers for the first time. They had been captured at the Battle of the Bulge. One of them from Detroit spoke Polish. I asked who had taught him Polish and he said his grandma. We were liberated by the Welsh guard of the British army in April 1944. The bad guys disappeared. A striking detail is that we were well dressed with US Army uniforms of World War I which had been sent by the International Red Cross. The day after, the tanks broke the fence of the camps. The English tried to feed us and a week before the end of the war we met with elements of the Polish army, the 1st Division. They were happy to see us because there was a need for soldiers. I enrolled in the 2nd Polish Corps. I served in Italy from May 1945 until November 1946. I went to military school and we were invited by the Canadian government to come to Canada and work on the farms. I declared myself of farming origin and in November 1946, I found myself in the port of Halifax. During that time, the Knights of Colombus welcomed us. I was not a farmer by origin and I could not answer questions related to farming but I worked in Alberta in a farm for a person named Jespersen, who in spite of the name, was of German origin. He and his wife did not want to talk about Germany and the old land. He wanted me to learn English which I had learned a little on my own. He prayed in the morning and listened to the English radio and I started a normal life again. I spent twelve months there; I worked for a meat and wood company and I began to study at night. In 1948, I was accepted at the University of British Colombia and my life began to be "normal" again. From thereon, I obtained a full tuition fellowship from the French government. I was chosen in spite of my foreign origins and I began to study seriously. I was living in Paris in the City University Canadian House on Boulevard Jourdan. I began to study and I obtained a certificate for teaching French and then I began a doctorate. I wrote a thesis on Russian philology; the influence of the liturgy on the Russian language.

ETM: What should we remember from your experience?

PFD: It was gratifying to live in France. I had studied French early in life. We had relatives in France through marriage and meeting French soldiers at the

Stalag was very important to me. America represented for us the Red Cross and generosity, because they saved the health of a lot of people. Every four weeks, we would also receive a packet that came from Switzerland and that also counted. In general, France, the US and England represented the outside world not controlled by Russia. It is only later during my studies that I met the Communists. During the time I was in France, there were two types of French people in the late 1940s: the Communists and the Catholics. Naturally, there were other people but I never met them. The communists were impossible. During my trip in 1953, I had the satisfaction to learn that Stalin had died. Another Polish boy from Paris and I went out and saw 35,000 French people gathered in a large convention hall. They were crying and we understood that we should not say a word. They were in mourning. I understand now that for many French people, Stalin represented the end of the war, the father of the Russian people whose army had destroyed the German army. In any case, the Americans, the British and the French represent for me the real world, outside from Eastern Europe. I participated and witnessed French politics at the time; for example, when we repeated with Maurice Schumann who said that the communists were not "on the left but in the East." That was true. Unfortunately, based on my experience in France, they considered too easily the anti-communists as fascists.

ETM: What are, in your views, the most important challenges today in the area of International relations, after having experienced Nazism?

PFD: We must live according to life, not ideology. The crimes committed by the Nazis were fatal and they were based on a pre-established ideology. Also, the world should not be built on abstractions. I think when I look at my life that the current world recognizes the necessity to proceed through practical agreements. I have seen in my life a move toward a great "de-politicization" and idealization of life. We should discuss in a united Europe. I was touched by the fact that Europe now exists in Central and Eastern Europe. I think that if Europe had been created in 1913 there would not have been the First World War; and the Second World War is a postscript to the first one. Because of the existence of Europe, one cannot envision this old dream to take Warsaw once again or allow territorial expansion. I feel strongly American in spite of my personal experiences that are not truly American; but these experiences led me to discover this world.

ETM: What does it mean to you to be American?

PFD: It means that I have a certain loyalty for this country and that I do not see a conflict between my country of origin and America. If there was a conflict between the two nations, I would stay American.

There is also in the minds of Americans a certain "no nonsense" on the one hand, and a lack of "preconceived" logic on the other; but also a sense of morality. For example, with respect to Iraq and to ancient ideologues and tyrants, the Fascist-Communist Saddam Hussein presented himself on a white horse as the "father" of Society, and pretended to be a descendent of Saladin, the chief of Arabs at the time of the Crusades. He (Hussein) probably did not know that Saladin was Kurdish. These people who create a sort of myth around them are opposed to American values.

ETM: So, is America a chance for the world?

PFD: Yes, for me yes; not because it is the best country in the world but because there are no others with the same capacity. The experiences of World War II for the Europeans were such that the French lost the battle, the British became disenchanted after the war, and the Americans, because of a renewed economy, were in a position to make decisions. One must understand this; there are a lot of French people who understand it and I do not take the form of anti-Americanism that is "stupid" too seriously. It can be compared to the anti-Gallicism, anti-France, of primitive Americans. It is not really thoughtful nor is it deep in France, when you witness it. In France for example, a lot of anti-Americanism is expressed among intellectuals who find life without the Soviet Union difficult. These intellectuals looked at the Cold War as if it were a ballgame between two opposing teams. We must have clear ideas but we must question ideology. Regarding my patriotism, I was completely blind when I was young and excited by the bad German conduct. I am now a friend of Poland but I don't cry when I see the red and white flag. This is the past. Patriotism should be the expression of love for others without the exclusion of others. We do have much in common, and I think that in this respect this country has shown a lot to the world. So, I am happy to be American with a Polish experience and tradition.

Harry Deal

HD: My folks originally came from Kent, England. In the vicinity there's a little town called Deal, and they come from that area. I was born in Dallas, Texas in 1921. My father worked at building cotton gins at a large company called the Continental Gin Company. He started to work there in 1913. The plant was built in Dallas around 1900 on twenty acres of land. Since my father was one of the supervisors, we lived in a company house by the Baylor hospital where I was born. My father was born in Dallas, Texas in 1885 and my mother in Cincinnati in 1895.

ETM: What was your experience of the Depression in Texas?

HD: I hadn't started high school yet when it began. We lived in south Dallas and we grew up in that depression, my sister and I, and it was pretty tough. My daddy still had his job. He was working one day a week, making nine dollars. But they shut down the plant. They just quit building cotton gins and that's the only work he could get. Cotton gin looks like cotton. They made the whole gin, and sold it to different places around. They separated the saw and the bush. Then, they took it and bailed that up and it went to different supply of vendors and they cleaned it and they got cloth out of it. So, during the Depression my father was working in this factory one day a week and he had to sell his car and he took my bicycle to go back and forth that one day a week, working part time for whatever he could get.

ETM: And how did you get involved in World War II?

HD: American aviation built airplanes and moved into Dallas from Grand Prairie, Texas. I got a job with them in the sheet metal department making the firewalls for these training planes they called the SNJ, the AT 6, and the Harvard Trainer. We built them for the Navy, the Army, and Britain. I stayed with them until August of 1942 when I joined the Navy with friends of mine I went to high school with. We all decided we were going to do our part so we joined the Navy together. I had bought a car, a nice little Chevrolet coupe, and we decided to go to Galveston because we had never seen a ship. We didn't know what the Navy was all about, so we got in my little car, 200 and some miles from Dallas, and went to Galveston. Then we were sent to New Orleans to catch a ship, a tanker, and while we were there we went through gunnery school. We took training in fighting fires and what not. The ship was finished in January of 1943. We went aboard; it was a 20,000 tons ship, about 550 feet long. It was a big ship, and it was new and fully armed with about 14,000 barrels of oil. We put the ship through the Mississippi River, went to Galveston and to Corpus Christi to pick up some more oil. Then we went through the Panama Canal toward Guadalcanal, in the Pacific Solomon Islands.

ETM: What do you remember from your experience on this ship?

HD: We joined the Third Fleet which consisted of four battleships, the Mississippi, the Texas, the Maryland, and the Pennsylvania, eight cruisers and twelve destroyers. We had the tanker that supplied oil to that group. There were three battleships that took all of our oil and we never went back to get oil. We stayed there and other tankers brought it to us out of San Jose, California. We followed the fleet around; we would be tailgating them and wait for them. When our group got into Bougainville, I remember that we were attacked by Japanese planes. This was for me the first round of action. Then after the invasion of Saipan which became one of our bases. We covered different islands until we hit Iwo Jima where we had several ships and a lot of planes shot down with quite a bit of action. Then I was transferred to a destroyer and went from Iwo Jima to Okinawa where all the destroyers sat out there and waited for the Japanese fleet to come through. We lost 13 ships and destroyers there because of Kamikaze suicide bombers. We didn't get hit, thank goodness, and we made it through.

ETM: Seeing these ships go down and sailors get killed made Truman think that something had to be done. What was your feeling about the Kamikaze at the time?

HD: Well it was a terrible feeling, you know, you look up. You are on board a ship and you get your guns, and you can shoot them down but they're coming pretty fast. They're coming at you head on; all you can see is a propeller coming at you, and they're not shooting at you. They have a bomb, usually one 500 pound, maybe 1,000, and their job is to die, and to take in the process as many ships down as they can. So they come into you and they explode, and that was it. Usually a lot of people died.

ETM: Have you lost someone close to you, a friend during the war?

HD: Yes I lost several of my friends, two of them from high school. They died at Okinawa and I have two others who died at Iwo Jima, Raymond Pope and Edgar Hyatt. When we returned in 1946, we docked in San Diego. I had my time in at sea, I was ready to go home; they sent me on a train to Norman, Oklahoma, and I was discharged. Then I went home and went back to work at the gin.

ETM: What was in your mind when you were in battle?

HD: It was to do our job and to survive. My sights set on a 5 inch 38 gun; that was on the stern of the ship. I had my big steel hat on, and my earphones, and I got my orders from the bridge. I was to measure how much wind there was, and the elevation. We were also shooting at aircrafts. And usually, they would bang down whatever the target was. We had submarines after us several times but we would navigate in circles. The fact was that the Japanese had attacked us. We didn't dive in, and our job was to defeat them before they go into our country. As young men (we were all boys), our job was to prevent them from destroying our way of life. We wanted to maintain our way of life, especially with what the Japanese had to offer us. But they shouldn't have been messing with us. You know we didn't attack them.

ETM: Have you forgiven the Japanese for what they did?

HD: Yea, yea, we get some good friends; we get some veterans coming here all the time. We have no problem with race; blacks, whites, Asians, they're our allies now; most of them. People are people. You know you've got to consider the fact that with this enemy we have today, it's a very different battle and a different type of war. We really don't have a great big reason other than the fact that they blew up our building and that their leaders told them to kill as many Americans as they could in that one whack. So I felt that we should fight back. Either that or get our asses out of the way and let them have it.

ETM: Are there parallels between the two conflicts?

HD: We were attacked in Pearl Harbor and on September 11. But now we have a different enemy and a different way of fighting. I'm not anti-Muslim. In fact we had some the other day, evacuees from New Orleans. There were quite a few Muslims and they left me a Bible, the Koran. I'm going to read this book. And I have one in the library here too. I have no quarrel with them. I don't have any quarrel with their religion. I'm a Christian. I belong to the Methodist church, but I have no quarrel with Mohammed. He's a prophet and he probably was a good one. But I don't think he taught them to kill like they're killing and desecrating bodies like they are; no I don't believe he taught them that.

ETM: You talked earlier about the American way of life. What is it about the American way of life that deserves to be defended?

HD: And possibly die for. Well, the American way of life is just what you see. I don't know how long you've been in this country, but we have a lot of freedom. We have laws, and we have taxes you know, like any other nation, we have to pay our fare and do our duty, but we have a lot of freedom in this country. We do what we want to. We organize the way we want to. This is a club, a private club, and we have a lot of fun running it together. We're taking anyone who wants to come in here and eat when we eat. They have to be a veteran. We also organize events with the veterans of foreign wars. We're building a park and we're going to make a memorial. We bury our dead; we do a lot in regards to the veterans.

ETM: Freedom seems central to the American experience and way of life.

HD: Freedom of press, freedom of religion, and you can criticize your people in power. I can criticize Bush even though I'm a conservative and vote republican. We don't like our administration at times. I'm what you call a swing voter. I'm an independent. Right now, I'm a republican, but I go for the man rather than the party. The party doesn't matter. I also criticized the democratic government when Clinton was running. That's our freedom. That's our privilege, being critical.

ETM: What do you criticize about this government?

HD: Well, it got us in a war. He attacked the Iraqis because he thought that this would be the best way to keep the insurgents and the terrorists out of our country. But we have yet to win the war. We're separating the good Iraqis from the bad Iraqis. They are surrounded by people who don't want democracy in their country, so they're just taking it hard. But two thirds of the Iraqi nation wants democracy and we're there I guess now to help them get it and we teach them how to take care of themselves and live in a free and democratic country. In many cases, that's worth dying for. You take all these boys in the pictures on the wall; you see here service men and most of them are dead now. Some of them died in battle. Some of them didn't. These are veterans from all wars, veterans of foreign war. All these people were different, sailors, marines, soldiers and coast guardsmen, and they have done their job which makes it possible for us to have this little club, Veterans of Foreign Wars. And we just get together, we have a social club, you might say. Your buddies and your friends died for this, for us to be able to have this conversation today.

ETM: So that we may be free to live, to grow, to learn, to live a happy life, and that is not true of everybody on this planet.

HD: Not everybody, not every country, no.

ETM: Who is for you an iconic figure of the American story?

HD: My favorite president is probably Lincoln; he had a real tough situation, the blacks and the whites, and slavery that had to be abolished. He made a great sacrifice. But in modern times, I'd say the president would be Franklin D. Roosevelt, a democrat. My father voted for him. At that time I didn't vote. I was too young to vote. He had a hard job. We were attacked by the Japanese and he had the burden of doing something about it. A sleeping country which was having a lot of fun in its democracy was all of a sudden at war. Japan attacked us and he accomplished a miracle. He turned this country around and we started building more war goods than the world had ever seen. We had three aircraft carriers and one of them was sunk. We ended up with twenty before the war was ended and thirty battleships. We were the biggest country in the world and we still are. Roosevelt came in the 1930s with ideas and he set up programs. They don't have these ideas today. He set up the NRA, the National Recovery Administration, and the CCC, the Civilian Conservation Corps. He put people to work. My father went back to work you know two days a week, three days, then four, then five. He went back to work and we had a better life. Once you got factories rolling, you're doing it. You're doing the job.

ETM: What would you say to the people abroad or in this country who oppose the war in Iraq and say let's send the troops home?

HD: I find that they have the freedom to do so, the opposing, but they should realize what we're up against. Right now, they don't bother us anymore in this country. They don't come over here and run airplanes into our buildings. We stopped that. With respect to France, one of my heroes when I worked at Continental Gin Company was a Frenchman named Evel. His ancestors came in this country when the French Huguenots landed at Galveston from Nova Scotia. Some of them settled in Dallas. My daughter was educated in France. Once she got out of New York University and got her masters in arts, she went to Paris and worked at the George Pompidou Center and then received a Ph. D. or its equivalent from overseas. She stayed in Paris, I think two years. She speaks good French.

ETM: What is your hope then with respect to what is taking place in Iraq?

HD: I hope that they're able to maintain a democratic regime if they want it. If they don't, let us get the hell out of there and go home.

ETM: This is a book about your experience during the war?

HD: It is about what I felt like talking about in my travels throughout the ocean, you know; putting 100,000 miles on a boat, you see a whole lot. There is an anecdote I could share with you. We were on our way from Iwo Jima, and our flotilla of destroyers, four destroyers, was doing "bird dog patrol." This is a patrol where you scatter out, you zigzag, and your job is to pick up any down pilots or any survivors from a sunken war ship. It was called bird dog patrol, and we were the last ship in the flotilla. We were about three miles apart doing this job, and we were heading for Han Shu, off Japan, searching in the water for down pilots. We got a lot of bombing there with the B 19s and the B 51s and so forth on the coast of Japan. Anyway, there was a star up there. I didn't know it was a star. It was real bright, called Venus, and it made a lot of light on the water. You know, we were blacked out, but this lit up the whole ocean. You could see the water. It was kind of calm. It wasn't rough, and I had the watch on the bridge, on this destroyer, on the starboard side of the bridge, and I had been talking to a guy on the other side. He was kind of loud you know. He really wasn't supposed to; we didn't have any lights on. We were blacked out.

ETM: Because of the bombing?

HD: Because of the Japanese planes flying over, and I hollered at the officer who was on the bridge at the wheel: "What is it? Is this a Japanese plane coming in?" He said: "No, that's Venus." It was mighty something, this part of the ocean, quite bright, and it looked like it was going to fall on you, but it was not. It just stayed on. So, as I stood there, on my watch, I was trying to figure out what we could do with that much light. We were wide open and I looked to my side of me and there was someone standing there, an apparition. It was a young man in a uniform. It looked like it might have been a navy uniform, not a navy, but a, how do you call . . . a medic. And it was really a ghost, an apparition. I hollered out: "What are you doing here?" And they heard me and the guy on the other side of the bridge said: "What are you hollering at?" I said: "There is someone here." He said: "There's no one there." I looked over and he was gone.

The apparition was gone. So I just feel that was a soldier, a medic, or marine who had just been killed in Okinawa and that was his body floating over. He was going over. . . . I could see the water was dripping on the other side of him so I knew it was a ghost. He was next to me, but he didn't answer my question. Who are you and what are you doing here? That fellow just may have been killed the day before. A sword or spear was floating over, on his waist, and that was the end of that. I will never forget it.

ETM: What has it meant to you?

HD: To me that, you know, you don't die. If there's a place for you to go, your spirit goes. It is returned to God. So he was passing over. That is the way I'll put it. I've talked to some about it, not too much. They think you're nuts. I couldn't recognize the face or the profile. It wasn't one of my friends. This was in 1945, June, or July, it was before the Armistice, before the Japanese surrender.

Hank Stein

HS: My parents came from Europe, my father from Zhitomir in Russia and my mother from a small town in Lithuania. They came to the United States separately, met in Chicago, and were married in 1920. There was my older sister, Sylvia, and younger sister, Ethel, and we were all redheads although my parents were not. I grew up in the South-East side of Chicago on 79th Street in an Irish-Polish neighborhood. My father was a tailor and we were all Orthodox Jews. In fact at the age of 5 or 6, I studied at the Hebrew school and I also started at a public elementary school called Myra Bradwell in the South-East side of Chicago. Being the only Jewish family in this particular neighborhood, it was very interesting for us as a family and we got along very well. As a family, we certainly felt the suffering and pain of the Depression era. But I really enjoyed the neighborhood. I became very friendly with my Irish and Polish friends. In fact, my parents spoke four different languages, including Yiddish, Russian, Lithuanian, and Polish. So I heard all these languages at home. And many of my friends, who were in fact all the friends I had in that neighborhood, were Catholic.

ETM: Could you tell us about your family?

HS: My mother spoke several languages and the Polish women who lived right across the street from us would get together and speak in Polish with her. I did not understand much of it, but it seemed that they were talking about life in Poland or in Lithuania. It really helped my mother because she never learned how to read or write English. She had not been able to go to school because she had to begin working at the age of 15 when she came to the United States. I always felt kind of sad about that when I reflect on it because my mother was a very bright woman, a great housekeeper and a great cook. I learned quickly that my mother and my father were very serious Jews and I had my Bar Mitzvah and got through all the rules and regulations of the Jewish religion. In Hebrew school, I learnt a lot about reading and writing Hebrew, as well as a lot about the history of the Jews, going back to the beginnings. During my high school life, we lived in the back of the tailor shop at 3026 East 79th Street, and that building is still there. In fact there is a sign that my father painted on the side wall, which said: "Max Stein, expert tailor." I just happened to drive by there a few days ago, and sure enough, the sign of "Max Stein, expert tailor" was there on the wall. So that brings back some very interesting, painful and also wonderful experiences that I had, living in the back of that store.

ETM: What was the discussion like at home about the events in WWII Europe?

HS: The Jews and other minority groups were confronted with prejudices because of their religion or beliefs. The Nazi regime under Hitler was taking power and seizing territories in Europe and they were trying to eliminate as many Jews as they could. We heard about that in the late 1930s and early 1940s in the United States. My parents were very upset because they had relatives living in Lithuania and the Ukraine where Jews were being transported to so-called "safe places," to eventually fall into German hands, and end up in concentration camps. The same thing was happening to Jews in Germany. There were discussions on the subject and family members were trying to figure out how to get them out of Europe and bring them into the United States or other countries in North and South America. There was a strong effort on the part of the Jewish organizations in the United States. They were not always successful, but they were able to bring in many Jews through all kinds of means.

ETM: What was it like going to school, what did it mean to be a student in school during the time of war?

HS: My friend Jacky Kelly, my Irish friend, we were out shoveling snow, on December 7, in fact, and the bombing changed everyone's lives, including the Kelly family, the Stein family, and every family in the United States. It was really chaotic. I was going into high school in 1942, South Shore High School, and I had done very well once I had gotten over the fear of being separated from my Jewish parents and learning to speak English very well. I was always a good student, very active in sports and education. During these years in South-Shore High School, a lot of my friends were being drafted into the war. In fact, one of my friends belonged to a Hi-Y club; it was a sports club of the high school kids. I was the only Jewish kid in the Hi-Y, but a kid named Dan Osterman, I can't forget the name, was drafted out of high school; he was a junior. He took basic training and was sent to France where he was wounded very seriously. He came back to the United States within a year with a medical discharge. I was still in high school at that time. As a junior at South Shore High School, I thought I may want to enlist because I felt so patriotic and I felt that I should get into this war. However, my parents thought otherwise and I did finish South Shore High School in 1946. My mother was very insecure. I remember once we had a conversation and we were seated in the back of the store and she said "I want to go back to Lithuania!" I said "Ma, there is a war going on in Europe!" This was 1944, people were killing each other, Americans were dying, and I used to look at cartoons where Japanese airplanes were dropping bombs over China and other places in Asia. And so I told her: "You can't go back to Lithuania; it's impossible! You'd be dead before you even got there, probably!" So I too felt insecure about the whole thing. I completed half a year of studies at Wilson Junior College, and during the summer of that year I decided to join the army.

ETM: Were you working while you were in high school?

HS: I worked part-time through high school in downtown Chicago at Becks Shoe Store and Maurice Rothschild's retail store. I also worked for the last year and a half of my high school studies at the Railway Express Agency, loading freight after school from 5 o'clock to 11 o'clock at night, everyday including Saturday and Sunday. My classmate Louis Collosky and I worked there. Also, they had a bunch of recruits from Great Lake Station come in to help because a lot of the manpower was not there. I have an interesting anecdote. At my job, there was an older Irishman who was a superintendent in the railway express. And he looked at me and he said: "Kid, what's your name?" I said "Henry, Henry Stein." At that time I had curly red hair, freckles, green eyes, and he looked at me and said: "Stein?" And he kind of "quizzingly" asked me: "Are you Jewish?" I said: "Yes, I am Jewish," and he looked at me again, shook his head and said: "You have the map of Ireland upon your face!" I said: "Oh!" and that was the end of the conversation, a kind of interesting little tidbit that I will never forget! Of course, we worked because we were all very poor, living in the back of the store without hot water, and we all had to work. My older sister, my younger sister, myself, always had part-time jobs throughout high school. I later got into the army and that was probably one of the greatest turning points in my life, because I really got kind of separated from my family; I was really on my own and it was a great experience.

ETM: What was your experience in the army?

HS: I went into service when the war had ended but I was still offered the GI bill. I was stationed, originally, at Camp Polk, Louisiana, in the middle of the summer for basic training; it was three months of really tough hard work. It was very hot, and I learned how to become a soldier. I was then sent to Fort Custer, which is near Battle Creek, Michigan, and was attached to an army hospital called Percy Jones General Hospital. That originally was a building owned by the Kellogg Company, which is located in Battle Creek and the army bought it during the war, as an amputee center primarily, but also for other ailments that were sustained by soldiers during wartime. I worked as a member of the Military Occupational Specialty, as an occupational counselor. My job was to write up histories on these patients being discharged who could not speak because of injuries caused by shrapnel wounds, or serious medical problems like psycho-logical disorders. They were sent to the Veterans Affairs hospitals or sent to special families if they were able to sustain their lives in that capacity.

ETM: What were the conditions of the patients?

HS: Many of these veterans, the soldiers, were in a very, very poor physical, mental or emotional condition, because of what they had gone through fighting the war. Some cases that I remember particularly were young men, probably in their twenties, who suffered from speech pathologies such as Aphasia. They could no longer speak. They would nod or shake their head, and my job was to interview these people, to try to help them get their discharge and do the paperwork to satisfy the military rules. It was difficult, but I was able to glean enough information and I got kind of a sense of the needs that a given individual had and hopefully get some assistance for him. Some had been hit by shrapnel in the neck area; their nerves had been cut off and that affected their ability to speak. It was sad meeting these young soldiers. Yet, I hoped that they would still live a good life and learn sign language and other things. I remember that a soldier I interviewed had holes in his head, he had one arm missing, he had one eyeball missing and the other eye was completely closed; yet he was able to speak and he talked about his experiences in France and part of Germany, and the terrible destruction that he saw, and the horrible things that had happened to him and to other GIs fighting in this war. At first, when I started this job, I was an occupational counselor. I was only 19 and I didn't have a great deal of maturity. However, I learned quickly that you could show sadness or too much empathy. At the same time, it was important to be empathetic with these people and I tried to do the best that I could in terms of giving them information and advice about the GI bill, what rights they had as veterans, and what support they could receive in VA hospitals in terms of their physical trauma or emotional disorder. And I thought, in terms of the response I got from my superiors, that I had done and was doing a good job. There were three others that worked in our separation center and they became very good friends of mine. One, in fact, ended up going back to the University of Notre Dame and we are still friends, 60 years later, and we are still in contact. It was gratifying not only helping these wounded, traumatized war veterans, but also just working with some of these great guys I met in the service. I also had a great admiration for these veterans who were seriously injured, physically and emotionally, in all kinds of ways, and were still able to fight, go on and carry on with their lives.

ETM: These soldiers, injured and traumatized, had made great sacrifices.

HS: I think this experience can help us learn to care for everyone, not only ourselves, our family and loved ones, but people throughout the world. These are human beings who had much suffered and given. I went on and tried to do the best I could for the many people in my life, in the army, in college, as a teacher also for many years in Chicago, in schools with students of different races and ethnicities. It did not matter. My job was to teach and I thought, considering the response I got from the parents and the students, that I did a good job; this made me feel good. I still volunteer in the local public schools, including the Ray School in Chicago, and a number of organizations in the Hyde Park area, to help the community and the people who come here from all over the world.

George and Claire Zenie

GZ: My parents were both born in Beirut; however my father came here in the United States at an early age, maybe 8 or 9 years old with his mother. My grandfather had left to go to Brazil, thinking that he would establish himself there and then bring his family, but after he got on the boat and left, nobody ever heard from him again. They don't know what happened to him. This was my paternal grandfather. My grandmother decided she wanted to come to this country because her brother had come here and she decided she wanted to come to America also. She brought the little boy with her and they came to live here. I would have loved to go to Lebanon to visit because it is described as such a beautiful country although it went through a civil war which wreaked the whole country. My grandmother who came from Beirut never returned there. She lived with us for quite a long time, and she used to describe how beautiful it was with the mountains and the sea. I would have liked to go there, but I never did.

ETM: You showed me a letter earlier dated June 11, 2001. Could you tell me about it?

GZ: There was an article in the newspaper that said that if someone had participated on the D-Day landing, they should contact the French consulate; so I sent them my name and transcript, telling them what I had done there and they sent me this diploma as a token of gratitude. I was very proud to get it. The French also gave us the *fourragère* which we wore on our uniform, you know, for all the troops that landed and did their work in France. I want to tell you some more about the French people. After we had landed on D-Day and had moved on up, there was a breakthrough at Saint Lô and we were moving quite fast, the division I was with and the whole army that I was with. And, we went sweeping through France and then stopped. There were pockets of Germans left behind. Now, I was given the job of going back and seeing if I could make them surrender to a Prisoner of War camp or get them out of the way because we didn't want them to cause any harm. I had a squad of men which was ten men plus a half-track with a 50 caliber machine gun mounted on it and I was in charge. I was a sergeant at the time.

ETM: Did you have some knowledge of French?

GZ: Very little, I was good with languages and my mother, being from Lebanon, spoke French besides Arabic, and I could say, "Avez-vous . . . voulez-vous?" this sort of thing. But I was able to communicate a little bit with the people. Now when I went back to find these groups of Germans that were left behind, I spoke to the French people on the way, especially the French resistance who were so helpful. They would tell me: "They're over there, and there are so many of them and so forth and so on." We would come around them and encircle them and tell them get out, you know, hands up. In the majority of cases they surrendered and we sent them to the prisoner of war camp. We had two incidents where we had a fire fight and fortunately only one of my men was wounded and we killed quite a few of them. They didn't want to surrender. The French people were so helpful; of course they were thankful to the Americans because we were there and they wanted to get rid of the Germans.

ETM: Could you tell me about your experience growing up in this country?

GZ: Oh sure. I was born in Brooklyn in 1920, right here in New York City. My mother and father met and they were married here. My mother had four children, four boys. Unfortunately, two of them died very young and then there was my brother and myself. When I was just 8 months old, my father died in an accident. So, I grew up without a father. He was coming back from some place on the subway. He leaned over the platform; he was nauseous. The subway train came, hit him and killed him. My mother was a seamstress. She had a rough life too; she had been in an orphanage in Lebanon and then was taught how to sew and she came to this country because she had a cousin here. After marriage, my father was a street car conductor and he also worked in the garment industry. When my father died, we didn't have any money. So, after that she had to work full time. When we were very little, my grandmother came to live with us because, at that time, they all stayed together as a family.

ETM: Was it different for you as a person of Lebanese decent to live in the United States, did you experience discrimination?

GZ: No, I tell you why. The neighborhood that I lived in was integrated; we had Syrian and Lebanese people there. But there were also Italians; as a matter of fact my best friend was Italian. We had Irish and we had so forth and so on. Then the reason why I wasn't stuck with just Syrian people was because I lived in downtown Brooklyn. But in Brooklyn Heights, when we needed help, my mother went to our church, the Melchite Church and they were poor and they couldn't help us. There was a Protestant church, an Episcopalian church, a Grace church right near by. They found out about us and they said that they would help us. Therefore, I got involved with this Grace Episcopalian church. I used to sing in the choir, they would send me to camp and that sort of thing, and I got to know the people. So actually I was Catholic, and I was integrated into all these different things.

ETM: How did you come to be enrolled in the Army?

GZ: I enlisted in the Army because after I lost both of my jobs during the Depression, I didn't want to be a burden on my mother; so I was 20 years old and I said to her: "I'm going to enlist in the Army of the United States." At the time, France had fallen but still, given my age, I had not really appreciated what was going on over there. I enlisted in the army but I wanted to find a place close to Brooklyn. I was placed at Fort Hamilton which was in Brooklyn and I could get home when I had time off by taking the subway. At the time, they were forming an anti-tank company; it was something new for me and I was learning. I was a truck driver. I learned how to take care of my truck, about guns, about all that sort of thing. And later on, they sent us down to Puerto Rico for amphibious training to learn how to land from ships to shore. Then, they brought the whole division back to Massachusetts, and it was there, at Fort Devens that we learned about December 7, 1941 and the beginning of the war. We were one of the first divisions to be sent overseas after we received additional training in Florida where we learned a lot of good. I say thank God I learned them because it saved my life many times.

ETM: What was it that you learned that you feel saved your life?

GZ: I learned that you had to take care of yourself, watch what was going on; always be vigilant. Help your buddy and he would help you. Of course, there were times when you couldn't do anything about that. They taught us how to dig fox holes, how to find the best terrain to hide in when there's artillery coming over. The officers of the 1st Infantry Division at that time were either from West Point or from the old army. They then sent a lot of our men to train new Divisions. But I stayed with the 1st Infantry Division and we left England in 1942 before we made the landing in North Africa outside of Oran. We fought at one place called Medjez-El-Bab and then at El Guettar. Rommel tried to break through the British and the Americans at El Guettar. He brought in his tanks and his artillery pieces and we were stationed in the hills up above. I was in an anti-tank company; our guns were looking down on them. When we got up that morning, after the fog lifted, there were tanks and trucks all over the place and they were moving, as a matter of fact, they moved beyond us. We were firing down on them, but our missiles, our projectiles, could not penetrate these German tanks because they were very thick. Fortunately, their guns could not aim high up to where we were with precision.

ETM: This was your first military engagement?

GZ: Yes, that's right. It was amazing to see all of this going on. I probably was scared, but we had things to do and we did them while the artillery was going on; two of the squad that I was with were wounded and evacuated them, but we were so pleased that we were able to do something by firing on them to stop them. We also had heard of the Free-French force in the area and were told that they were a very good force. After the Tunisian campaign, we went back to Algiers to train before we made the landing in Sicily in July of 1943. The Germans had quite a few planes at the time. We didn't have the cover that we had later on. When we landed, the ship that carried our heavy equipment was hit by a bomb; it had explosives on board and the whole thing went up in flames and we lost everything that we owned outside of what we were carrying. And then, we were attacked by tanks and we didn't even have our guns to fight back. We helped the artillery by bringing up the ammunition since our equipment was at the bottom of the Mediterranean Sea. Patton was in charge and our goal was to get the Germans out of there as fast as possible; the British on one side and we were on the other, and we moved up the Island. It was an infantry fight and we were up and down the hills fighting until the Germans left.

ETM: Did you meet or see Patton at the time? What was his reputation among the troops?

GZ: Well, I recall the one time we met Patton. He had slapped one of the men from my division in the hospital. He happened to be from my division. So, when the Sicilian campaign was over, he apologized to the whole division. We were all lined up, and he came up. I had seen him before. Not that I had met him, but I had seen him going and coming, but this time he came out in front of the 1st Infantry Division and he apologized for slapping the soldier. The incident had taken place in a hospital. The soldier was not wounded, but he was emotionally distressed and disturbed and he made a comment that Patton did not like. He thought he was a coward and he slapped him and of course the doctor at the hospital was very agitated about that whole thing, and so Patton came to apologize to the whole division. We all lined up and he apologized. He said that he was very proud of us and that we had done a good job (this was after the campaign was over) and that he was sorry that he had lost his temper to the point where he had slapped the soldier. We never liked Patton and when we landed in Normandy, I was very happy to be under Bradley rather than under Patton. They called him "blood and guts." That was Patton's nickname, because he didn't seem to care about what happened to anybody as long as he achieved what he wanted to do.

ETM: How did you learn that you would land in Normandy?

GZ: When I first went back to England from Sicily, I had malaria and I was put in the hospital for a while. When I got out of the hospital, I found that our outfit had been put into a stockade place so that we wouldn't mingle with the people because we were getting our guns and trucks and whatnot ready for D-Day. They didn't want to give away where we were going to make a landing and I think they succeeded in telling the soldiers that we were going to land in Calais which we never did. The first day we went out, which was on the 4th; the weather was bad, so we stayed on the ship and then the next day, they told us that we would go that night. We took off and we could hear the planes going over with the paratroopers and the gliders that came over and when I got out into the water, I could just see ships all around me, big ones, tremendous war ships and all the landing crafts; that night, we moved out. It was dark but I could see all the shapes of all so many ships all around, and when we woke up on the morning of the 6th, the ships were firing their big guns, the planes were bombing the area and the first assault troops were landing. I didn't land until noon. We were told that we would have to get our anti-tank guns on land and get off the beach so that we could stop a counter invasion from tanks which they were sure were right there and they were going to do that. Our big job was to get those guns that we had, the anti-tank guns, off the beach and into position. They told us where the position would be so that when they did attack, we would help to stop the tanks.

ETM: Could you tell us what you witnessed when you when you reached Omaha Beach?

GZ: When we first landed, we had to wait until the landing crafts that were ahead of us landed, and drop their people and then get out of the way because the beach was jammed with wrecks and all kinds of others things so that there were few landing spots. As soon as our spot was open, we rolled up there with our platoon on board. The intensity of arms fire had diminished; however, there was artillery and mortar shells landing on the beach and the driver of my half-track was hit on the right side of the face as we reached the shore. He was not killed but the side of his face was torn, so I put a bandage on it, moved him over, because I had to get him out of the way, and I drove the half-track on up to the beach, following the others. The situation on the beach was chaotic. There was, I remember very vividly, a gasoline truck that was on fire. There were dead bodies lying all around and wounded were everywhere. Some of the first units that had landed earlier had moved up. There was a hill in front of us and they had moved on up to the hill and reached the places from which the Germans were shooting at us. There was a gully beside the hill. I moved the half tracks as close to the gully as I could because that was the safest spot at the time, right near the cliff. They were using bulldozers to try to open up that area and every once in a while the men on the bulldozer would get hit and wounded and someone had to replace them. They were unbelievable because they were directly exposed to the enemy fire. After we positioned our guns, my platoon leader, the lieutenant in charge, asked me to go back on the beach to find more men. So I took a rifle, I went back and brought a few up to the hill above. One of them stepped on a mine. I felt very bad about our losses. When I landed on D-Day, I saw the casualties by the hundreds. We couldn't get off the beach for five hours and during these five hours we were being hit and artillery came down. There was a question: are we going to make it? We lost half of our company of 200; either killed, wounded, or missing. But we had to move on.

ETM: At the end of the day, having witnessed all this, what was your feeling?

GZ: Thank God that we were up where we were supposed to be. Thank God that we had enough men there to handle the guns in case there was a counter attack; and maybe take a couple hours to sleep because we hadn't slept the night before. This was my feeling anyway. But I had gone back to the beach and I had seen what was there, and it was an awful, awful, awful feeling, chaotic and bodies laying all over and people wandering around, but, by that time in the evening, they had started moving up and getting things organized.

ETM: What images do you recall of Normandy today?

GZ: I see the beach and the destruction and the chaos that was on the beach and then the hedge rows where we worried that the enemy was on the other side; and the French people we did see were all helpful. I remember the hedge rows more than anything else because they were obstacles but also a refuge. We lived very primitively of course because they would bring us something to eat once in a while from the back and we would move forward. I realized later on that we had landed on D-Day; that most of the country over here, the United States, had gone to churches to pray for us because they felt that this was an important thing and they were praying that we would do the job and that their sons would not get hurt or killed. Now, I understand what the landing and D-Day meant that the Americans and the Allies were going to go into Europe and they were going to take Europe away from Hitler.

ETM: How about the sense that America was on the right side of history.

GZ: Oh yes, definitely. We were on the right side of history. To me, it was the Allies as a whole, the British, Canadians, the Free French, and the Poles and so on. We were all doing what needed to be done. That's one of the most important things that happened during World War II. It was for a good cause. I was wounded once in the city of Aachen and when I returned on January 1, 1945, my lieutenant was wounded and they didn't have anybody to replace him. They said to me: "This is your platoon. You take it and you run it and we will tell you what you're supposed to do." They wanted to make a lieutenant out of me. So they gave me a battlefield commission and transferred me from one platoon to another. I was blown up in a jeep in March in the region of the Hartz Mountains in Germany. Then, I returned and became executive officer of the company until I came home.

ETM: Where were you May 8, 1945?

GZ: We wound up in Czechoslovakia when the war was finally over. We were outside of Prague making prisoners of all the Germans who didn't want to be captured by the Russians. They would much rather be captured by the

Americans and our job was to steer them in the right direction and put them in a big enclave with barb wire around. One after the other, they came through. Later on after the war, I did occupation duty in Germany until October 1945. While I was doing occupation duty, I was put in charge of a camp which had mostly displaced Eastern European people who had fled from the Russian army, and had to be sent back to their country; but for the time being, they were in this camp. My job was to take care of these people by getting them food that we found in the surrounding countryside. I would have the German people there send in milk, bread and vegetable. There were about 250 people there, mostly women and children, men also but not young.

ETM: You also saw a lot of destructions.

GZ: Oh yes, yes I did. I saw many villages and towns that were completely leveled. They were all destroyed. War is a horrible thing. I want to say if there is any way out of it without going to war, it would be the better thing to do because too many people get killed, get hurt, too much destruction goes on and, actually it doesn't solve the thing unless there's a complete surrender like there was in World War II. That was a good war but in the Vietnam War, we didn't have that sense. We really didn't. War should always be the last option.

ETM: How has America changed since 1940–1945?

GZ: When we went to war against Germany and Japan, everybody was doing things to help the war effort. Today it's the exact opposite. Most of the people are saying this war is not a just war; that we shouldn't even be there, that we should get out of there and you don't see people flocking to go to war; but in World War II everybody helped. In response to September 11, we did very well by going into Afghanistan, by knocking the Taliban out. They were covering Bin Laden, and if the current president had continued in that direction, if he had sent our troops into Afghanistan, taken over the area, and really tried to get Bin Laden, that would have been much better than what he did. I don't like dictators but they are also in other parts of the world. They could have used the troops and money and everything else in a much better way.

CZ: I'd like to say something. You know, my father was originally from Iraq. I received a letter from relatives that said that, even though they come from a wealthy background, one woman in that family has breast cancer and she can't even go to the hospital for treatment. The other one wants to go to the supermarket to get some food and they're afraid to go in the street and she says: can't Bush do something to at least make us a little safer? But it's a shame what they did to that country. That was a beautiful country; Iraq was beautiful. They had a great culture there and they had everything. I agree that the head of Iraq was a dictator but once they got him down, Bush didn't have to go on wrecking the country, and that's exactly what he did. How many of our boys have been killed? It's horrible, every single month it's a little bit more. And then he says things are getting better. How can things be getting better? How can they leave that man in power? I don't understand it. This is a democracy? Who wants a democracy like this? It's a shame what he did to our own country.

ETM: It is probable that the people of this country were misled. I also think that September 11 played a very important role into what happened all the more since many believed that Hussein was involved. Since your father is from Iraq originally and your mother from Lebanon, you probably think that there is a great misunderstanding in this country about the Middle East, a region that is rarely presented in a positive light. There are many moderate followers of Islam who would favor democracy in this part of the world. Perhaps we need to differentiate between American leadership at this moment and the American people, and consider that the core value of the American people has not been altered. It seems to me that a reflection about the American experience in World War II can enrich our thinking about America today, but also about the war today, the question of civilizations and dialogue between cultures, the dialogue between religions, and that needs to be at the center of our preoccupation today. How do you, how do we respond to September 11 bearing in mind that it may be the tip of an iceberg?

GZ: I agree with that, yes. We certainly do, we absolutely need to question the whole thing. When you have these young Arabs and Muslim people who are willing to blow themselves up in order to kill somebody else, there is something very definitely wrong with the way they are being treated or the way they feel they are being treated. Very definitely wrong, because nobody really wants to kill themselves and the reason they're doing this is because they feel that they're helping a cause, which is not a right cause. If we could speak to these countries, if we could get them to talk to one another, it would help. Many people in the Middle East are probably hoping for such as dialogue and like you said, many of them don't want war because it's not in their favor.

ETM: What kind of leaders do we need today in this country, from your point of view?

GZ: I thought Truman did a very good job because when he saw what was going on in Europe after World War II, he decided to help rebuild these countries in order for them to be democracies and to be part of the democratic world. He also implemented the Marshall Plan. So, this is a leader that I thought was very good in both ways, when he wanted to stop something and when he wanted to do something to help people, he did it quite well. This president is not reaching out to other people. I don't know where he's getting his advice from. I feel that he wants to continue this until he's out of office so that he can say that he wasn't there when all this happened, whereas actually, he contributed to the whole thing. I do think that the best candidate at the moment is Edwards.

CZ: I do have the impression that the United States as a whole, I don't know whether you can say individual people, but you know, our country has done some pretty awful things, but even the immigration policy right now, which is simply horrible. They had to close three hospitals because they couldn't accommodate all these people that are coming in and that are so sick. The jails: 27 percent of the people in the jails are immigrants. What do you do about something like that? What Bush has done to the country and what he has done to our boys is terrible. How are things getting better?

GZ: That's just it. He keeps saying things are better and things are not better. Even his generals told him and he had to replace all of the generals who were running the Iraq war; he had to replace them because they were telling him things are not moving. And if you ask the American people today, more than 50 percent are against the war. That's what the polls indicate. What has happened in Iraq has not helped the situation between the ethnic groups which were living together peacefully. They got along fine and now they want to kill each other. I honestly believe there will be a civil war there regardless of whether we stay or whether we don't stay. They will fight because of religion, and because of the oil. I honestly believe that. We should have been more patient to bring along more countries involved at the beginning. There are people in all of these countries who have a feeling that if you talk you can get things done rather than go to war and kill people trying to achieve something.

ETM: What does it mean to talk? Does it mean to understand how the other feels?

GZ: That's one, to understand how they feel, to know what their needs are, to maybe help them with what they need. There are countries like Saudi Arabia that have all this oil and could get more involved; instead of pushing for the Sunnis to be the top people over there, maybe they can reach out to the Shiites. Why can't the Palestinians and the Israelis have a decent dialogue? They seem to hate each other so badly it would take a long process of dialogue in order for them to come around and to not hate one another. Why can't they think along these lines: what can I do to help you and what can you do to help me?

ETM: And even right now there are problems in Lebanon. Can Islam and democracy be compatible?

GZ: They are compatible because there are good and moderate Muslims. Traditionally, Islam is not a religion of war but of peace.

CZ: My mother always said that when she was in Lebanon as a little girl, she didn't go into the territory where the Muslims lived. Each had their own place and they all lived in peace. My mother was Catholic. There is a Christian community in Iraq, they are suffering very much and they do not like Bush. They don't think very highly of him; let me put it that way. Years ago, two young boys from Iraq, distant cousins, came to this country and they went to college here. One of them became an engineer and one of them was a professor and that's who I talk to. They write letters to their families. One of them passed away unfortunately, but the other one writes to me and tells me what his family is going through.

GZ: I don't think that the United States wants to colonize Iraq but many Iraqis feel that we're occupying their country. They really feel that way.

CZ: A senator recently came back from Iraq and he said that 75 percent of the people don't want us there. They hated Saddam Hussein I am sure but there are plenty of other ones that are just as bad and that we have supported. Are we going to make a democracy of their country; and if this is a democracy, who needs it? Well, look what has happened to the hospital in Washington, to the returning soldiers who aren't even being treated right. Bush should take a look over there and see what he is doing. He's wasting all of this money and lives and everything else, when we could be doing so much more with it right here in this country and in other countries where we could be helping instead of destructing. And they showed a family with three children where he's taking not the mother or the father, but both of them. Now, they never did that in World War II because I remember I had a very dear friend in the service and his sister died. They brought him back and they left him there with the family. But take the mother and the father from three little kids? I know that they stay home and they pray and they hope that everything is going to be alright. But they're on edge all the time because their loved ones are in danger and any day somebody might come knocking on the door and telling them that they have been killed or something may have happened to them. That's very hard on people, very hard on them.

ETM: Are you hopeful about the future of this country?

CZ: Well absolutely, just as soon as some people get out of power. I think it can't be any worse. It's bound to be better; it's absolutely bound to be. It really is a shame. I remember my mother when she was alive, I'd often say to her, wouldn't you like to go to Lebanon and see what it's, and she would tell me, "No, this is my country. There's no place like this."

GZ: Absolutely, 90 percent of the people in this country are proud to be Americans. They're proud of what we have accomplished so far and they want to continue doing that and they want to help people, but they don't want a war, they don't want destruction. There was one senator talking the other day. He said if we took a part of the money that we're using over there and help the people in Africa, help the people in South and Central America that need this money to progress, we would be doing so much more. There's no country like the United States where there is freedom. You can be a rag picker one day and a millionaire five years later. That can happen in other countries today, possibly, but not the way it happens here. If you look at Bill Gates, he started out with nothing and he's a billionaire. And now, he's helping; he's using his money to help a lot of people in Africa and around the world.

CZ: Well even George and I, when we got married in 1946, what did we have, 75 dollars in the bank? And he had a job where he was making $30 a week and I was making, I think $40. Eventually, we had a beautiful house in West Hempstead, a big English Tutor. We had three children. They all went to college; they all got their Master's degree. I mean, we had nothing to start. And my mother didn't have a husband either, and at that time, there was no Social Security or anything. I think people should think of religion too. I don't care what kind of religion but we have to bring up our children with a certain amount of religion and morals. The golden rule, we're back to the golden rule: Love one another.

GZ: We want our country to continue to be better, we want our country to help other countries, we want our country to do the right thing for everybody, all religions and everybody else and if we did that, I think we would be so much better off than trying to impose on anybody by war or any other way how we want things done. That's the way I feel.

Jean-Baptiste Feuillye

JBF: I grew up here in Fresville, just next to Neuville-au-Plain, where we are right now. My parents owned a small farm. I was 13 when the landings occurred and it is an event that affected me profoundly. When you are 13 you are not prepared for too much whatsoever, but this event affected my life, since even today I spent time in the company of veterans that fought in my village, on June 6, 1944, in order to liberate it, about less than an hour ago. They have been here for two days with a team from the American Discovery Channel. They were making a video about the story of a famous soldier who was parachuted in on the night of June 5. I believe his name is Bob Bearden. He is from Texas. He came back here for the 50th anniversary, but on his own, not in a group. His son was a pilot for American Airlines or for TWA, and he told him: "Dad, one day I will take you back to Normandy, about which you talked so much during my entire life. One day, I will take you back." And the promise was kept. For the 50th anniversary the son obtained a flight for his dad. He landed one beautiful morning on the beach of Fresville, stayed at Désirée Duchemin's house, and since then, we kept in touch. He is now 83.

ETM: In what way has this event affected your life?

JBF: First of all, there was the surprise effect. We knew quite well that something was going to happen, but we didn't know by whom or how. One must remember that at that time my parents were not rich farmers; there was no electricity, there was no radio, there was nothing. So, we were not expecting the Americans at all. I am talking about the people in Fresville, in my village. They were flying very high, in flying fortresses. It was amazing to see. But in our minds, we thought that the English would free France, under De Gaulle. He was the Phoenix, the hope; everybody was talking about De Gaulle. He was the liberator; he was the Joan of Arc who was expected to free the whole of France and Europe as well. But we didn't know exactly which form this liberation would take, nor about the armies available in England. We knew that the Germans were a little nervous. I remember that they had commandeered the school in the month of March, and it was just a little before I got my school diploma. They occupied the school as of their arrival and we took refuge at Désirée's parents' house. Taking into consideration the Germans' attitude, they knew that something was going to happen; they were more nervous in spite of their age, and they made more night patrols. Their primary concern was about the light. They didn't have much problem since the three quarters of the farms didn't have any light. We lit our homes with oil lamps or candles. But they required us to paint the windows with blue paintings. They feared the bombing, of course.

ETM: Do you have any stories about what you saw on June 6, 1944?

JBF: As for everyone, and especially for me, since I was a child, what I found really surprising was the way the parachutists came down just like that. We were not expecting it at all. We were used to strict discipline coming from the German army; one could recognize the Germans from three hundred meters with their studded boots and their songs. They had a certain kind of severity in them, and they made their presence felt. And suddenly there were those very brave men landing, a little cow-boyish, silent, very silent, individualist and brave, very brave. During the first hours of the landing they had to make themselves known, with a lot of difficulties.

ETM: You talked about courage, bravery, referring to the American soldiers.

JBF: Yes, because I think that when you are prepared to jump from an airplane in the middle of the night in an occupied country that you don't know, and the language of which you don't speak, that requires some hell of courage. They were well prepared, but for many of them this was their first experience in a battle. As for the 505, they had had the chance to tangle with the Germans in Sicily and in Italy. They were aware of what to expect, but for the others this was their first battle. Normally, the 82nd was expected to land in Saint-Sauveur-le-Vicomte. Their mission was to cut the peninsula as fast as possible, and this way seizing Cherbourg, so that everything would happen for the best. But it was after they learned that the 91st German Division that had fought so tenaciously in Russia, and that had just been reequipped, reformed, and reorganized in both soldiers and equipment was coming, that the Americans decided to cancel the landing in Saint-Sauveur-le-Vicomte. It was a week or two before June 6 that they had to rethink the attack and remake the maps. The fellows from the 82nd knew that they were going on a dangerous mission.

ETM: And it is through these troops, these parachutists, who were just a little older than you that you discovered America? What aspects of America did you see in them?

JBF: I was quickly influenced, because this small part of the region became 80 percent American, physically as well as militarily. There were camps everywhere. So there was this situation that made possible direct contact with Americans. I was lucky to have a company of combat engineers coming right next to my house, the 307th. Their mission was to build bridges. It is then when, by accident, I came in contact with an American soldier, after I had a flat tire on my bicycle; he took the tire and then repaired my bike. Needless to say, that next day I went to that place, I saw the soldier again, and in the end I remained with them. I had become their mascot. This company was washing the dirty linens, it was a laundry company. They had some enormous trailers with huge washing machines, and they were washing the linens of the country hospitals, the sheets, the towels, and everything that was needed in a hospital; at the same time they were also doing the laundry of the soldiers fighting on the front. The latter arrived by trucks, most of which were driven by African Americans, called "Red Ball Express." Those trucks were on each front, and the "Red Ball Express" existed until the Battle of Ardennes.

ETM: What did this experience teach you about life?

JBF: It allowed me to head towards a completely different lifestyle. I entered in a world of adults who could serve as mentors for me since my father was quite old when I was born. By the time I was ten, my father was already sixty. Thus his behavior was more that of a grandfather than that of a father. Those guys, however, were about twenty, twenty-five. I decided to go with them. I went with them all the way to the German border, and I didn't return before the end of 1945.

ETM: You accompanied them all the way to the German border?

JBF: Oh yes, I went with them, and I had to get my parents' permission. They had to have a lot of confidence in me. Would parents in our days let their children leave like that in search of adventure? It was with the 681st washing company. There was a sergeant called Donald Jacobi. He had a child who died in the United States. I could actually feel paternal affinities toward the soldiers of the company, affinities that, to put it like this, I never felt before. I can't say that my father didn't show me any affection; it's just that I didn't feel that type of affection that bonds a father and son. I felt that with Don Jacobi who became an ideal father. When they left to the United States, they brought me home. I cried a lot, because I wasn't only losing a father, a second father, if you prefer; I was also losing all my friends. He wanted to adopt me, but it was out of the question. However he didn't give up, so as the years passed, in 1951, when I was eighteen, I obtained, thanks to him, a visa that was later extended.

ETM: Had you learned English before your trip to the United States?

JBF: I was working with them, but the English that I learned certainly wasn't literary English. However, one can learn very fast at 13. It was by that time that Air France opened an office in Los Angeles; the consultant offered me a job there, and to become an American citizen, if I wanted. But towards the end of the two years, I received a letter from my brother saying that my father wasn't doing very well, and that it would be a good thing to go back to see him. He actually died shortly after that. Then I got in touch again with the person who later became my wife, and whom I knew prior to my departure. I started a family, but I always remained in touch with my American friends. I went back over there a few times. I saw Don Jacobi again. My children went to see him too. He died five or six years ago. For me he was a second father and I think that for him I was a son. While I was in California I often helped him in his work as an American Greetings Card representative. And I still write letters to his second wife. So, I consider Jacobi's family my second family.

ETM: When you hear about problems in French-American relations, how do you react?

JBF: I was very apprehensive when I was invited to attend the 82nd Airborne Convention at a time when there was the most friction. I could not decide whether to go or not. It was in Atlanta. I thought that they were going to eat me alive there. I was expecting the worst. As was expected, I was invited, I went, and I carried a message. Honestly, when I left I was quite nervous, because it really was a difficult moment; it was three or four years ago. So I arrived in Atlanta and you know the American receptions. It was Don who planned the conference, and it actually went on quite well. I met people that I knew before. Since I was the representative of Normandy, I was seated at the head table, along with Barbara Gavin; there was also the Archbishop of New Orleans. In a word, there were a lot of esteemed people. The ceremony of flags and of the honor guard took place. They knew that I had a message, and I had to read that message from the mayor of Sainte Mère Église. I added some of my own thoughts to what I read, and finally I received a standing ovation. That softened the mood; there was no trace of discontent. I was expecting the worst, but it was completely the other way around. They stood up to applaud me. I don't mean to sound boastful, but I really think I found the right words to say. It all came out extremely well and I realized one thing: there was much more said on this side of the Atlantic than on the other side. We used to say that they were throwing the wine in the streets, and then there were also the freedom fries. Next day I took the plane to Detroit. And what do I find? There was this French bakery, and in the hall there was an exposition on Manet. However, forget the French fries; there was nothing said about them. That was nonsense! Here we made up things that honestly were not said on the other side. It takes more than the fries to turn us Normans against the Americans for whom we feel friendship and gratitude. And I believe this reflects the feelings of all the inhabitants of Normandy. I think that the Normans are really touched by the landings and by the courage of the American soldiers.

ETM: So, there has to be a distinction to be made between what is said among governments and the reality of human relationships between French, Normans, and Americans.

JBF: Also, there are many young people here who want to be steeped in this experience, and who regret not having lived in those times. Looking at the teenagers from here and from all over France, and seeing them so passionate, coming every year for the landing in Sainte Mère Église, you can feel in them some kind of nostalgia for not being able to take part in those events. The number of veterans is now decreasing, but there are the young children who come and who will continue coming even more. There are also exchange programs that are absolutely amazing for the students. I had the chance to accompany a group of teens quite recently. They were a select group chosen from among the best schools in the Far West, Montana, Wyoming, Oregon; one child for each state.

ETM: The veterans of Normandy have returned in the years that followed.

JBF: Their priority was to found a family and to find a place to work. They continued with their lives; they started all over again. I accompanied groups of veterans that came back here during the first years. But it is mostly for the 50th anniversary that couples came here. Ceremonies, banquets, and speeches took place then. But when you take each of them (and I talked about this many times), the women were pleasantly surprised, and I would say even shocked, because their husbands never told them anything about it. And all that made me ask them questions: "So since you returned to the United States, you never told any stories?" "No." And I asked why, and they would answer: "They wouldn't have believed me." And that was unanimous; almost all of them gave me the same answer. "This was one moment in life when we didn't want to talk even to our close ones." On the other side, I had women that came to me and asked me: "I didn't know that for forty years I slept with a hero. I didn't know that my husband was a hero." It is precisely us, the Normans, who showed them the truth, through the reception, the banquets, the welcoming we gave in their honor. We made it obvious that we had such a huge admiration for them, and that we owed them a lot, no matter what the rank or the person; we owed them a lot, and they never claimed or pretended anything. Even today for many of them, it is hard to talk about it.

ETM: For those who didn't live through the war it is difficult to imagine the horror that it produces, and to understand the heroism and the risks at their true value.

JBF: When I came back from that trek as a troop-kid, there were three cemeteries at that time in Sainte Mère Église. One of my neighbors from Fresville worked there. One day he came to see me and my parents and told us that the sergeant responsible for the cemetery, Espinoza, was looking for a person, a Frenchman, willing to work in the cemetery to receive the first visitors, and then to rise and lower the flag each day. He thought that might have interested me. Of course, the next day I went to see the sergeant. I went to the cemetery, and there Espinoza considered that my English was good enough, and that I could start next day in the morning. It is then that I joined the service of military graves, in October 1945. At that time, there were only wooden crosses, and a lot of Frenchmen came simply to drop flowers on the first tombs. Many officers, soldiers, and parachutists came, because, I should mention that the 82nd was during that period in Germany. They were the honor guard of Eisenhower's headquarters. They considered that the 82nd deserved this distinction. They had been to Berlin, Stuttgart, Mayence, and many of them, at the time of their return to America, in 1946, came to say a last goodbye to their comrades. Then, after 1946, American families started to come.

ETM: What was your experience with the first families?

JBF: I remember that the first person was a lady from Washington State, whose name was Ms. Arouet, I believe. You have to know that at that time there were no hotels, there was nothing. So this woman was housed at Ms. Renaud's place, she came several times to my house. She stayed for fifteen days. I remember that the priest of the village came to drop her off at Sainte Mère Église. And she went every day to the tomb of her son who was killed on June 13 at Amfreville. She came every afternoon to the tomb of her son. Then she left for the United States, and we communicated for a long time. When the tombs were uncovered in 1948 to be placed into a larger cemetery, her son's body was sent back to America. As a mother, she wanted her son to be buried at Saint Laurent with his men, because he was a captain. One of his men had also been killed on the same day, and his mother, as well, wanted him to be buried in Saint Laurent. But he was married and his wife was pregnant with a baby that he never had the chance so see, because the child was born after the landing. The wife had priority in deciding whether to repatriate the body or not, as the widow; after her came the parents, the brothers and sisters. And the decision could only be made once. It was like this: "Yes or no? Do you want the body of Captain Harvey to be brought to the United States in order to be buried wherever you please, or do you prefer to bury it permanently in the cemetery of Saint Laurent sur Mer?" Since the mother couldn't contradict her daughter-in-law, who had priority, the body was repatriated. And the daughter-in-law was from North Carolina since they were living in Fort Bragg. The child was born, and she remarried an air cadet. The poor guy was sent down to fight in the Korean War. And the last time I had contact with the mother of the captain who died on June 13, was in the United States. I went from California to Washington State to see her. I spent two days there. She told me that her son died a second time. Because of the fact that her daughter-in-law was from North Carolina, her son was also buried there, and his tomb was abandoned anyway, as far as she was concerned, a second time. She died of sorrow six months later, but she did everything she could so that her son's body would be unburied and taken to the cemetery in Saint Laurent, at her own cost. This news reached the State Department, but she was told that it was too late. They didn't want to create a precedent for that. She communicated for a long time with Ms. Renaud. She came to say goodbye in the place where her son was killed. And for forty years I've been trying to find out what happened to her grandchild, since I knew that the son of Captain Harvey was somewhere in the United States.

I wrote to many places in order to find out where Captain Harvey was buried, because I knew that Ms. Harvey did everything possible for her son to be brought back to Washington State. There is a military cemetery at Takoma. They told me it was quite a recent cemetery, so there were no veterans of the Second World War there. However, they put me in touch with an agency in Washington, and they confirmed to me that he was still buried in North Carolina. But I knew that the son existed, and every time there were visitors from Washington, I asked them about it. About two years ago, a man, Mr. le Votre, called me and told me: "Mr. Feuillye, I have news for you. I have someone who wishes to meet a certain Bobby that was translator in the cemetery of Sainte Mère Église." "Well, I told him, that's me." So he tells me: "Imagine that there is a man in a travel group going to Italy. But he will leave the group tomorrow to come to Normandy where his father was killed and buried in the same place where that Bobby worked." I told him that it was me. And it was Harvey. So I said to him: "I have been looking for you for forty years." He knew about me from the letters of his grandmother, and also from his mother. Things happened this way because he was in touch with Le Votre who was in charge of the 90th division. The Internet can make miracles these days. And it was amazing; it was an absolutely fabulous meeting. I asked him how come I've tried for forty years to look for him. So he answered me: "I am a military man, so I traveled a lot. Right now I am a retired colonel." He was in Korea and in Vietnam, and he even went to Germany for two years. I never knew anything about him, because I didn't look for him in the 90th Division.

ETM: That is a great story that crosses over people from different places and generations.

JBF: There are many veterans who would say that Normandy is their second country, if not even the first one. Some of them claim a close ancestry. Of course, they don't say: "My mother-in-law is from Neuville-au-Plain." They tell you: "I have family in Normandy." For some it is true that we came to be really close. The Americans have had an important impact on this region. We came to know them as they really are. We were able to come very near their inner selves because we were extremely close to them. The soldier who came here to fight came with an ideal; he came with faith in himself and in us. That has nothing to do with America's image as a super power. What they did is very unique as is what they inspire in others. They changed our lives. They defended their flag but they also defended an ideal that is ingrained in them since childhood, and that we don't find in any other place. I don't think the word "indoctrinate" exists in their culture; but they do have the words "courage" and "duty."

ETM: America is a story, a land, and a spirit held together by an ideal, and in the center we find freedom.

JBF: In the end, it's you, it's us. The pioneers were in search for freedom. Some of them needed to flee in order to find their freedom. There are three quarters of veterans who come to you and say: "Normandy . . . Normandy is our second home." They come to a place that they identify with without having a certitude that their ancestors are here. They are of many origins. And our way of being, our entity if you want, corresponds to what they wished to discover. This land that they liberated is theirs. They somehow made it theirs. For me, it's a great pleasure to accompany these veterans, like for the last two days that I have spent with Bearden. On Tuesday, there is one veteran coming from the same group, from the 505. He had never come here before, and he is very surprised that we are so close through memory to June 6, 1944; and most of all for our gratitude. I am waiting for a confirmation of his visit on Tuesday. They are five all together. I also found another one who came with his niece, and a guy named Spencer who is coming with him. And there is another one who is a glider pilot. In a few days they will probably confirm their visits.

George Daniels

GD: I was born in 1917 on Long Island. I have lived at my present address for 85 years, in the same house. We moved here when I was about 5 from Maspeth in Queens to New Hyde Park. When we moved from Maspeth to New Hyde Park, the town was largely farm land and the house that we purchased had farms both in front of it and to the side of it. To the north we had a potato field, and in the front we had a corn field going down to Floral Park. We have all races here and a great variety of cultures, but at the time I was growing up it was largely people from Europe. We were a large family of eight people and so we had plenty of company in the house. My step father was in a laundry business; he was a partner in a company called the Big Five Laundry in Ridgewood

ETM: On D-Day, you said that you saw the gliders leaving for France. Could you tell us about your experience that morning?

GD: I was based in Deenethorpe, England at the time, and when I came out of the house, I saw these little blue lights slowly moving in the night sky. They told me that it was D-Day. That was about 3:30–4:00 in the morning. I sensed it when I saw the gliders going around. Of course we had an idea that D-Day was near; we were getting close to it but we did not know exactly when it would happen. As a matter of fact, I learned what was happening when I went to the briefing room. The first thing that we did was go to the mess hall for breakfast. After that, we went to a small theater where there was a map on a stage, to tell us where we were going that day, our target. Well, that morning, Colonel Bowman said to us: "Gentlemen, this is the day that you will tell your children and your grand children about. This is D-Day."

ETM: What were your regiment and the nature of your engagement?

GD: I was with the 401st Heavy Bombardment Group, 615 Squadron. I was a left waist gunner and we had ten men on the crew: pilot, navigator, bombardier, co-pilot, engineer, ball turret gunner, left and right waist gunner, and the tail gunner. I may have left out one I am not sure. At the time we were flying we had command of the sky, but the flights were tremendous. The Germans were throwing thousands of shells at us to knock us down and they were very successful at times. They knocked out sometimes twenty or thirty bombers per flight. I once saw three planes in front of us go down. I should say that I did not actually see the explosion. Here is what happened: a single German fighter flew down though our formation and picked up the three of them simultaneously. The man who actually saw this happen was in the upper turret; he was the engineer and he had his guns strained on him, but they jammed so he was not able to get his shot. But I did remember seeing the bodies go by, the crewmen. Most of them were alive I believe. Some had parachutes, some did not. That must have been thirty men, just gliding by in the sky.

ETM: What were your feelings at the time, hopelessness?

GD: I felt what a terrible thing this was. What a horror war was, you know. It is hard to say what all of my thoughts were at the time. There was horror up there. A lot of men lost their minds as a result of these missions. The stress was terrific. It would vary anywhere from fifteen to forty minutes. The explosions were right next to you. They would actually lift up the ship. The anxiety, as you can imagine, would be enough to drive you out of your mind. And many did; there were many thousands of mental cases. The engineer of our plane was institutionalized, and he has been in and out ever since. He lives in Jeffersonville, in upstate New York.

ETM: How did the stress come about?

GD: It came progressively. This varied depending on the individual but after the missions, you realized what an awful thing this was and the effect it had on you. I remember waking up for several years, seeing pictures of those men flying by from their bombers that had exploded and seeing other planes go down. I used to wake up, but then it went away. It must have been horrible for them.

ETM: And you probably felt for the people below too?

GD: Absolutely, especially the innocent people. I remember on one occasion we were a lead plane. I forgot where we were bombing, but anyway, our bombs did not release; the bombing mechanism had been shut out. So we arranged for a deputy plane to come in. We were going to hit a secondary target, but the salvo bar on our plane had been shot. We fell off the formation very gradually because of the weight of the bombs and some of us on board were trying to knock them off. But nothing came, and on the way back we just flew gradually over the open countryside of France; and there was a little village there I saw with orange roofs. The officers and the engineers were trying to release the bombs since one could not land with them and finally they went away, but they accidentally dropped right in the center of that little village and blew it apart. I saw one house that seemed to slide from one part of the street to another. It was terrible.

ETM: And so, what did you learn from this experience after all these years in terms of war? War is absolutely a tragedy and is catastrophic.

GD: Yes, that, and I also learned that God is with us all the time, whether we realize it or not, because I prayed up there, as I am sure others did. One of my prayers was "God save us." It was not something I thought about, it would just come out of me. But when I looked at the other planes flying with us in formation, I said to myself: "Why should God save us?" Someone is going to have to pay a price for this war. So I decided to change the prayer, and I said: "Dear God, no matter what happens to us, just be with us." Well, I had scarcely said the last word "us" when I felt this powerful presence larger than life starting from the top of my head, working down through my shoulders to my whole body. Then I knew that God was with us, not that we were not going to be killed or injured, just that he was with us. That was amazing. And I said to myself I don't have to believe that there is a God, I know there is a God.

ETM: Did you have a special thought with respect to the people being liberated and the sacrifices of the soldiers?

GD: Oh yes, well, I believe it was General Eisenhower who said that had it not been for the bombing of the Air Force, the price to be paid would have been much higher. He said that men probably could not have gone on with the conflict. Because we bombed everything from submarines, highways, railroads, yards, industries, and oil depots, everything, but that was the price that had to be paid. The price was 26,000 men killed, 28,000 taken prisoners of war, and about 9,000 of our planes shot down, a staggering number of planes. Our losses were twice that of the Marines, four times that of the Army, and seven times that of the Navy. When I finished with the missions, I thought that was the worst thing off my shoulder. They called me "Pap." I was 27 years old at the time.

ETM: Have you returned to France since the war?

GD: I returned in 1991. I had flown over many times, mainly in Northern France. I think we even saw Paris in late 1944. We were at a pretty high altitude when we were flying, and many times you could barely make out the outline of the city. I had never been on the ground before but I had a sense of the countryside and the land from above.

ETM: What was the experience?

GD: I liked it, the countryside was beautiful and I went to Chartres Cathedral. I was especially interested in that because we had an organist here at the Garden City Cathedral who won the *Grand prix* for an International competition for organists. So, I was very anxious to get there. I went inside and learned about the history of the place and looked at the stained glass windows. Of course, I did not have much time, you know, but I was impressed by the work of art and the gargoyle on the outside which depicted the world outside. Inside it was heaven; it was beautiful. And while I was there, there was a young couple who were going to be married. They went into the Cathedral and I heard the organ so I rushed back inside to listen. It was wonderful, and the bells were towing from the top of the edifice.

ETM: What did you witness during the Normandy landing? Did you fly that day?

GD: Sure, we flew on D-Day. They sent out about 2,000 planes that day. But it was a very hectic thing. I was told that we missed the target by about 13 miles and the bombs were dropping and almost hitting some of our own planes. There was a lot of confusion. We hit the coast before the men landed. We tried to knock out the targets there. I forget the time but it was very early. As we left the English coast, I just had a glimpse of the ships and it was tremendous to see.

ETM: What did you make of the disagreement between France and the US on Iraq? How did you react when France decided not to go along in Iraq?

GD: I don't know. I cannot tell for sure because I had mixed feelings about the war, about going over there. The Middle East is a totally different part of the world: the religious and ethnic groups, the culture, the whole thing. Of course, we are still not out of that place yet; we don't know, there may be a civil war there. It was a dangerous action to take. At the same time, when I heard in the media that they had weapons of mass destruction, about Saddam Hussein and the way he treated his people, I leaned toward getting involved in the war. But I cannot say that I felt different toward France or any other country because I know the English people were not too happy about it either. After the Second World War, we had a Marshall Plan, loved our enemies; we helped Germany get back on its feet, and saved the West from Communism. So, we did good things but if people do not accept your love, and I don't know whether they would over there, that is a different thing; then you have to fight them. There are also different people over there, different opinions. And the challenge is to distinguish between those who want progress, who want democracy to prevail, and those who want to prevent its advance. They do not have the same mind over there. It is a very complex situation, to say the least.

ETM: What do you think is the legacy of your generation?

GD: Well, I would say, try to avoid war as much as possible. Try to talk things over. Take the middle way because you have extremists on both sides and that is dangerous. Whenever you have extremists, one side or another, they are going to go for the jugular. In this life, we live in a world a few hours apart from each other, and the best you could do is to try to compromise, and come to a moderate middle ground so that you can get along with people. We are going to have to live with other people as long as we live, people who don't share our ideas or values, but we've got to try if possible, if it is humanly possible to get along. We fought the war; we defeated the enemy, an enemy led by a madman who wanted to take over the world. There is so much to this,

ETM: Are you rather optimistic for the future?

GD: Oh yes, I have to be. Yes, I am. I think that if you are Christian you have to be optimistic no matter how bad things look. But we are in the atomic age now and we have to be very careful that we don't have a proliferation of these atomic bombs; we have to try to prevent that as much as possible. Because when things begin flying back and forth, that will be the end of civilization as we know it.

ETM: What did you do after the war ended?

GD: I took a job in construction. Then after a year, I sold men's furnishings in New York for Franklin Simon in 1946 for about a year, and then I met a friend of mine who came in the store, and he was looking for a transportation manager, so I took that job. But I think I missed my vocation; I think I should have been an actor. Because this is the thing I used to do as a child. I used to read poems and get up in front of four people and make my show. This reminds me of an episode of the Johnny Carson Show when a little kid of eight years performed in front of the audience. One of them was dancing on stage once and Johnny asked him: "Where did you learn that?" and the kid said "It is a God given gift!" My father died of influenza in 1918 and I think had he lived, I would have gone to school and into other careers because I had an IQ of 132, which is not bad. As a matter of fact, the psychologist who gave me the test said that I scored 7 points higher than the average of the doctors who took that test.

ETM: Do you recall any specific moment from your youth?

GD: When I was about ten years old, I went to Curtis Field one Spring morning. It was about noon and I saw a small group of people, possibly ten or twelve huddled together, and I was curious to see who was there. I had heard that Lindbergh was planning to cross the Atlantic. He was waiting for the Weather Bureau to give him the ok, which as fate would have it, was the following day. In fact, I should have been at school that day but I wanted to see this and I knew the time was approaching. He was ready to go. I was by myself and was a little hesitant to getting close to the group because I knew I should not have been there. Nevertheless, I got close to the group and I saw Lindbergh talking with the people surrounding him. And I recall looking at the hangar where the plane was based and it looked like a tiny bird getting ready to fly. At that time, he did not realize that he was going to get a call from the Weather Bureau and he had made plans to go to New York City. However, he received word that the weather was going to be good the following day for take-off. Either late in the day or at night, they moved the plane to Roosevelt Field because the runway was longer.

ETM: Looking back 80 years later, what was in your view the significance of this crossing?

GD: There, in this big hanger was this tiny plane, and they knew nothing about what the weather would be like over the Atlantic; they only knew that it would be good for take off. It was the first solo successful flight. It was a pathway and a stepping stone for great things to come in aviation. It was a very significant event in world history. The anticipation was great and the event was filled with anxiety. Prayers went up for this courageous young man. They said that when his plane approached England and he could see fishermen below, he swooped down and called to them saying: "Which way to Paris?" and they motioned the direction. He arrived there in the dark, brought the plane down safely, and immediately the people rushed to the plane and carried him out as a hero. It was such jubilation here; and we were so happy that he had made it.

Looking back, I think this means that it lies within mankind to achieve greatness and doing what seems like the impossible.

ETM: How would you compare 1927 and 2007?

GD: In terms of daring, I don't think that it is any less today than it was then. It is such a different world. The world has become smaller with communication, and we are far more knowledgeable today than we were then. I have had one year of high school; this is the extent of my formal education. I remember in one of my classes Economic Citizenship that the teacher, after presenting an important part of the course, asked one of the students to rise and respond to a question. The student apparently had not been paying attention and gave an irrelevant answer, to which the teacher replied: "X=23, sit down!" When someone questions your knowledge today, you are aware of what technology can do; it can improve all matters in life if used appropriately. It also depends upon the moral integrity of those who possess the knowledge.

ETM: Lindbergh's crossing embodied the spirit of America, the notion that we can extend ourselves and go beyond our limits.

GD: The willingness to dare, to challenge the unknown. I think that people captured to some degree the spirit of America by that event. They also looked at it with a great sense of expectancy for it could have ended in a failure. And so, it is an instance in which America showed the way to the future, triumphed over the unknown and it brought the world together. The people have not changed. They have become more knowledgeable and more aware of our power, as well as that of other countries. I think that our greatest challenge is to find some way to use nuclear energy and other resources for the betterment of all mankind, through experiments in space travel, communication, and technical improvements.

ETM: What do you make of September 11?

GD: I slept late that morning. My radio was on and I heard that a plane had flown into the World Trade Center. I immediately assumed that it was an accident. However, shortly thereafter, another report came over the radio that a second plane had struck the other tower. I knew instinctively that it was the work of terrorists and not an accident. It made me feel terrible. I did not know what to think at the time. Today it tells me that evil is very much alive in this world and that we must constantly be on guard against similar acts. It could be jealousy or a sincere hatred of our culture, since Islamic culture seems so opposed to ours. At best, they are wonderful people since there are good people in every culture and nationality, but at worst, those who committed the crime are diabolically evil.

ETM: Should we seek to establish a rapport with the moderate voices in the Arab world?

GD: Absolutely, because there are people of good will, there is no reason not to; and I think that eventually, goodness always triumphs over evil. I have been a Democrat since the days of Franklin Delano Roosevelt because I believe that the party best represents the interests of the middle class and the poor, whereas the Republican Party mostly represents the interests of the very affluent and the rich. And history bears that out. Edgar Hoover was a good man, a humanitarian, but he did not seem to grasp the enormity of the problems the American people faced after the stock market crashed in 1929. He thought it best to wait for the private sector to catch on, which it never did. In other words, he had to realize that government needed to step in.

ETM: As a Christian, how do you think we need to act vis-à-vis the poorest countries, some of them Muslim, around the world?

GD: Based on our ability to help, the poor should be our number one priority wherever they are; they are the same people that Jesus associated with in terms of their need, whatever the need. He associated with the oppressed, the poor and rejects of human society. Those were his primary answers. He put this before all else; he chose to do it. Of course, it gives the example today of how we should behave in all respects, prudently and with generosity, nationally and internationally.

ETM: What meaning do you give to the sacrifice of the American soldiers on D-Day?

GD: To me, it is a significant part of World History that the Nazi regime was destroyed. When you think of what Hitler was saying in *Mein Kampf*, you cannot let evil go unopposed. We watched the *Anschluss*, the invasion of Czechoslovakia without reacting because the democracies had permitted him to arm himself without any resistance. Their sacrifice was well worth it, whether it would have been me, them, or anyone else, once this monstrous evil was exposed. When I think that this originated in a predominantly Christian nation, and was allowed to proliferate, I cannot comprehend it. Hitler was a leader and the German people who were having terrible times were looking for a leader; they were proud people who could not accept having been crushed after WWI. When we saw that Nazism meant the hatred of others, the idea of a superior race, we were so intent to put an end to it that we felt it was worth our sacrifice. The system had to be destroyed.

ETM: What should be our answers to September 11?

GD: "Eternal vigilance is the price of freedom." I don't remember who said this. A few days before D-Day, General Patton said the following to the troops who were about to land in Normandy. He said "this business of dying for your country is BS, let the other son of a bitch die for his country." I would say that first, you have got to stand for what you believe in and be willing to pay the price for freedom. But we need to keep an open mind, listen to new ideas, and never try to coerce the conscience of any human being. Public television is priceless from this standpoint because it is educational and it allows you to explore all points of views. We are limited in what we can do. We have to gain the confidence of all governments abroad as much as possible by being a good example, and I am afraid that we are not in many respects. If we are a good example, they are going to be influenced by us so we have to treat them as equals. We have to take care of the poor in our country too, and if there is evil, don't hide it. We have to live though our example in terms of how we conduct ourselves.

ETM: Just recently, I saw a program with Bill Moyers which showed how the Administration had leaked false information to the press about Iraq's nuclear capabilities in order to make the case for war. What do you make of this?

GD: I hate to say it but I think that our current government is thoroughly corrupt. It is dishonest. It is about anything they can gain for their own agendas. And what it needs is a cleansing of corruption and the ongoing investigation is the best possible way to bring about change in the way our government conducts itself. Money and power have the ability to corrupt and they do.

ETM: What about the relation between France and the United States. Do we share in your views common values, and should we have common goals?

GD: We certainly do and we certainly should. We should also question our policies. I think there are times when civilization and civility are thin veneers over what is wrong in human beings. They are relative to a time period and a location because we know that people can be corrupted wherever they are. And contrary to what one hears at times, there is nothing wrong with being a "liberal." If you look at the definition of the word in the dictionary, it means to be progressive, open to new ideas, and caring for the less privileged wherever they might be. As God reveals himself to us, we can better understand the meaning of our existence "Love your neighbor as yourself": I do not know any humans who can achieve this, but it is a calling. War occurs because we do not keep the Ten Commandments and honor the significance of God's sacrifice. War is a transgression. However, if forced upon you, you have no choice. We live in a world of past knowledge, in a world in which we are still learning. This gives rise to differences of opinions. If you look at our past and present civilizations, Mesopotamia, Egypt, Greece, Rome and Europe, human beings are learning to live together. Hopefully and by the grace of God, we will continue to strive for peace. If we only go our own ways, we will fail, and there will be no life at all without any reliance upon God and the spirit.

Index

NB: The persons interviewed in the book are identified with (*)

About the Author

Eric Touya de Marenne is originally from the south of France. He received his *Diplôme d'Etude Approfondie* from the University of Paris, Sorbonne, and his Ph.D. from the University of Chicago. He is currently Assistant Professor of French in the Department of Languages and Literatures at St. John's University in New York.